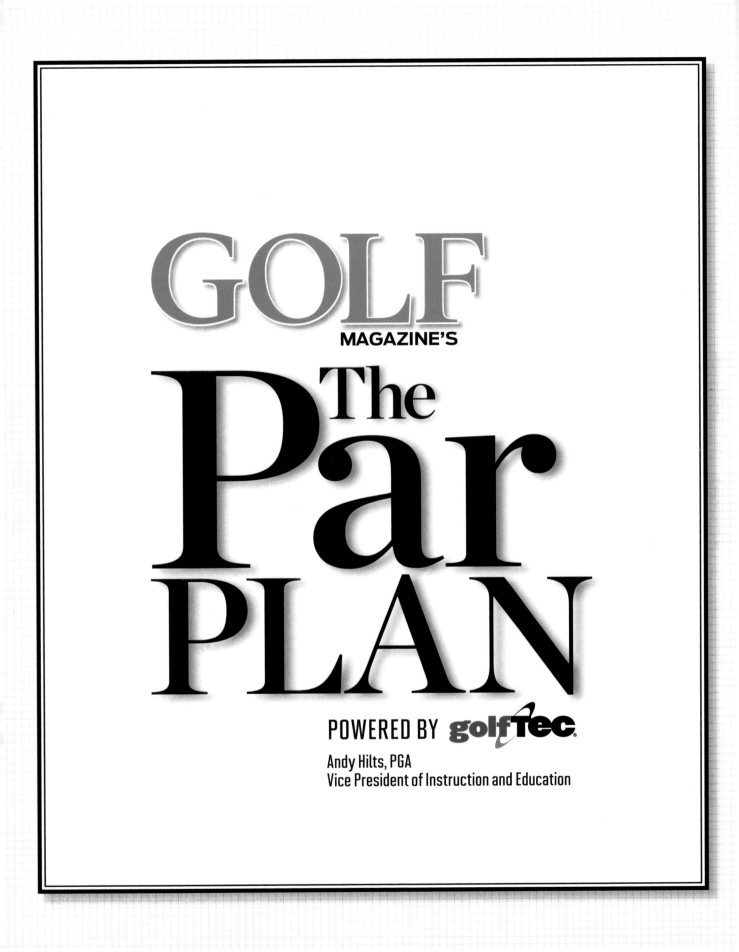

GOLF
MAGAZINE'S

The
Par
PLAN

POWERED BY **golfTec**

Andy Hilts, PGA
Vice President of Instruction and Education

Published by Time Home
Entertainment Inc.
135 West 50th Street
New York, New York 10020

Instruction material in this book
previously published, and is reprinted
with permission by GolfTEC. For more
information, call (877) 446-5383.

ISBN 10: 1-61893-050-8
ISBN 13: 978-1-61893-050-7
Library of Congress Number:
2012954602

We welcome your comments and
suggestions about Time Home
Entertainment Inc. Books.

Please write to us at:
Time Home Entertainment Inc. Books
Attention: Book Editors
P.O. Box 11016
Des Moines, IA 50336-1016

If you would like to order any of our
hardcover Collector's Edition books,
please call us at: (800) 327-6388
(Monday through Friday, 7 a.m.–
8 p.m. central time or Saturday,
7 a.m.–6 p.m. central time).

Cover/book design: Paul Ewen
Cover/book photography:
Angus Murray

GOLF

MAGAZINE'S

The Par PLAN

A REVOLUTIONARY SYSTEM TO SHOOT YOUR BEST SCORE IN 30 DAYS

POWERED BY golfTec

Edited by David DeNunzio

A **Sports Illustrated** PUBLICATION

■ CONTENTS

The Par PLAN

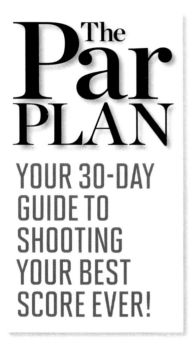

YOUR 30-DAY GUIDE TO SHOOTING YOUR BEST SCORE EVER!

golfTec

MY PRO TO GO

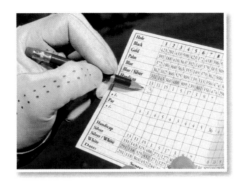

DAY ZERO

PREP FOR THE PLAN

How to define your goals and level of commitment to get the most out of the plan. Plus, tips for using the My Pro To Go app to assess and improve your skills.
Page 6

DAYS 1–5

DRIVE IT FARTHER AND STRAIGHTER

Stop penalty shots in their tracks by grooving the moves that consistently put your tee shots safely in play.
Page 14

DAYS 18–22

IMPROVE YOUR IRON CONTACT

You don't need a new full swing to hit solid iron shots, just one that makes the right kind of divot with every club in your bag.
Page 100

DAY 23

TAKE NEW SKILLS TO THE COURSE

How to transfer what you've learned to your actual rounds and save a few strokes by using your head.
Page 120

DAYS 6-9

NEVER THREE-PUTT AGAIN

Improve your speed and directional control for putts that always roll close—if not in.
Page 34

DAYS 10-13

TIGHTEN UP YOUR WEDGE SWING

Learn the easy way to dial in the right distance with each of your wedges for short shots that never leave the pin.
Page 60

DAYS 14-17

THE SECRETS TO SCRAMBLING

Stop your scores from ballooning after you miss the green by using the tried-and-true keys for expert chipping and pitching.
Page 78

DAY 24

FINE-TUNE YOUR GEAR FOR SCORING

Follow these checkpoints to make sure your gear is allowing you to take full advantage of your best swings.
Page 132

DAYS 25-27

EXPAND YOUR SHOTMAKING

An easy-to-follow plan for building a basic arsenal of specialty shots to escape trouble and work the ball into better scoring position.
Page 144

DAYS 28-30

SIMPLIFY YOUR SAND GAME

How to turn a trouble situation into a scoring opportunity by focusing on the proven keys for consistent sand escapes.
Page 166

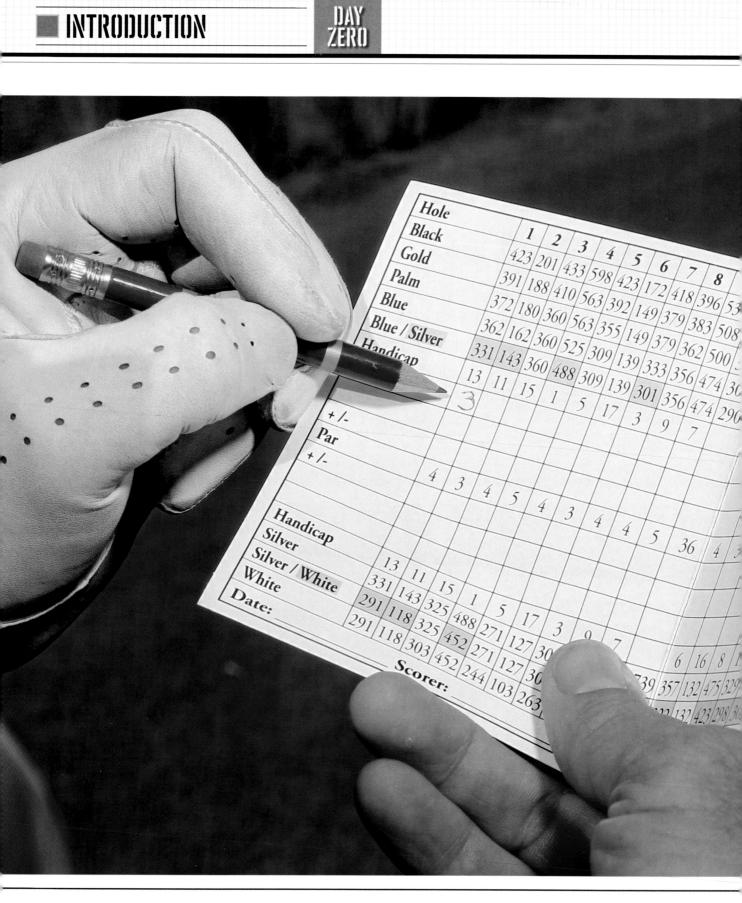

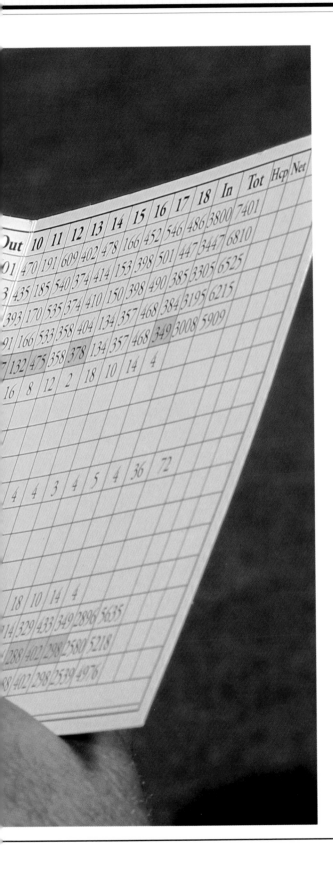

DAY ZERO

PREP FOR THE PLAN

*How much you put into the plan
determines how low you'll score*

INTRODUCTION by **DAVID DeNUNZIO**
Managing Editor (Instruction), *Golf Magazine*

You're about to begin a 30-day journey to your lowest score ever. Along the way, you'll be asked to take a good hard look at your swing (and overall technique) in various situations and perform a number of drills and exercises to make small—but important— improvements in nine key areas of your game. It's an expertly devised plan formulated by the company that teaches more than 500,000 lessons every year, but it's only going to work if you commit to the plan and put in the necessary time and effort.

On the following pages you're going to learn about the methodology behind the plan and how to attack each of its components. You'll also get an idea of when and how to start your path to improvement and the types of things you're going to work on as you follow it. And you'll experience a revolutionary digital product that will assist you in performing key self-assessments. These evaluations are a critical part of the plan and help make it a one-of-a-kind learning experience for golfers of all skill levels. Best of all, the product is free and works with the smartphone or tablet already in your possession.

You've been shooting numbers higher than you should for too long. Turn the page to start becoming the player you've always wanted to be.

THE PAR PLAN SMALL IMPROVEMENTS FOR BIG SCORING GAINS

You don't need a swing overhaul—you need to limit your mistakes

A common bond among all golfers is a scoring goal—a magic number every player has in his or her mind that represents a successful round. For some, that number is in the 70s; for others, it's simply anywhere in the double digits. The fact that you're holding this book in your hands is evidence that you have yet to reach yours. The truth is that nobody ever does, because as soon as you reach your ideal number, you immediately set a new one. The game is truly one of successive achievements.

Lets, however, deal with the here and now: You're shooting numbers higher than you'd like to. Enter *The Par Plan*—a revolutionary day-by-day guide developed by the nation's largest network of teaching professionals to help you assess the weak spots in your game and improve upon them so you don't keep committing the same mistakes. The widely held belief among amateurs that you need to be a shotmaking machine to shoot in the 70s just isn't true. Plus, it's an unrealistic goal for the vast majority of recreational players—most people don't have the time, patience, money and resources to develop a Tour-level motion. As you proceed through the plan, all you'll be asked to do is to take an honest look at nine parts of your game—each of which can gain or cost you strokes—and make a concerted effort to improve each. Getting better across a broad spectrum of your game is easier to do—and manage—than trying to rebuild your swing from the ground up.

The nine critical areas (listed in order of importance and how they're presented in this book) are as follows:

1 DRIVING Better driving is your number-one priority because putting your tee ball safely in play eliminates penalty strokes and takes pressure off the rest of your game.

2 PUTTING You can make up for a bad full-swing shot sometimes, but a missed putt is a stroke lost forever, especially when you're three-putting more often than you should.

3 WEDGE SHOTS Any shot within 100 yards of the green should be considered a scoring shot. Mistakes here mean wasted opportunities to lower your score.

4 SHORT GAME Getting up and down from off the green normally won't help you gain on your score, but can certainly stop the bleeding when you get into trouble or fail to hit the putting surface.

5 IRON PLAY You don't need to hit every green in regulation to post your best score ever, just more than you're hitting now. At the very least, you need to learn how to miss in the right spot when you fail to hit a green in regulation.

6 STRATEGY Playing smart is the difference between your best score and your second-best score, especially when you're grinding it out because your A game just isn't there.

7 YOUR EQUIPMENT It's a fact that properly fit gear—from driver all the way down to your putter—helps you hit it farther and straighter, which are the key requirements for posting your best score ever.

8 BALL CONTROL Learning to hit the ball higher and lower—and intentionally making it curve to the left or right—on demand is the savvy player's secret to saving strokes here and there during a typical round.

9 BUNKER PLAY As soon as you realize that taking the safest route and using three shots to get up and down from a bunker is perfectly acceptable, the less frequently you'll need four shots or more.

This may seem like a lot, but remember: The goal is to improve a little in all areas, not master them. That can come later. These lessons focus on singular moves and feels that are easy to digest and that have a positive effect across a wide range of skills. For example, you don't have to completely retool your wedge swing to consistently knock it closer from 100 yards. Instead, all you need to do is practice the feel of the shaft leaning forward at impact to instantly decrease the frequency with which you hit skulls or screamers. You'll simultaneously increase the likelihood of a solid shot. If you follow the plan (including the self-assessment tests, weekly practice regimens and targeted at-range and in-home drills), you'll go out in 30 days and have an excellent chance of shooting a number that you're proud of. Golf is like fitting together the pieces of a puzzle: it's important to get each one right to see the whole picture. Improving in the nine key areas just enough to cut one or two strokes per skill set is the key.

"Golf is like fitting together the pieces of a puzzle: it's important to get each one right to see the whole picture. Improving in the nine key areas just enough to cut one or two strokes per skill set is the key."

GETTING STARTED

Let's be honest—if your average score is 98, this book won't make you a single-digit handicapper by the end of 30 days. Nobody's trying to fool anybody here. But the plan can certainly get you to the point where you're easily scoring in the 80s and in position to really take your game where you want it go. It'll only work, however, if you dedicate yourself to the plan, find the necessary time to complete the drills and lessons, and use the assessment tools to accurately determine if you're ready to move on to the next step. Obviously, the more time you dedicate to the plan and the greater your level of commitment, the more you'll improve.

STEP 1 SET A DATE

The first step on your path to lower scores is to decide when to start. Check your calendar and find the weeks when you're not busy with family commitments or work travel or unable to consistently get out to your course or practice facility. (Keep an eye on the weather, too.) You're going to spend several hours a week at your practice facility as well as rehearsing at home or in your office.

STEP 2 REMAIN IN "PRACTICE MODE"

Don't substitute playing for practicing while in the midst of the plan. You won't do yourself any favors by taking the skills you have right now to the course. You'll get more benefit by finding some answers in the practice facility dirt. Turn a deaf ear to the call of an afternoon round or the pleas of your golf buddies to join their Saturday foursome.

STEP 3 STAY POSITIVE

There will be some hiccups as you proceed along the plan, but you'll also find that you don't need as much work as you think you do in some areas. This will allow you to dedicate more time to your real trouble spots. The plan is neatly spread over the span of 30 days, but it's more than likely that you'll deviate from this structure now and then and borrow time from less-critical areas to nail the skills that are giving you fits. That's perfectly okay as long as you don't fall too far behind. If you find yourself playing catch-up, then stretch out the plan to a more comfortable time frame or seek the advice of a certified personal coach. (We provide a list of every GolfTEC improvement center in the U.S. and Canada on page 186 to assist you in your search for the best professional help possible if and when you need it.)

THE PAR PLAN ATTACK
LESSONS, VIDEOS AND MY PRO TO GO

This book is a breakthrough lesson guide in that it's the first of its kind to create a learning experience across three platforms. The first is *The Par Plan* book. You can also watch videos of the majority of at-range and in-home drills featured in *The Par Plan* at golftec.com/parplan to make sure you're performing the exercises correctly and to see exactly how they're meant to be executed. Lastly, you can assess your technique and check your progress using the free app from My Pro To Go (available at the iTunes store and Android Marketplace to download to your smartphone or tablet). The My Pro To Go app includes a state-of-the-art swing-capture program that allows you to look at and analyze your technique using quick-and-easy drawing tools that show if you're making the correct moves or not. My Pro To Go was developed jointly by *Golf Magazine* and GolfTEC to bring expert video analysis to everyday golfers and is an essential component to completing the plan. The My Pro To Go app allows you to honestly assess your skills to see where you need to focus your improvement efforts. (You'll be asked to do this numerous times as you proceed through each of the nine key areas.) There isn't any cost to using the app to capture and analyze your swings, and it's an innovative and fun way to see if you're on the right track and keeping up with the demands of the plan.

The real benefit to the app, however, is that it allows you to upload your swing to My Pro To Go for an expert analysis by a GolfTEC certified personal coach. While this analysis isn't a requirement to complete the plan, it's available to those who want to make absolutely sure they're where they need to be in each section. There's a fee for this service, but My Pro To Go is offering a special discount to *The Par Plan* readers. Visit *golftec.com/ parplan* to register for a 50 percent discount on My Pro To Go lessons as well as fittings at any GolfTEC improvement center.

Video is an important part of the plan because it provides you with facts and truths that your sense of feel or a friend's eye simply can't catch. Pros know this, which is why video now dominates Tour practice tees. Thanks to new technology like My Pro To Go, using video is easier and more comfortable than ever. If you follow the advice on the opposite page, you'll actually be able to get your swing back on track even when you can't see your pro. Keep in mind that video isn't a useful tool only when assessing skills or when things go wrong. One of the best times to capture your swing is when your ballstriking is at its best. Taping good swings gives you a model to compare with when your game inevitably goes a bit off.

MODERN MARVEL MY PRO TO GO
Download the free My Pro To Go app to take full advantage of the plan. Visit *myprotogo.com* for details.

HOW TO RECORD YOUR SWING

Use the ***My Pro To Go*** swing-capture app to assess your technique and pinpoint your weak spots. The secret is to capture your swing from the position that allows you to most accurately review your motion and to make full use of the menu of drawing tools. As you proceed through the plan, you'll be asked to capture swings from two powerful angles. Here are some quick pointers:

DOWN-TARGET VIEW (BEHIND GOLFER)

This perspective allows you to see (among other things) your swing plane, clubhead path, address and in-swing posture, and clubface angle. Position the camera (i.e., your smartphone or tablet) about 15 feet behind the ball—make sure there's plenty of room above your head so you catch the upper parts of your backswing and through-swing. Use the on-screen brackets and positional image to frame your body so you can capture your swing in full from start to finish.

Also, make sure the operator positions the camera in line with your hands and sets the camera at about waist height. Check that your right arm and right leg and foot hide their left-side counterparts. That ensures a true down-the-line perspective.

● *Camera in line with hands.*

● *Camera positioned at waist height.*

● *Left side hidden by right side—a pure down-target view.*

FACE-ON VIEW (CADDY PERSPECTIVE)

This perspective allows you to see (among other things) the length of your swing on both sides of the ball, spine tilt, arm and hand position throughout, shaft lean at impact and lateral movement (if any). Position the camera about 15 away from the ball and use the positional image to correctly frame your body. Set the camera in line and even with your belt buckle.

Try to be consistent with the height of your camera. Keep it at waist height. The worst place to position the camera is at eye level, as it significantly changes the angles of the club during the swing. A steady camera also is vital in making an accurate analysis of your swing. Use a tripod or clip on your bag to produce a steady video instead of one that jumps or moves.

● *Camera in line with belt buckle.*

● *Camera positioned at waist height.*

● *Make sure you can see the club on both sides of your swing.*

GOLF MAGAZINE AND GOLFTEC A WINNING COMBINATION

When *Golf Magazine* came up with the idea for a 30-day guide to help recreational players get the most from their games and shoot their lowest scores ever, teaming with GolfTEC—the world's largest and most experienced golf-improvement group—seemed liked the perfect fit. For more than 18 years, GolfTEC has been helping golfers of all skill levels play better and enjoy the game more with a five-pronged attack that fuels maximum improvement and lasting results. The attack includes: 1) fact-based diagnosis, 2) sequential lessons, 3) advanced retention tools, 4) video-based practice, and 5) precision clubfitting. Every year, thousands of golfers just like you shoot their personal-best score thanks to the GolfTEC approach to learning and sustaining improvement.

GolfTEC Vice President of Instruction and Education, Andy Hilts, incorporated much of the company's teaching philosophy into the *The Par Plan*. This includes video analysis (via the My Pro To Go app), lessons that build on one another so that you seamlessly produce correct overall motions (look for the Lessons, Fixes and Drills throughout this book), and access to more than 500 instructors at 160 improvement centers across the U.S. and Canada. In addition to using the swing-upload service with My Pro To Go, you'll get the most out of the plan by scheduling a lesson at the GolfTEC Center nearest you at the conclusion of each section. While the My Pro To Go app is an efficient way to assess your skills and to check if you're making the necessary improvements in the nine key areas, a one-on-one lesson is the ultimate way to make sure you're on the right track.

"Video is an important part of the plan because it provides you with facts and truths that your sense of feel or a friend's eye simply can't catch. Pros know this, which is why video now dominates Tour practice tees. Thanks to new technology like My Pro To Go, using video is easier and more comfortable than ever."

THE BOOK ON GOLFTEC

- GolfTEC teaches 25 percent of all U.S. private golf lessons annually and delivers a consistent 95 percent success rate.
- Since 1995, GolfTEC's certified personal coaches have taught more than 3.5 million lessons to more than 250,000 golfers.
- Each GolfTEC coach helps at least 25 students per year shoot their career-low round and gives more than 1,300 lessons annually.
- There are 500-plus coaches at your disposal at 160 centers across the U.S. and Canada, including 11 PGA Section Teachers of the Year.

MEET THE PAR PLAN PROS

Golf Magazine recruited three of GolfTEC's most experienced and valued instructors to develop the nuts and bolts of the plan, including the key skills you need to work on and the drills and exercises to help you build them into your swing. These are the teachers you'll see in each section of the book and in the supplemental instruction videos at **golftec.com/parplan**. Together they have more than 40 years of professional teaching and instruction experience and have taught more than 50,000 lessons.

IMPROVEMENT CENTER DIRECTORY

See the list on page 186. For more information on GolfTEC locations, rates, programs and instructors, visit *golftec.com*.

ANDY HILTS

*Vice President of Instruction
and Education*

The architect of *The Par Plan*, Hilts is a graduate of the Professional Golf Management (PGM) program at Mississippi State University (1999), and taught over 11,000 lessons in his first seven years as an instructor. A PGA Master Professional in instruction, Hilts was named the Colorado PGA Section Teacher of the Year in 2005. Since then, he has trained and mentored more than 1,000 GolfTEC coaches worldwide. Hilts has also been a member of the Instruction Committee for the PGA of America since 2011 and is recognized as one of America's Best Young Teachers by *Golf Digest*. The Golf Range Association of America named Hilts one of the Top 50 Growth of the Game Teachers.

DOUG STRAWBRIDGE

*Houston Regional Manager
and Director of Instruction*

Strawbridge graduated from Mississippi State University's PGM program in 2002. He worked at Old Waverly Country Club in West Point, Miss., and Camelback Golf Club in Scottsdale, Ariz., before joining GolfTEC in 2002. During his 11-year career with GolfTEC, Strawbridge has worked with more than 1,500 students and taught in excess of 17,000 lessons. He has won numerous awards with GolfTEC, including Outstanding Achievement in Instruction nine times, Center Manager of the Year (2010), and Regional Manager of the Year (2012). In 2010, Strawbridge was a finalist for the South Texas PGA Section Teacher of the Year award.

PATRICK NUBER

Manager of Teaching Quality

Nuber also is a graduate of the PGM program at Mississippi State University (2004), joining GolfTEC the following year. He taught over 12,000 lessons in his first seven years with the company, winning GolfTEC's Outstanding Achievement in Instruction award four times. In 2006, Nuber became director of instruction for a new GolfTEC location in Golden, Colo., and achieved full PGA certified professional status in both instruction and general management in 2010. Currently, Nuber oversees the quality of instruction provided at over 160 improvement centers and by more than 500 certified personal coaches.

DAYS

1-5

DRIVE IT FARTHER AND STRAIGHTER

Better contact leads to greater accuracy and more distance, and you get it by swinging on the right path and with the correct angle of attack

LONG & STRAIGHT

A quick look at key PGA Tour driving averages:

289.1
PGA Tour Driving Distance (yds.)

60.7%
PGA Tour Fairways Hit Percentage

113.0
PGA Tour Clubhead Speed (mph)

167.2
PGA Tour Ball Speed (mph)

1.48
PGA Tour Smash Factor

2012 season
Source: PGATour.com

In your quest to post your best score ever 30 days from now, your goal in this section of the plan is to straighten your drives by working on the two main components of centered contact: swing path and angle of attack. Straighter drives lead to fewer penalty shots, which are probably a big part of your current scoring problem. Plus, every missed fairway is a chance to lose strokes. Eliminating these blunders will drop your handicap without your having to put a ton of effort into improving your technique.

That's not to say you won't be asked to make a few swing changes here and there. In this section you'll learn how to improve your contact with a series of easy at-range and in-home drills that will put you on the right swing path while helping you approach the ball on the correct, ascending angle. You'll also learn how to take an educated look at your driver to make sure it's helping you squeeze the most yards out of your motion. Attacking your driving game in these areas will not only help you hit more fairways and put you in better position to go for the green, it'll give you the distance you've been missing as well.

FIND THE FAIRWAY MORE OFTEN

Eliminating costly penalty strokes off the tee is step one on the path to lower scores

You crave distance, and why shouldn't you? A 285-yard drive is now near the bottom of the PGA Tour average distance list, and most of the guys you watch on TV can pound it over 300 yards without blinking an eye. That makes you and your 210-yard pokes seem a little puny in comparison, so your infatuation with distance is understandable.

Here's a secret, however: Driving the ball farther is more about improving contact than trying to swing out of your shoes. You'll find yourself deeper down the fairway when you learn how to catch the ball on your driver's sweet spot more consistently—even with the speed you have now. Distance *will* come, but developing the skills that produce a straight ballflight is more important to your scores than developing ones that only produce extra yards.

A lot of research has been performed over the years on the importance of keeping tee shots in play. Check the performance chart (*below*) that we use in our improvement centers to educate students about the relationship between fairways hit and scoring. The chart shows that in order to break par, you need to hit at least 10

fairways per round (about 71 percent). That's slightly less than what the best players on the PGA Tour can do. It also shows that hitting fewer fairways typically results in a higher score. More important, the performance chart gives you an idea of the number of times you need to put your tee ball safely in play in order to post a particular stroke total. For example, if you're trying to break 80, you need to hit somewhere in the neighborhood of eight fairways per round. If you're doing that already, yet still unable to break into the 70s, then you probably have a deficiency in one of the other key areas of your game. (You'll find out where as you assess your skills in different situations throughout this book.) On the other hand, if you find, after consulting the performance chart, that you're not hitting your ideal scoring number because you're hitting fewer than the required number of fairways, then you need to work on your tee-box technique stat.

Now, there are a lot of ways to hit more fairways without spending minute one working on your skills. You can aim up the left side of the fairway so that your fades end up in the short grass, or aim up the right side of the fairway if you tend to draw the ball.

You can throttle down to a 3-wood, the extra loft of which produces more backspin and, as a result, less shot curvature. (You'll learn more about these shortcuts in section 6.) If you're serious about improving, however, you're going to have to fix the reasons why your driver swing isn't putting the ball in play often enough.

TWO KEYS FOR BETTER DRIVING

Most amateur's driving problems have to do with inaccuracy, not a lack of distance. If you take a moment to reflect on your tee shots, you'll probably come to the realization that you've paid more in the price of penalty shots than you spent having to hit longer irons into most par-4 greens. Improving your accuracy means improving the quality of your contact, and you do it by focusing on two very important keys:

1. Swing Path You need to approach the ball from inside the target line, not from the outside.
2. Angle of Attack You need to approach the ball on a slightly ascending arc. You never want to hit overly down on the ball with a driver.

Most good drivers swing from the inside out and hit up on the ball. Poor drivers tend to swing from the outside in and hit down on the ball too much. With the correct angle and path, you're more likely to make contact on the sweet spot. That's where the greatest transfer of energy takes place, so shots struck here travel farther without your having to swing harder. That's why improving contact is so important—it simultaneously improves distance and direction.

PERFORMANCE CHART

golfTEC

GOAL SCORE	71	73	75	77	79	81	83	85	87	89	91	93	95
Fairways You Need to Hit Per Round	10	9.6	9.2	8.9	8.5	7.8	6.9	6.0	5.5	4.9	4.3	3.6	2.9

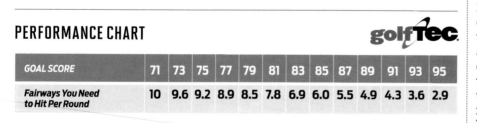

Discovering the number of fairways you need to hit to reach your scoring goal shows you how much—or how little—work you need to put into your driving game.

"Most amateur's driving problems have to do with inaccuracy, not a lack of distance."

LESSON IMPROVE YOUR SWING PATH

An outside-in approach has no place on the path to improvement

Modern ballflight-measuring technologies and the extensive use of launch monitors throughout the teaching community have led to several important discoveries over the past few years, the most important of which is that the angle of the clubface at impact (the amount it's square, open or closed relative to the target line) accounts for roughly 85 percent of your shot's starting direction, while the clubhead path relative to the face angle at impact contributes mostly to the curvature. This is the polar opposite of what was believed for the better part of four decades. That shouldn't, however, diminish path's role in your quest to hit straighter shots, or put into question why improving it was inserted as the first lesson in this book. Research shows that swing path is a major factor in how the ball curves. It works in tandem with face angle to determine how much your shots bend to the left or right. The greater the difference between your face and path angles, the more the ball will spin off line. Shots that initially start to the left or right of your target are one kind of problem; those that continue to curve to the left or right are another altogether.

A GAME OF OPPOSITES

Swing path problems among the amateur ranks typically take the form of too much outside-in action, or a swing that cuts across the ball from the outside (right of the target line) to the inside (left of the target line). Most teachers will agree that an outside-in path is more of a challenge to fix than an open clubface because it involves changing the golfer's misguided logic, reasoning and technique. Although it seems to make sense that, in order to stop the ball from going right, you need to swing more to the left, the exact opposite is true. Swinging more to the right negates left-to-right (slice) sidespin, and swinging more to the left only magnifies the curvature.

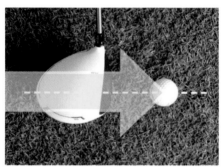

A square path (along the target line) produces minimal sidespin independent of face angle.

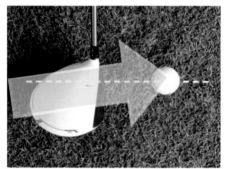

An outside-in path produces left-to-right (slice) sidespin, the amount of which is determined by how open the clubface is at impact relative to the path.

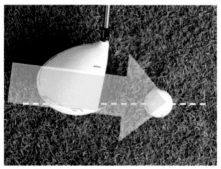

An inside-out path produces right-to-left (draw) sidespin. This is the ideal path to generate solid contact and max distance.

A *Golf Magazine* research project analyzing drives hit by a robot proved that an open clubface causes the ball to curve to the right even when struck with a square path (albeit left relative to where the face was pointing at impact). It also showed that the amount of slice increases when you pair an open clubface with an out-in path.

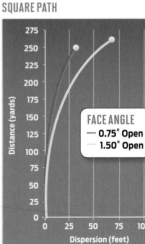

SQUARE PATH

FACE ANGLE
— 0.75° Open
— 1.50° Open

Distance (yards): 275, 250, 225, 200, 175, 150, 125, 100, 75, 50, 25, 0

Dispersion (feet): 0, 25, 50, 75, 100

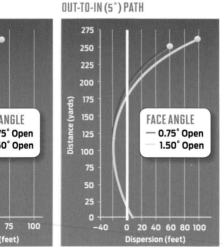

OUT-TO-IN (5°) PATH

FACE ANGLE
— 0.75° Open
— 1.50° Open

Distance (yards): 275, 250, 225, 200, 175, 150, 125, 100, 75, 50, 25, 0

Dispersion (feet): -40, 0, 20, 40, 60, 80, 100

ASSESSMENT CHECK YOUR SWING PATH

Use My Pro To Go to determine how much work you need to put into reshaping your swing

How do you know if you're cutting across the ball or striking it with the preferred inside-out approach? Instead of relying on feels or the untrained—yet good-intentioned—eyes of your playing partners, capture and analyze your swing using My Pro To Go for a clear picture of the quality of your swing path. To do it, film your swing from a down-target view following the guidelines presented on page 11. Capture it from address to finish, then follow the steps below.

Setup

Tap the My Swings button and launch the video. Select the line tool from the drawing menu and, using your finger, draw a line from the hosel through your belt buckle (*photo, above*). This is your swing plane line, which gives you a good idea about the path your clubhead is on as it moves into impact. Step the video forward frame by frame to the moment when the clubhead is at waist height in your downswing.

YES! Your Swing Is on Plane

If the clubhead is on or very close to the line, then you're on plane, which also means that you're tracing the appropriate swing path. Ideally, you want to match this position at the same point in your backswing, but it's not as critical. There are plenty of golfers who take the club back below or above plane, but only the great ones are on plane—and on the right path—in the downswing.

NO! Your Swing Is Above Plane

If the clubhead is significantly above the line, then you're above the ideal plane, which also means that your downswing is too steep (an error that creates an out-to-in path). You're making at least one of many errors that lead to an above-plane downswing. Regardless of how you're doing it, consult the drills on pages 22–23.

NO! Your Swing Is Below Plane

While it's okay to swing a *little* below plane, overdoing it comes with its own set of serious problems.

> ### Hear It From a Pro!
>
> **Upload your swing to My Pro To Go for an in-depth video analysis of your path and plane. Details at *myprotogo.com*.**
>
>

FIX SWING OUT TO THE RIGHT

Simple imagery is the strongest tool you own

I f someone asked you to shoot a free throw or toss a Frisbee, you wouldn't have too many problems getting the ball or disc to travel in the right direction. That's because you're used to tapping your natural athletic instincts when performing familiar tasks. That all seems to go away, however, when you wrap your hands around the grip of your driver. Suddenly, what should be a smooth athletic motion becomes a tangled mess of hard-fought positions and angles. Before you attempt the drills on the following pages (each of which is designed to help you *feel* the right moves instead of worrying about mechanics), it's important to understand that you can teach yourself to correctly swing on a slightly inside-out path by simply telling yourself to do so. If someone offered you $1 million dollars to make your next swing move more from the inside out than the outside in, you'd find a way to do it. You'd certainly be able to do it if you didn't care where the ball ended up, and that's the kind of mentality you need to adopt when working on your path issues as part of the plan. The immediate goal isn't your best drive ever. It's swinging more out to the right.

A SIMPLE SWING THOUGHT

Instead of coaching the positions that lead to an inside-out path, we find it's more effective to put a feeling or thought in players' minds to get them to react to the target like in the example above. Try this: When you're at address with a driver in your hand, imagine that you're standing in the batter's box on a baseball diamond. If the My Pro To Go analysis on the previous pages showed that your swing is above plane, then your current swing path is biased toward the third base line. Ideally, you want to swing over the pitcher's head and toward second base, but since bad habits are hard to break, you should feel like you're swinging toward the first baseman. Exaggerating the feel of

> **"You can teach yourself to correctly swing on a slightly inside path by simply telling yourself to do so."**

an inside-out path by trying to swing toward first base will help you find the happy—and correct—medium.

Another way to accomplish this is to set a target for your path. Instead of focusing on where you want the ball to land or the shape of the swing itself, focus on the back-inside quadrant of the ball at address (*photo, right*). Picture the center of the clubhead ramming smack into the heart of that quadrant. If you think about it hard enough, the image of a subtle inside-out arc through impact will be extraordinarily vivid.

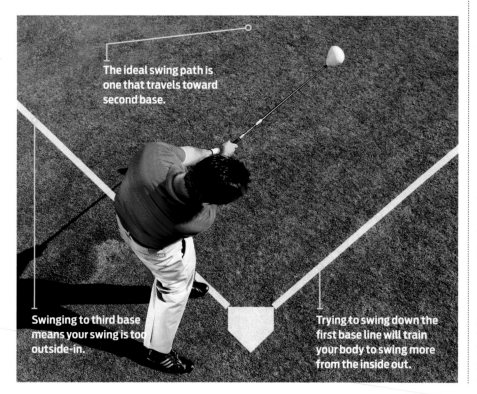

The ideal swing path is one that travels toward second base.

Swinging to third base means your swing is too outside-in.

Trying to swing down the first base line will train your body to swing more from the inside out.

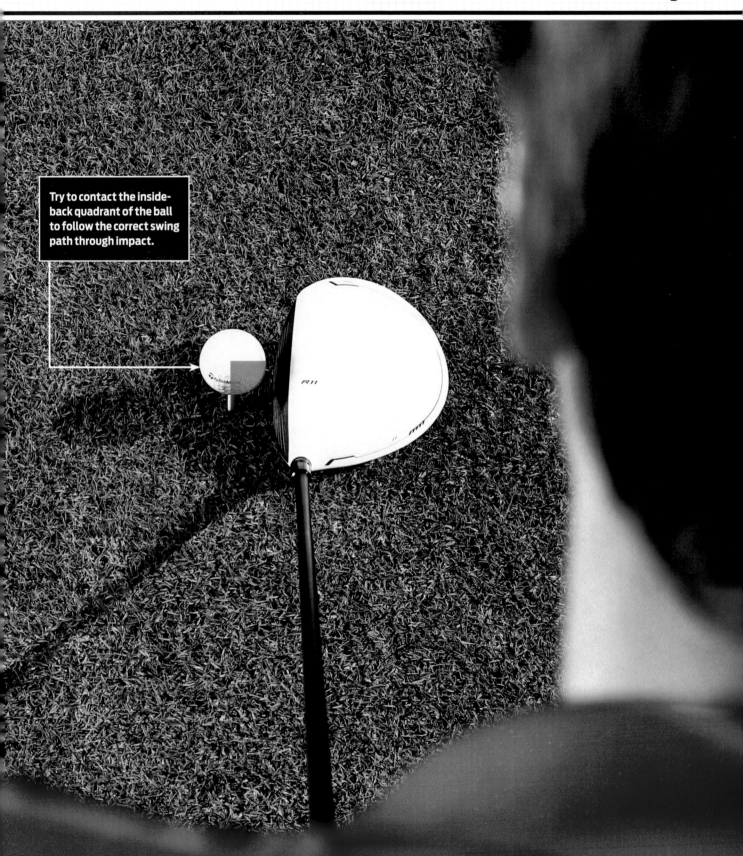

Try to contact the inside-back quadrant of the ball to follow the correct swing path through impact.

PRACTICE EASY WAYS TO IMPROVE YOUR SWING PATH

Use these drills to change your slice-prone outside-in motion into a power-packed inside attack

DRILL 1.1

Three-Tee Reroute Drill

When Days 1, 4 and 22
Where Practice facility
How Long One half-bucket (30 balls) each session (about 45 mins.)

HOW TO DO IT

Tee up a ball and lay your driver on the ground next to the tee (with the same amount of shaft length on both sides of the peg). Set a tee in the ground parallel with the top of the grip (call this Tee 1), and one 10 inches to the left of the handle (Tee 2) and another 10 inches to the right of the tip of the shaft (Tee 3). Angle Tees 2 and 3 so that they point at one another. A line drawn between them should bisect the shaft at about a 25 degree angle (*photo, below*), After you complete the setup, follow the steps at right.

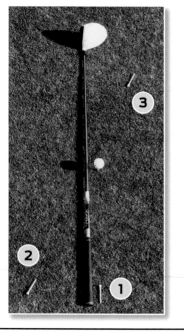

STEP 1 Grab your driver from off the ground and address the ball like normal. Your goal in this drill is to swing the clubhead over the tees in numerical order to groove the correct inside-out swing path.

STEP 2 Take the club back over Tee 1 (the one behind the top of the grip). If you're an over-the-top swinger, then you typically take the club back over Tee 2, so this might feel strange to you.

STEP 3 After transitioning from the top, swing the clubhead over Tee 2. This will give you the feel of the proper inside approach.

STEP 4 Continue through impact and move the clubhead over Tee 3 before swinging the club to the left and up into your finish.

IMPORTANT! Perform this drill slowly at first. Your goal is to correctly swing over the tees in order, not hit crushing drives. Only after you get comfortable with the drill should you increase the speed of your swing. (You'll know you're doing it correctly if you start seeing more of a draw look to your shots instead of your usual slice.) By the end of Day 5 you should be able to trace the correct path at full throttle.

BONUS LESSONS!
Watch videos of these drills at *golftec.com/parplan*.

DRILL 1.2
Advanced Reroute Drill

When Days 1, 7 and 17
Where Practice facility
How Long One half-bucket (30 balls) each session (about 25 mins.)

HOW TO DO IT
Tee up a ball and set an alignment stick (available at your local golf shop) on your target line and another one at a 10 degree angle off the first (*photo, above right*). Set a third stick along the line where your toes will be when you take your address. (This stick should run parallel to your target line.) Now, hit some drives at half pace. Your goal is to start the ball between the first two sticks. If you use an overly outside-in swing, the ball will start left of the first stick. If you overdo your new moves and swing too much from the inside out, the ball will start to the right of the second stick. Once you can consistently launch the ball between the two sticks with your 50 percent swing, go at it at full speed.

DRILL 1.3
Gravity Drop Drill

When Days 2 and 3
Where Home or office
How Long 20 reps each session (about 10 mins.)

KEY MOVE

1 2 3 4

HOW TO DO IT
Use a wedge for this drill. The shorter shaft length will ensure that you don't bang any walls or knock over your favorite lamp. Your goal here is to keep your shoulders from turning too early in your downswing, which is the number-one cause of an over-the-top, outside-in swing. Simply take your address, swing to the top of the backswing and stop. Without moving anything else, let your hands, arms and club drop down to about waist height. Don't pull down. Let the whole structure fall in response to gravity (hence the name of the drill). From there, swing through impact and into a full finish. Work on blending the stop-action into a fluid motion. Make sure to drop—don't let your shoulders turn.

TRY THIS! golfTEC

Use an Intermediate Target to Improve Your Path

Wayne Sciscio, PGA: GolfTEC—East Hanover, N.J.

A lot of golfers use an intermediate target to aim and align at address, but it can also help you visualize the ideal swing path when hitting a driver. The next time you practice, stand directly behind the ball and select an intermediate target roughly six feet in front of the ball and on your target line. Mark the intermediate target with a head cover. Take your address position, turn your head to the left and look down range. Notice how the head cover appears to lie significantly to the right of your actual target. (This alignment discrepancy is greatest with the driver because with it you stand the farthest distance away from the ball.) Since the ideal swing path is slightly inside-out relative to your target line, focus on swinging on a line slightly to the right of your intermediate target (i.e., the head cover). If you swing directly at your target, you'll produce a swing path that's too outside-in relative to your target line. It's an easy trick that really works. With enough practice, you'll start seeing the head cover even when it isn't there and get a clear picture of the appropriate path.

WINNING NUMBER 0.47

The average number (in degrees) skilled players (−5 to 5 handicap) swing inside-out relative to the target line through impact. Higher-handicap players (> 15) average 2.75 degrees—in the opposite direction (outside-in)!

Source: TaylorMade Golf

LESSON IMPROVE YOUR ANGLE OF ATTACK

Pair your new inside-out swing with an ascending attack to maximize tee shot accuracy and distance

I f all you had to do in order to improve your contact (and hit straighter and longer drives as a result) was to improve your swing path, you'd be well on your way to a better driving game and lower scores. But your swing moves in multiple dimensions, not just left or right of the target line. It also moves up and down to complete its circular route from the top of the backswing to your finish. A key segment of this circle is the point where your swing arc bottoms out and begins to rise up again down near the ball. When you're hitting an iron, you want the bottom of the arc (or low point) to occur after the ball. In other words, you want to hit down on the ball when it's in the fairway (more on that in section 5).

But since you tee the ball up when swinging your driver, you must make contact with the ball *after* it reaches its low point, or when it's on the ascent. If you hit down on the ball with a driver, you're going to pop it straight up and kill your distance every time.

THE CASE FOR HITTING UP

To hit the ball the farthest with your

Most research on launch-condition optimization shows that hitting up on the ball with the driver is ideal.

driver you need just the right balance between your ball speed, launch angle and spin rate. Ideally, you want to combine high launch with a low spin rate without sacrificing ball speed. The problem is that it's very difficult to increase your drives' launch angle without also increasing the spin rate, so simply using a more lofted driver (say, switching from 10.5 degrees of loft to 12 degrees) doesn't quite cut it because spin increases with clubhead loft (the reason why you can back up shots hit onto the green with your wedges but not with your 3-iron). Your only way out of this problem is to optimize your angle of attack by hitting slightly up on the ball.

Numerous studies have shown that optimizing your launch conditions (launch angle and spin rate) by hitting up on the ball the correct amount can increase the average recreational player's driving distance as much as 30 yards. The problem is that hitting up on the ball isn't something you should "try" to do. There isn't a person in the world who can adjust his or her swing

> ## "Hitting up on the ball the correct amount can increase driving distance by 30 yards."

on the fly to make sure they attack the ball on the correct angle every time. The best way to think about it is that your driver impacts the ball after it reaches the low point in its swing arc, which you can make happen with ease if you set up for an ascending strike in the first place. Getting into a fundamentally solid address position with a driver can help you avoid the errors that cause you to hit down on the ball when it's on a tee. One of the most common of these is coming over the top and swinging down on too steep a plane. That's why we worked on your swing path first—approaching the ball from inside the target line fuels the correct upward strike.

ALWAYS!
ASCENDING HIT
Launch-monitor research shows decisively that if you hit the ball on the upswing, you'll hit longer drives with less spin—without any increase in your swing speed. This ascending path creates the optimal launch angle and spin for most swing speeds because it increases club-to-ball energy transfer.

SOMETIMES
FLAT HIT
It's logical to assume that the clubhead travels parallel to the ground through contact. However, striking the ball this way can rob your drives of extra yards, especially if you're not a fast swinger, but it's better than hitting down on the ball too much.

NEVER!
DESCENDING HIT
When you hit down on the ball, even as little as 5 degrees, you have virtually no chance with a standard driver to achieve the launch angle and spin rate required for max distance, especially if your swing speed is 90 mph or less.

ASSESSMENT CHECK YOUR ANGLE OF ATTACK

Test your swing to see how much you're hitting up or—gulp!—down on the ball with your driver

It's critical to see if your current driver swing leads to an ascending strike on the ball. This very well may be an area that's costing you yards and accuracy off the tee. While the majority of skill assessments in this book involve the use of the My Pro To Go app, here you'll use the driver itself as the assessment tool. You'll need a dry-erase marker to complete this analysis.

A dry-erase marker is a great assessment tool.

HOW TO DO IT

Color in the face of your driver with the marker (use up-and-down strokes rather than side-to-side ones for a smoother application), then hit some drives. Stop after a few, then check the impact marks on the clubface using the guidelines below.

SECONDARY ANGLE OF ATTACK CHECKS

If you don't have a dry-erase marker handy or are unable to get to the course

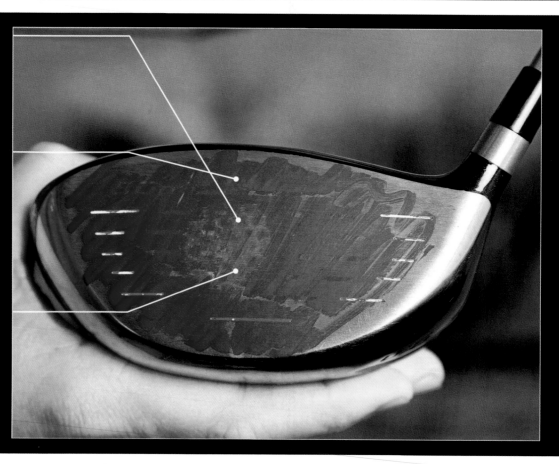

YES!
Impact marks in the center of the sweet spot are ideal. You're correctly hitting up on the ball and with a good swing path.

OK
Impact marks slightly above the sweet spot but on the centerline of the clubface are okay. Not great, but okay.

YES!
The more clearly you can see the dimples of the ball the better. This indicates a clean strike, not a glancing or brushing one.

to test your attack angle, there are clues all around you when you play that tell you if you're hitting down on the ball instead of up. Think back to your last round and ask yourself the following questions:

1. Did I break a lot of tees? Snapping pegs is a sign of too much downward action through impact. Watch the pros on TV—their tees often spin straight up into the air.

2. Did I leave any divots on the tee box? Taking a divot is good when you have an iron in your hands. Taking a divot when you're hitting driver is bad. Really bad.

3. Did I hit any pop-ups? It's a game of opposites sometimes, so if you're popping the ball up it means you're hitting down on it too much.

Tee-box divots are telltale signs of a steep angle of attack.

Broken tees also are indicators that you're contacting the ball before you reach the low point in your swing.

TRY THIS!

Tuck and Straighten for an Ascending Strike

Nick Clearwater, PGA: GolfTEC—Oak Brook, Ill.

Hitting drives with a minimal amount of downward strike is crucial to maximizing launch and distance. In addition to establishing the correct body angles when you make contact with the ball (*see next page*), straightening your legs and tucking your hips just before impact and into your follow-through keep the club from crashing downward. If you look closely enough, you'll see this straightening and tucking move all day long on the PGA Tour. To learn how to coordinate the correct motions, start by addressing a tee with no ball and make a swing at 50 percent speed. Don't swing all the way to the finish—end your swing at hip height in your follow-through with both arms and your left leg straight and with your shoulders tilted to the right. Once you can get into these positions consistently, start adding some speed to your swing and then try to incorporate the moves into longer and longer motions. You'll know if you're doing it correctly if you catch only the top of the tee. If your driver hits the ground, you need to exaggerate the straightening and tucking moves even further.

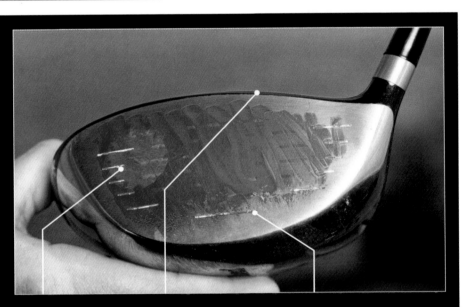

NO!
Impact marks away from the center indicate both a poor path and attack angle. Hitting the ball off the toe area is especially damaging to your distance potential.

NO!
Impact marks on the crown of the club are big-time indicators of a poor attack angle. Catching the ball here means you're swinging down on the ball way too much.

NO!
Marks left on the lower half of the face can mean that you're hitting up on the ball too much or trying to scoop it off the tee, but more often than not they're the result of an overly steep attack.

WINNING NUMBER 39

The average number (in degrees) PGA Tour players tilt their shoulders (right below left) at impact, a move that sets up an appropriate strike. Amateurs average only 31 degrees of shoulder tilt at impact.

Source: GolfTEC

FIX SET UP TO HIT UP

How to use your address position to ensure the proper ascending strike

Correctly hitting up into the ball boils down to positioning it after the low point of your driver swing (or positioning the low point of your driver swing behind the ball). While you might think this involves a lot of intricate in-swing maneuvers and positions, you can make it happen automatically by setting up to the ball correctly. Copy the positions at right and check them every once in a while in front of a mirror to make sure you don't fall back into bad setup habits and unwittingly set the foundation for a downward blow.

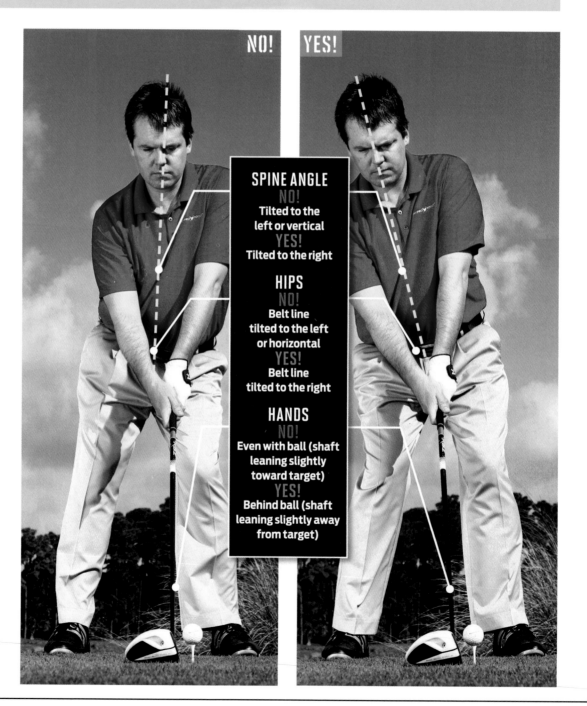

NO!   YES!

SPINE ANGLE
NO!
Tilted to the left or vertical
YES!
Tilted to the right

HIPS
NO!
Belt line tilted to the left or horizontal
YES!
Belt line tilted to the right

HANDS
NO!
Even with ball (shaft leaning slightly toward target)
YES!
Behind ball (shaft leaning slightly away from target)

PRACTICE EASY WAYS TO IMPROVE YOUR ATTACK ANGLE

Here's how to establish the foundation for hitting up on the ball and making the right kind of impact

DRILL 1.4

Double-Tee Drill

When Days 2, 4 and 13
Where Practice facility
How Long One half-bucket (30 balls) each session (about 25 mins.)

HOW TO DO IT

Tee up a ball and set a second peg in the ground 5 inches in front of it and on your target line. Tee the second peg higher, and try to drive the ball off the first tee and clip the second. Touch the tops of the tees, not the stems. This will help minimize your downward strike.

HIT THE BALL... ...THEN CLIP THIS TEE.

DRILL 1.5

Shoulder Tilt Creation Drill

When Days 3 and 8
Where Home or office
How Long Five times each session (about five mins.)

HOW TO DO IT

Bend forward into your golf posture and hold a club against your torso as shown. Tilt your spine to the right (away from the target) until you feel the clubshaft strike the inside of your left thigh. This gives you the right idea of how much tilt you need at address so that you can properly hit up on the ball at impact.

BONUS LESSONS!
Watch videos of these drills at *golftec.com/parplan.*

Start here.   Tilt like this.   Never tilt like this.

LESSON FINE-TUNE YOUR DRIVER FOR BETTER PERFORMANCE

The last piece of the driving puzzle is tweaking your club and shaft specs to create optimal launch

By the end of the first five days of the plan you should see marked improvement in your ability to swing up on the ball and on a slightly inside-out path. (Continue to use My Pro To Go to assess your technique, and don't forget to take advantage of the swing-upload service, offered to *The Par Plan* readers at a discount.) You should also see a noticeable improvement in your accuracy and maybe a few more yards of distance. The cold, hard truth, however, is that your swing can only do so much, especially if you're limited by improperly fit gear. While there's a chance that you can compensate for a driver that doesn't fit you, there's a greater possibility that you won't make the appropriate compensations consistently. A properly matched clubhead and shaft, however, give you the best opportunity to maximize your outcomes off the tee. If you bought your current driver straight off the rack, you can bet that you're wasting this opportunity.

In order to take your driving game as far as it can go, your first course of action is to spend an afternoon at your local retailer or fitting center (check the fitting programs at the GolfTEC improvement center near you as well—see directory, page 186) during the next 30 days and, at the very least, make a few swings on a launch monitor under the trained eye of a fitting professional. This will give you an idea of the very basic elements of what you're getting out of your swing. Launch monitors like Flight Scope and Trackman and the ones we use at every GolfTEC improvement center have become very powerful tools for fitting and instruction. They not only provide important information about how your tee ball flies through the air, but also how you're delivering the club into the ball and causing it to fly the way that it does. When you're on a launch monitor, you should know exactly what's being measured.

1. Launch Angle The initial angle on which the ball leaves the tee. Launch angle is affected by the loft built into the clubface, clubface angle at impact, and your angle of attack.

2. Spin Rate The number of revolutions per minute the ball makes as it spins backwards. Spin rate is

VOLUME
The larger the clubhead, the easier it is to hit.

FACE ANGLE
Adjustable drivers allow you to set the clubface square, open or closed.

C.G.
A low and deep center of gravity tends to launch the ball higher.

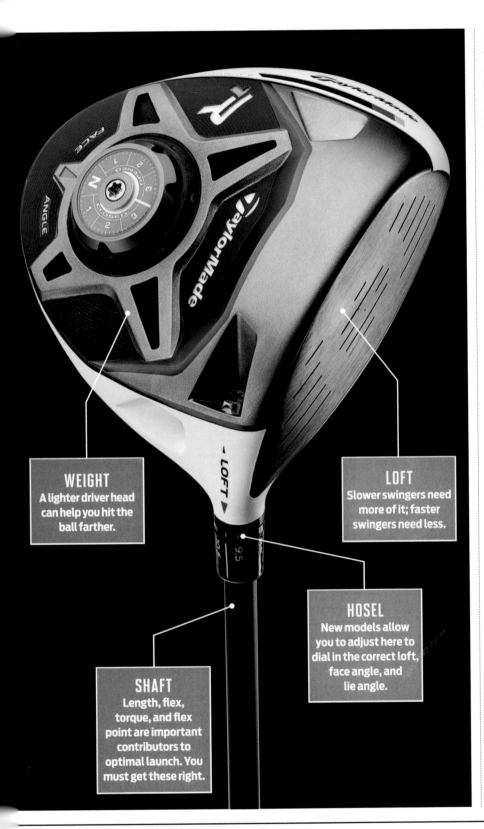

WEIGHT
A lighter driver head can help you hit the ball farther.

LOFT
Slower swingers need more of it; faster swingers need less.

HOSEL
New models allow you to adjust here to dial in the correct loft, face angle, and lie angle.

SHAFT
Length, flex, torque, and flex point are important contributors to optimal launch. You must get these right.

affected by the loft of the club, the weight of the shaft, the flex of the shaft, your angle of attack, clubface angle, and the type of ball you use. The longest drivers are typically those that produce the right amount of spin for their ball speed.

3. Clubhead Speed A measurement (in miles per hour) of how fast the club is moving at impact. Clubhead speed is affected by your physical strengths and weaknesses, club length, shaft flex, hand speed, swing technique and overall club weight.

4. Ball Speed Initial miles per hour at which the ball leaves the face at impact. Ball speed is affected by solidity of contact, clubhead speed, shaft flex, the spring-like effect of the clubface and the type of ball you use.

5. Smash Factor An efficiency rating based on your ball speed versus your clubhead speed. Smash factor determines how solidly you make contact with the ball. It's measured by dividing your ball speed by your clubhead speed. For example, if your club speed is 100 mph and your ball speed is 120, then your smash factor is 1.2. A perfectly efficient smash factor with a driver is 1.5.

The trick with any fitting is improving these numbers by determining the clubhead and shaft specifications that create what fitters call "optimal launch." For every clubhead speed and face angle combination there's an optimum launch condition (the perfect marriage of launch angle and spin) that gives you the max possible yards, and there's one for every golfer. As a rule, slower swings require higher launch angles and faster swings require lower launch angles. (Both swings require less spin that what you're probably producing right now.) In helping you find the perfect combination, your fitter may or may not tweak the specs listed here.

FIX JUDGE FOR YOURSELF

Look at your ballflight for clues to whether you're optimizing or limiting your launch conditions

Keep in mind that a fitting doesn't have to be time-consuming or expensive. In fact, you can use just your eyes to see if you're getting anywhere close to your optimal launch. Think back to your last practice session and ask yourself the following questions:

1. *Did my drives seem to travel too high or stop almost immediately after hitting the ground?* This could mean that your launch angle or spin rate is too high.

2. *Did my drives seem to travel too low or roll out excessively once they hit the ground?* This could mean that your launch angle or spin rate is too low.

Deciding on what's too high or too low without the help of a launch monitor is difficult, especially if you're a new or inexperienced player. If this

is the case, then think of optimal launch as the way water flows out of a hose when you're washing your car or watering your plants. When you point the hose straight up, the water streams out on a high arc and falls near your feet. When you point the hose straight out (parallel to the ground), the water shoots out with very little arc and doesn't travel very far unless you press your thumb against the nozzle. Hopefully you're starting to understand that too much or too little arc (i.e., launch) isn't the ideal situation. Hitting the ball too high negates roll (the distance the ball travels on the ground), while hitting the ball too low negates carry (the distance the ball flies through the air).

SET YOUR SIGHTS ON THE SHAFT

If you're like most golfers, the only thing you know about your shaft is its flex (regular, stiff, x-stiff). The

problem is that one manufacturer's R flex rating might be another's S, because industry-wide standards on flex simply don't exist. You're likely playing a driver with a flex (among other specifications) that's inappropriate for your swing. Swapping a new model for the one that randomly came with your driver can dramatically improve your launch conditions, accuracy, and distance. Here are four areas in which the shaft influences your ballflight:

1. WEIGHT

Today's driver shafts range in weight from 40 to 80 grams. Weight is a big deal because the lighter the shaft the more the ball will spin and vice versa. Plus, a lighter shaft is easier to handle for most players. Shaft weight also affects swing weight. A shaft that's too heavy for you will rob you of your feel for the clubhead when you swing.

PICTURE A PERFECT BALLFLIGHT

TOO HIGH

Too much launch, like the flow of water from a hose held straight up and down, limits the distance your drives can travel.

TOO LOW

Low launch, like the flow of water from a hose held parallel to the ground, negates distance by limiting carry.

JUST RIGHT

Optimal launch is created when you dial in the right gear specs for your swing and approach the ball on the upswing.

2. PROFILE

Tweaking this specification can help you more consistently square the clubface, launch the ball higher, spin it less, and swing your driver faster. It can stop you from doing all of those things as well. Just because a manufacturer says its shafts are tip-stiff doesn't mean they are. Stiff compared to what? All the other shafts they make? All the shafts on the market? The expertise of your fitter is invaluable in clearing the air when it comes to the shaft profile that best fits your swing.

3. FLEX

The flex of a shaft is a rating of its stiffness, which can help you get a better feel for the weight of the clubhead (thereby helping you control it from start to finish) or negate your feel altogether, especially if you're playing a shaft that's too stiff. The proper stiffness will also allow the shaft to load and unload at the proper time in your motion to maximize your distance and accuracy.

4. TORQUE

Torque is a measurement of a shaft's ability to resist twisting around its own axis (torsional stiffness). A good rule of thumb is that the stiffer and heavier the shaft, the lower the torque (and vice versa). As clubhead size has increased, torque has decreased in response to stop these 460cc-sized clubheads from rotating too much so you have a better chance of catching the ball with the face square.

FINAL ARGUMENTS

If you're one of those players who think that optimal launch, properly fit gear, and angle of attack aren't very important, check the example below. It's the story of two prominent PGA Tour players with identical swing speeds (124 miles per hour) and identical ball speeds (183.1 miles per hour). Both have swings with a very efficient smash factor of 1.48. Launch-monitor analyses of Player A's swing show that he hits up on the ball with his 7.5 degree driver about five degrees. Launch-monitor analyses of Player B's swing show that he hits down on the ball with his 7.5 degree driver about 3 degrees. The clubhead loft/swing combination of player A helps him outdrive player B by almost 20 yards and launch the ball almost 2 degrees higher at impact.

GOAL 1 *Improve Your Path*
Assess swing plane using My Pro To Go, then perform the Three-Tee Reroute, Advanced Reroute and Gravity Drop drills using the suggested schedule on page 184.

GOAL 2 *Improve Your Angle of Attack*
Check your impact marks, then perform the Double-Tee and Shoulder Tilt Creation drills using the suggested schedule on page 184.

GOAL 3 *Improve Your Equipment*
Have your swing analyzed on a launch monitor by a qualified fitting professional. Balance the cost of a driver upgrade with the perceived value of extra yards and accuracy that come with a proper fitting.

CHECK YOUR PROGRESS

Upload a video of your swing to My Pro To Go for a professional critique of your path and angle of attack (plus drills that target your weaknesses). Visit *golftec.com/parplan* to register for a 50 percent discount, available only to *The Par Plan* readers. Purchase lessons at *myprotogo.com*.

FITTINGS BY

Visit your local GolfTEC improvement center for a one-on-one clubfitting session to find the shaft and head specs that create optimal launch for your swing. Visit *golftec.com/parplan* to register for a 50 percent discount on a personal fitting.

A TALE OF TWO TOUR PROS

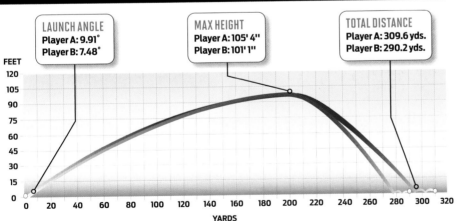

LAUNCH ANGLE
Player A: 9.91°
Player B: 7.48°

MAX HEIGHT
Player A: 105' 4"
Player B: 101' 1"

TOTAL DISTANCE
Player A: 309.6 yds.
Player B: 290.2 yds.

Player A's ascending angle of attack generates nearly 1,000 fewer rpm of spin than Player B's downward strike (2,381 rpm vs. 3,128 rpm). This extra backspin causes Player B's drives to reach their apex earlier and fall to the ground sooner with less roll.

DAYS
6—9

NEVER THREE-PUTT AGAIN

Get in touch with the keys that allow you to better control both the distance and direction of your putts so that you're always near the hole

When you miss putts, you probably chalk it up to a bad read or a bad starting direction. The real problem with the amateur putting game, however, is speed. While starting the ball left or right of your intended line or failing to get an accurate read of slope and break certainly contribute to your missing more putts than you should, failing to dial in the correct speed is more likely to blame for your three-putting, because poor speed control negates even the most accurate reads and strokes.

In this section you're going to first learn how to become much more adept at controlling speed on the greens. Then you'll work on improving your control of the putterface through impact. This combination will work wonders for your ability to roll the ball close enough to the hole to avoid a three-putt every time. You'll spend the last part of the section reviewing the factors that influence how the ball curves during its journey to the cup.

While it often takes time to work up the full-swing moves you need to hit better drives and iron shots, you can improve your putting in a heartbeat, but only if you work on the right things. Stick to the plan and you'll see a marked improvement at the end of 30 days.

SWEET ROLLS

A quick look at key PGA Tour putting averages:

37.7%
PGA Tour One-Putt Percentage

3.2%
PGA Tour Three-Putt Percentage

29.2
PGA Tour Putts Per Round

1.8
PGA Tour Putts Per Green In Regulation

2' 4"
PGA Tour Approach Putt Performance

2012 season
Source: PGATour.com

IT BEARS REPEATING: TWO PUTTS ARE BETTER THREE

There isn't a stroke more costly than a missed putt that you should have made

Golfers typically fall into two categories: those who take putting seriously and those who don't. Members of the first group are usually those who post decent scores even when their driving and iron games aren't functioning at full strength. Those in the second group need to be firing on all cylinders to shoot decent numbers, because when they're not, their putting skills aren't strong enough to carry them.

No matter how you slice it, the number of putts you take to complete your round will make up about 40 percent of your total score. You'll see deviations from this average from time to time, like when an accomplished player pairs hitting a lot of greens with uncontrollable three-putting, or when a less-skilled player chips in a few times or suddenly gets hot with his or her putter. For the most part, however, you can count on that 40 percent benchmark, which means that the less you putt the lower you'll score.

Check the GolfTEC performance chart for putting shown below. It tells you the maximum number of putts you can take and still shoot your goal score, based on the 40 percent rule. If you don't track your putts when you play, you should. It'll help you see where you stand with the performance standards and give you an idea of how much work you need to put in to your putting as you go through the plan. Even if your current putting stats are okay, it's never a bad idea to review the fundamentals for solid putting. If putting is a weak spot in your game, then this review is critical. Keep in mind that the goal of this section isn't to make you a one-putt machine. It's to limit your strokes to a maximum of two on every hole you play while increasing the likelihood of a one-putt. This is important because you probably can't continue to three-putt at the pace you are now and expect to shoot your goal score.

THREE KEYS FOR BETTER PUTTING

On the following pages you're going to learn how to improve your putting in three distinct areas: 1) speed control, 2) directional control, and 3) green reading. Better speed control is essential for getting the ball all the way to the hole and for handling slope and breaks in the green. You need directional control because putts that start off-line have almost zero chance of going in. Green reading acumen is needed to decipher the direction and speed you need to roll the ball so that it traces the correct arc to the hole in the event the putt breaks (which most putts do, especially if you're putting from more than three feet from the cup). You probably won't become an expert green reader in the next 30 days. (Experience is a necessary adjunct to better green reading.) You can, however, increase your skill in the areas of speed and directional control in a matter of hours, but only if you work on the right kinds of drills and practice the moves proven to result in better stroke mechanics. We have these teed up for you in the drill pages

> ## "You probably can't continue to three-putt at the pace you are now and expect to shoot your goal score."

in this section of the plan, as well as some quick-and-easy assessment methods using My Pro To Go to show you where in your motion your current technique is hurting you, and your chances of putting success, the most.

Better speed control will give you better directional control, which is why you'll work on this area of your putting game first. That's one of the secrets to your success in the plan: building skills that lead to the development of other ones. Gaining even a little more speed control will take your putting game farther than it has ever gone in the past.

PERFORMANCE CHART

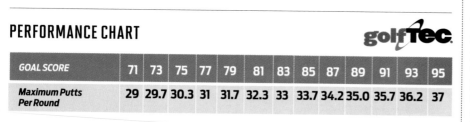

golfTEC

GOAL SCORE	71	73	75	77	79	81	83	85	87	89	91	93	95
Maximum Putts Per Round	29	29.7	30.3	31	31.7	32.3	33	33.7	34.2	35.0	35.7	36.2	37

Discovering the maximum number of putts you need to complete your round based on your goal score shows you how much—or how little—work you need to put into your putting.

LESSON IMPROVE YOUR SPEED CONTROL

It's a matter of tempo—not speed—to roll the ball the distance you need for the putt at hand

Putting is a unique—and very demanding—part of the game. When you're on the green, you suddenly go from selecting broad targets (a section of the fairway, an area of the green, etc.) to a very precise one (the hole),

Stroking the ball too softly causes it to come up short of the cup and break more than what you read into the putt.

Stroking the ball too hard causes it to roll past the cup and negate the break you read into the putt.

so you have to be exact in both your plan and execution. This goes for every putt you attempt and explains why mistakes made on the green (i.e., missing your targets) end up costing you extra strokes.

Although your putting stroke is small compared to the ones you make with your woods, irons and wedges, it involves many of the same features and gear considerations as your bigger motions, including path, arc, angle of attack, face angle and loft. So you can't ever take it for granted. That being said, putting eventually boils down to the simple act of swinging the putterhead back and through at a slow speed. That's why in this section we'll remove most of the clutter that comes from over-analysis by focusing on the big moves that exert the greatest influence on the quality of that little stroke of yours.

The first is speed control, which isn't necessarily something you do as much as it is something you develop by staying true to some key mechanics. Speed control not only involves the total distance the ball rolls after you strike it, but also how the ball reacts to the slope of the green as it travels toward the cup. This is the tricky part of speed control and the reason why you blow putts way past the hole immediately after coming up way short. Here are two very important putting facts:

1. The faster the ball rolls, *the less it will break.*

2. The slower the ball rolls, *the more it will break.*

When you get the speed of a given putt wrong, not only do you fail to roll the ball the correct distance, you fail to roll it in the right direction, because a ball that's rolling too fast will blow through the break, and a ball that's rolling too slow will drop below your intended line. The resultant miss looks like a directional or a green-reading

error, but it's actually a serious speed control miscue.

A MATTER OF CONSTANT SPEED

When golfers hit putts too far or short, they think of these misses as hitting the ball too hard or too soft. The word "hit" is a red flag. Hitting means you're actually applying or removing force, and that's a big-time putting error and at the root of most players' speed-control problems. *There's no hitting in putting.* The goal is getting the putterhead to meet the ball while traveling at a constant rate of speed. This sounds tricky, but the way you do it is by simply creating a pendulum-like feel in your stroke. In fact, step one is basically mimicking the swing of a pendulum when you putt.

Picture how a pendulum swings back and forth on a grandfather clock. It travels the same distance on both halves of the arc, which are in the same place on every swing. That creates constant speed at the moment the pendulum goes from swinging down to swinging up. This is what your putting stroke should look like. The secret to creating this look is to worry less about the pace part and more about the length. Just like the swing of a pendulum, you want your stroke to be even on both sides. Going from a long backstroke to a short through-stroke, or from a short backstroke to a much longer through-stroke, can cause havoc on your putting. In either scenario, you're trying to control the amount of force in your stroke at impact. Good putters dial it in by simply allowing the swing of the pendulum to do its thing. The length of your overall stroke (end of backstroke to end of through-stroke) can change, but it must always be even on both sides of the ball. Use longer—but even—strokes instead of more force to roll the ball faster and cover more ground on the green, and use shorter—but even—strokes instead of less force to roll the ball slower and cover less ground on the green.

ASSESSMENT GAUGE YOUR DISTANCE CONTROL
Use My Pro To Go to determine if you're putting with a pure pendulum motion

The fundamental key to producing a pendulum-like putting stroke (which you need to produce constant pace and proper speed control) is to match the length of your stroke on both sides of the ball. While it's almost certain that you can do this when you make a practice stroke or are just messing around in your living room, you need to find out how adept you are at doing it when you hit putts for real. The My Pro To Go app can help. Have a friend film your motion on a 15-foot putt from a face-on perspective following the guidelines on page 11. Capture your putting stroke from address to finish, then follow these steps.

SETUP
Tap the My Swings button and load the video, but before pressing Play, select the line tool from the drawing

NO!
Uneven (Accelerating) Putting Stroke

If the distance between the center line and your finish-stroke line is longer than the distance between the center line and your end-of-backstroke line, then your stroke is uneven and likely you accelerated during impact. (A shorter through-stroke than backstroke also is common. It's the result of a last-ditch move to slow the putterhead because you sensed that you took the putter back too far for the putt you're facing.) Because your stroke is uneven, it can't be a pendulum, and you'll have a difficult time producing constant speed.

menu in the upper right corner of the screen and use your finger to trace a line through the center of the ball. This line is the center point of your putting stroke (i.e., the bottom of your pendulum). Think of it as the midpoint between the end of your backstroke and the end of your through-stroke in a perfect pendulum motion.

STEP 1

Step the video forward to the point when your putterhead is transitioning from your backstroke to your forward-stroke and draw a line down the front of the putterface using the line tool.

STEP 2

Step the My Pro To Go video forward to your finish position (the moment your putterhead ceases to move forward). Draw a third line down the front of the putterface using the line tool, and examine the two end lines in relation to the center line using the checkpoints below.

"Match the length of your stroke on both sides of the ball."

Hear It From a Pro!

Upload your stroke to a My Pro To Go coach for an in-depth analysis of your putting motion and receive a lesson video and customized drills to accelerate your improvement in this section of the plan. Visit **myprotogo.com** for details.

YES!
Even (Pendulum) Putting Stroke

If the distance between the center line and your finish-stroke line is equal to the distance between the center line and your end-of-backstroke line, then your stroke is even. It also means that your stroke mimicked the action of a pendulum and maintained constant speed through impact. This is ideal. Once you can develop a stroke like this and repeat it consistently, you can adjust for distance by simply making your stroke longer or shorter (yet using the same tempo and keeping the length equal on both sides of the ball).

FIX FIND YOUR PERSONAL PUTTING TEMPO

It should take the same amount of time to complete every stroke you make

Developing a pendulum-like stroke is critical for speed control, but it's only the first part of a two-pronged solution. The second part is executing your pendulum stroke in a consistent time frame. That goes for short putts to long lags—every stroke you make should take the same amount of time to complete. Obviously, you'll have to move your putter at a slower rate of speed on short putts (because your stroke is smaller yet identical on both sides of the ball) and at a higher rate of speed for long putts (because your stroke is longer yet identical on both sides of the ball). As you draw out the seconds it takes you to make a short stroke (to match your time frame) and speed up so that a longer stroke lasts the same amount of time, you decrease and increase the force of your strike, giving you perfect distance control for putts of every length.

DIALING IN YOUR PERSONAL TEMPO

The amount of time that great putters use to actually make their stroke is extremely consistent. Using consistent tempo like this allows the athlete within you to sense the speed of your putts. Inconsistent tempo is a sure sign that you're trying to steer your putts. While it's impossible for an instructor to tell you what tempo—the pace of the "tick-tock" timing in your motion—you should use because it's highly personal, there's an easy way for you to get close.

Make three different strokes (*photo, above right*) and note the tempo of each motion. One of them will feel noticeably better for you than the rest. That's the stroke type you should use.

SHORT AND FAST
Putt a few balls with a short, quick stroke. The stroke length should be about the same as your stance width.

MEDIUM AND MEDIUM
Putt a few more balls with a medium-length stroke and medium tempo. The stroke should be a bit longer than your stance width.

LONG AND LANGUID
Now putt some balls with a long, slow stroke. The length should be well outside the width of your feet.

PRACTICING TEMPO

To really nail this section of your putting, download a metronome app to your smartphone and experiment with different speeds. Start at 75 beats per minute, then move up and down the dial. One of settings will feel better than the rest. Less than 65 beats per minute is getting a bit on the slow side and can lead to guiding the putter instead of swinging it. Faster than 85 beats per minute will likely make your stroke forced and punchy.

In addition to working with a metronome, try the following drill to practice putting using your personal pace while also grooving the movement of an even-length stroke: Set two tees about a foot from the ball on either side, just on the outside of your target line (so they won't interfere with your stroke). You can also perform this drill at home, using sofa pillows instead of tees. Practice taking the putterhead back and through, stopping at the back tee

COUNT "ONE"

Once you find your personal putting tempo, practice it by ending your backstroke on a hard count. Use two tees spaced equally apart to help you even out your stroke on both sides of the ball as you work on your tempo.

COUNT "TWO"

On your forward-stroke, time your motion so that you hit your finish position (and the second tee) on the next hard count. Keep practicing like this, timing the end of your backstroke and through-stroke to the beat of the hard count.

TRY THIS! golfTEC

Test Your Speed Control Prowess

Andrew Braley, PGA: GolfTEC—Nashville, Tenn.

Drills are great, but in the end you want to see if improvements in your putting tempo are helping you control the distance you roll the ball relative to your target. Here's how to gauge just how far you've come:

Find a flat section of the putting green and set tees in the ground at 5, 10 and 15 feet from the hole. Next, lay a club 18 inches past the hole. Grab three balls and putt each one from the tee closest to the hole. The goal is to make each putt, but at a minimum get the ball to stop somewhere between the hole and the club on the ground. If you make all three from 5 feet, move to the next tee at 10 feet. If you come up short or hit the club with any of the putts, start over. When you can roll all six putts from the first two distances either into the cup or into the safe zone behind the hole, move back to 15 feet. If you're successful at this distance, create a two-foot-wide "U" around the hole using three clubs, and repeat the drill. The goal is the same, and you must start over if any of your putts crash into the "U."

at the end of your backstroke and the forward tee at the conclusion of your through-stroke (*photos, above*). As you do this, count out a rhythm in your head. It can be as easy as "one, two." Count "one" as you reach the back tee and "two" as you reach the forward tee. You can use the "one, two" count, but it's best if you find your own timing phrase that allows you to establish a comfortable pace while also matching your stroke lengths. The late Payne Stewart used to say "Coca-Cola." Some students like to use "Let it-go," which is both a timing cue as well as a physical reminder to move the putter freely forward after the completion of the backstroke.

As with most putting fundamentals, there isn't a right tempo, just a right tempo for you. Even then, don't get hung up on trying to find the perfect one. Select a tempo that's comfortable and you'll be close enough to perfect. The key is the consistency of the overall timing of your stroke.

WINNING NUMBER 2.2

The number you get by dividing the average Tour backstroke time by the average Tour forward-stroke time (from the end of the backstroke to the finish). This 2-to-1 ratio creates perfect tempo.

Source: GolfTEC

PRACTICE EASY WAYS TO IMPROVE YOUR SPEED CONTROL

Use these three drills to change a herky-jerky motion into a flowing thing of beauty

DRILL 2.1

Gate Drill

When Days 7 and 15
Where Practice facility
How Long 20 balls each session
(about 15 mins.)

HOW TO DO IT

Sole your putterhead on the green and set a tee about a quarter inch from the toe and another a quarter inch from the heel, creating a gate just wide enough for your putterhead to pass through. Plop a ball down between the tees and make your stroke. Obviously, the goal is to hit the ball without hitting either tee. (Don't forget to make your stroke the same length on both sides of the gate while using your personal putting tempo.) Although this drill is commonly used to improve path, it's a good one for speed control because adding speed or removing it from your stroke often will cause you to move the putterhead off-line. So if you're hitting the tees, you could be having contact (and speed control) as well as path problems.

A CLEAN PASS
Putting through a gate will improve your ability to strike the ball with the center of the putterface. Consistent impact leads to consistent distances for all stroke lengths.

DRILL 2.2

Putt to the Fringe Drill

When Days 7 and 11
Where Practice facility
How Long Three reps each session
(about 20 mins)

HOW TO DO IT

Drop a dozen balls in the middle of a practice green. Putt in any direction and try to stop the first ball as close as possible to the fringe of the green. Rotate a few degrees to the left or right and roll the next ball, again trying to get it to stop close to the fringe. Continue to rotate and roll balls to the perimeter. Each putt should give you a different look, roll, break and distance, forcing you to adjust your speed control on the fly, which is a great asset to have when you're actually playing, because every putt will be different than the last. Once you can roll all of the balls to the fringe without coming up too short or rolling the ball too far, you're really starting to get a solid feel for putting speed.

Continuously roll putts to the fringe in different directions to learn how to adjust your putting speed on the fly.

DRILL 2.3

Look at the Hole Drill

When Days 9 and 24
Where Practice facility
How Long 20 balls each session
(about 15 mins.)

HOW TO DO IT

Set up for a straight 15-foot putt on the practice putting green and make your everyday stroke but while looking at the hole the entire time. (You can look down to make sure you set your putterhead properly behind the ball, but once you're settled in to your address position, shift your focus to the hole.) It's important that you rotate your head to look at the hole and not lift up and turn your body, as this will get you out of your putting posture. Putting while looking at the hole accomplishes a number of positive things. The first is that it shifts your attention from the ball to the target, which is far more important. Second, it allows your eyes to continually send signals to your brain to instruct your body to make the appropriate-length stroke. Finally, since you're less worried about impact and more concerned with the hole, you'll make a smoother, tension-free stroke, which is always a benefit.

BONUS LESSONS!

Watch videos of these drills at **golftec.com/parplan**.

BONUS FIX IMPROVE YOUR CONTACT
If you're still having speed issues, the problem is in your ability to make contact in the sweet spot

Putters are designed like any other golf club in that the center of the face is engineered for maximum energy transfer. If you strike the ball using any area other than the center, the putter will not only twist (causing the ball to start off-line), but it won't transfer all of the force you built up in your stroke to the ball and the putt will come up short. It's the same reason why shots struck near the heel and toe of your driver and irons don't travel as far as those that are hit in the center of the clubface. The real problem, however, is that a dead strike forces you to add speed to your next stroke even through your coming up short on the previous attempt had nothing to do with your stroke length or tempo. Poor contact is a speed-control killer, and if you're having problems with the drills and lessons presented thus far in this section of the plan, then you need to find out if you're making contact on the sweet spot or not.

HOW TO ASSESS CONTACT
To determine if poor contact is at the root of your speed-control issues, wrap a few rubber bands around the sides of your putter's sweet spot (*photo, right*). Stroke a few putts on the green (or in your home or office). If your current technique hinders you from making square contact, you'll know it in a second because the ball will rebound off the rubber bands and the contact will feel mushy at best. Putt at least a dozen balls this way, and if you're catching the bands on at least half of your attempts, you have serious contact issues, which are having a detrimental effect on your ability to control speed.

Putting with rubber bands wrapped around both sides of your putter's sweet spot is an easy way to see if your speed control issues are the result of poor contact and not poor tempo or stroke length.

THE CAUSE OF POOR CONTACT

While there are many ways to strike a putt poorly, the most common is with the shaft leaning away from the target at impact. Since you're supposed to address putts with the shaft straight up and down or even leaning slightly toward the target, getting it to lean away at impact means you're flipping the putterhead through the hitting zone with your hands. Overusing your hands like this means you're underusing your body, which, as you'll learn later in this section, is the correct way to power an on-line stroke.

MAINTAIN A FULCRUM

With the recent call to ban belly and long putters reaching a head in late 2012, the concept of fulcrum putting has become a hot topic. A fulcrum, as you know, establishes a stable and consistent pivot point. Anchoring a belly putter against your midsection or a long putter against your sternum creates a physical fulcrum, which makes it much easier to swing the putter back and through without your hands manipulating it off its natural arc. Even if you putt using conventional gear, you also employ a fulcrum, but more of a virtual one than a physical pivot point. Here's what we mean: If, at address, the shaft of your putter points at the left side of your torso, then it should point there the whole time, establishing a fulcrum in space (the point where the line extending from the grip hits your body). Flipping your hands points the shaft away from the left side of your torso, so you end up losing your fulcrum. When this happens, your strike pattern becomes inconsistent, and you'll have zero chance of accurately controlling speed.

NO! POOR CONTACT
Too much hand action through the ball causes you to lose your fulcrum, an error that leads to inconsistent strike patterns and poor distance control.

YES! SOLID CONTACT
Using your body instead of your hands to power your stroke creates a more balanced motion and increases the likelihood of making contact on your putter's sweet spot.

BONUS FIX IMPROVE YOUR CONTACT

Use more body than hands to put your speed-control issues to rest

The secret to eliminating excess hand action from your motion and improving your ability to make centered contact time and again is to train your shoulders to do the heavy lifting in your stroke. While you don't need your shoulders to work as much as they do in your full swing (we're talking tiny motions here), it's important that you view them as the engines of your putting stroke. Even if you're already producing decent contact and have a pretty good grasp of speed control, reviewing the following moves and positions will help solidify your motion so you can reach the improvement level you need to move on to the next section of the plan.

FIX

Rotate, Don't Rock

Moving your shoulders along, or parallel to, the target line seems like a good way to make a stroke, but in order to do this you need to rock your shoulders—right shoulder up in the backstroke and left shoulder up in the through-stroke (*top sequence, right*). All of this rocking makes it impossible to strike the ball squarely on a consistent basis. Instead, you'll catch the ball on the upswing on one stroke (adding too much loft to the putt) and on the downswing the next (taking too much loft off the putt).

The better way to motion your putter back and through is to rotate your shoulders, just like you do in your full swing. In the bottom sequence at right, you can see how turning like this points the shoulders slightly outside the target line on the backstroke and slightly inside the line on the through-stroke. This is ideal and will help you better maintain your fulcrum while also tracing a slight arc during your stroke.

ADDRESS

BACKSTROKE

FORWARD-STROKE

FIX
Remove the Angle in Your Wrists

When you're hitting your irons and woods, you want as much speed as possible. You add to your total speed by hinging and unhinging your wrists, which is why you address the ball with your wrists slightly cocked in the direction of your body. Since the last thing you want in your putting stroke is extra speed, and you've already learned that extra wrist action leads to inconsistent strikes, you need to deactivate your wrists at address so their motion is limited during your stroke. When you set up, position your hands on the handle so you create a straight line between the putter shaft and your forearms. If there's any angle between the shaft and your forearms, then your wrists are activated and free to move.

NO! Angle between both arms and the puttershaft.

YES! Straight line formed by the arms and the puttershaft.

FIX
Stop Your Flip

Even with proper shoulder rotation and the correct grip, you can still ruin your stroke by actively flipping your hands through impact. This is an error you need to eliminate from your game if you want to reach your scoring goal. Here's an easy drill to help train your wrists to remain quiet when you putt:

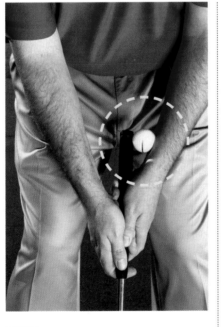

START
At address, wedge a golf ball between the inside of your left wrist and the grip of your putter. Don't pinch the ball—just let it rest there. Make your stroke.

NO! If the ball falls out of place when you make your stroke, you flipped the club at impact. Repeat until you can make your stroke without the ball dropping to the green.

YES! Keeping your hands quiet and using your shoulders to power your stroke from start to finish will keep the ball from dropping and allow you to make centered contact with the correct amount of loft.

LESSON IMPROVE YOUR DIRECTIONAL CONTROL

Starting the ball on your intended line sends your ability to sink putts through the roof

The old saying that the ball only knows what the clubface tells it to do is as true for putting as it is for any area of your game. Because the putterhead is moving at such a slow rate of speed (relative to the speed of your irons and woods when you're making full swings), face angle is king, contributing up to 95 percent of a putt's starting direction. Basically, you can expect any putt to start in the direction that the putterface is pointing when you make contact with the ball. If it's pointing left or right of your intended line, you're going to miss the putt regardless of your read or the quality of your stroke and tempo.

Problems with directional control don't just happen at the moment of impact. Setting up to putt with the face pointed in the wrong direction is just as damaging as overrotating the putterface during your stroke. Putterface aim is a critical part of putting that a lot of amateurs get wrong if only for the reason that they never learn what a square putterface looks like at address. In this section of the plan you're going to not only learn ways to strike the ball with a square putterface every time you make a stroke, but to address every putt with the putterface pointing down the line you've chosen after you make your read. Of course, you can still start putts off-line even when your putterface is square to your path if your path is wrong. Here's how to get everything flowing in the right direction so that missing putts from a makeable range becomes an anomaly, not the norm.

Fact: Putts start in the direction the putterface is pointing at impact.

ASSESSMENT TEST YOUR DIRECTIONAL CONTROL

Take two quick tests to gauge the severity of your putterface issues

Since even two degrees between square and open or closed can make a huge difference in your putts, you need to assess your skills using a results-based approach. The severity and consistency of bad outcomes using the exercises on this page will tell how much you need to put into improving your directional control when putting. You'll perform one of the assessments at your practice facility and the other in the comfort of your own home.

A chalk line doesn't lie when it comes to assessing your ability to start the ball on line.

ASSESSMENT 1 Stay on the Line

Run a chalk line on a flat part of the practice putting green. (If you don't have the tool to create a chalk line, get one. It's an invaluable practice aid that you'll use time and again in your quest for serious and lasting improvement.) Run the line for about a 10-foot putt, then roll a few balls. Your goal is to make each ball hug the chalk line from start to finish. (This is why it's important to find a perfectly flat section of the green.) If you can roll every ball perfectly down the line, then your face issues are minimal. If you have difficulty keeping your putts on the chalk line, then you have definite problems controlling either the putterface or your path. Take note of the side of line on which the majority of your putts roll. If they're falling to the left, you're closing the face or cutting across the ball. If they're falling to the right, you're opening the face or pushing the putts with a stroke that moves too much from inside the target line to the outside.

ASSESSMENT 2 Roll the Can

This drill will tell you how much you open or close the putterface relative to your path. This is important because hitting putts with a square putterface relative to the line can work even if your line is a little in-to-out or out-to-in. (You can adjust by aiming to the left or right, which a lot of golfers do anyway.) But as soon as you start mismatching face and path angles, you've got trouble.

Grab a soup or soda can and lay it on the ground perpendicular to your target line. Address the can like it's the ball, then make your putting stroke. If your putterhead is square relative to your target line at impact, the can will roll end over end. If it's open or closed relative to the line, the can will spin. If it spins on every attempt, then pay attention to the drills on pages 54 and 55. If you can roll the can straight every time, congratulations! This is not an easy task. If you have difficulty, set the putter next to the can and push it without taking a backstroke.

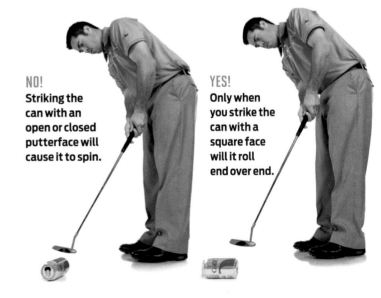

NO!
Striking the can with an open or closed putterface will cause it to spin.

YES!
Only when you strike the can with a square face will it roll end over end.

FIX MAKE SURE YOU'RE ALIGNED CORRECTLY

Work on your setup to point the putterface in the direction it should

Putting stances and address positions vary widely, even among the greatest putters in the game. There are very few hard-set rules. You can putt with an open, closed, or square stance. Most people assume that their stance is square when they address a putt, but more likely it's biased slightly to the left or the right. The trick is to know which type of setup you're using, because any discrepancy between how you think you're aligned and your actual alignment will cause one of the following to happen:

● *If you tend to aim to the right of where you think you're pointing the putterface,* you'll adjust by pulling across the ball and closing the putterface. You'll do this automatically as your mind interprets the difference between your aim point and the location of the target.

● *If you tend to aim to the left of where you think you're pointing the putterface,* you'll adjust by opening the face on the forward-stroke. Again, this is an automatic adjustment your body makes as it interprets your aim/target disconnect.

NO! Target

NO! Target

Golfers who aim too far left tend to compensate by opening the putterface during the stroke.

Golfers who aim too far right tend to compensate by trying to swing the putter to the left.

CHECK YOUR BODY LINES

The best way to check your aim is to attach a laser (available at your local golf shop) to your putterhead, aim at a target, then flip on the laser to see if you're pointing the putterface in the direction you intended. A simpler way is to have a friend check your alignment on a relatively short, flat putt. Although it's difficult to accurately determine where the putterface is aimed using the naked eye, he or she can look at the big picture and note where your body lines are pointing.

Have him or her check your forearms. If he or she can see your left forearm (from a down-target perspective), poking out above your right, the putterface is probably pointing right. If it's poking out below your right, then the face is likely pointing left.

MATCH YOUR EYES TO YOUR LINE

There are many great putters who set up to the ball with an open stance (Jack Nicklaus being the classic example), but the majority of players are better off setting everything (feet, hips, shoulders, etc.) square to the line, including the eyes. Setting your eyes level to the ground and parallel to your target line promotes a stroke that's stable, centered, and on plane. (It also makes it easier to establish and sustain a fulcrum for your motion.)

Setting your eyes level to the ground and parallel to your line is easy. You can nail this feature of your setup just by removing any excessive tilt in your neck and shoulders. The problem is losing your eye line when you go to take that final look at the target. A lot of golfers do this by lifting up and turning their head toward the aim point. That's a big-time no-no. Instead, give your target a final look by swiveling your head to the left. Rotate your head while tracing the line with your eyes (feel your right eye drop a little below your left). Rotate your head in the opposite direction to get your eyes focused back on the ball. Stop rotating when you feel that both eyes are the same distance from the ground. Now you're solid.

SEE THE LINE— LITERALLY

If you have trouble aligning to your target line, you can do what a lot of PGA Tour pros do and use a cheat. Draw a line on the ball across the equator. (You can buy a stencil at most pro shops). Once you've selected your line, point the line on the ball in the same direction. When you go to take your stance, simply set the putterface perpendicular to the line on the ball, and then your body lines perpendicular to the putterface. (The line on the ball also gives you a visual of the path your putter should travel on through impact.) The one caveat to doing this is that you need to point the line straight at your target or the cheat won't work. After you set the ball on the green, stand behind it to make sure the line is pointing in the correct direction.

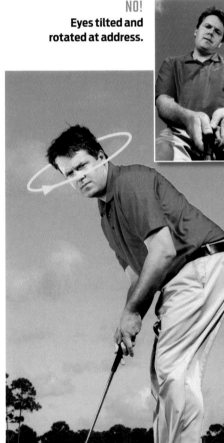

NO!
Eyes tilted and rotated at address.

YES!
Eyes level and square at address.

PRACTICE EASY WAYS TO IMPROVE DIRECTIONAL CONTROL

Work on the following drills to improve your ability to consistently start the ball on your chosen line

DRILL 2.4

Arm Hang Drill

When Day 9
Where Practice facility, home, or office
How Long Five minutes

HOW TO DO IT This one's easy. Take your address position to the side of a mirror and look for the following:

1. Parallel forearms Your right forearm should hide your left, and your forearms and puttershaft should form a straight line. Aligning your forearms like this gives you the best chance of swinging the putterhead down the proper line.

2. Eyes near the line While a lot of instruction dictates that you set your eyes near and parallel to the line, you don't have to be so precise. Just make sure your eyes are near the line. If you're standing too far away from the ball or too erect, you'll produce too much arc in your stroke and limit your ability to make a consistent strike. In any case, it's more important that your eyes are level to the ground and parallel to the line than anything else.

3. "Connected" arms The more you control your stroke with your body rather than your hands and arms, the greater your chances of centered contact and starting the ball on the line you've chosen. A good way to limit hand and arm action in addition to the ones already discussed is to set up so that your body and arms move as a single unit. If your arms are too far away from your body at address, they're free to manipulate the putterhead off-line during your stroke. Pinning your arms against your sides is equally damaging. Doing this fuels a rocking motion and actually negates the space your hands need to move the putterhead through the impact zone without your body getting in the way.

The best way to nail your arm position is to feel like only the top halves of both triceps are resting lightly against the sides of your torso. Connecting your arms to your body in this manner gives you the perfect blend of freedom and control in your arms and helps you engage your shoulders for your stroke.

NO!
Arms in too tight.

NO!
Arms out too far.

YES!
Arms hanging perfectly.

Don't just look at the hole (if it's indeed your target). Focus on a small spot at the back of the hole.

Practice Putting Like You're Playing

Kevin Kihslinger, PGA: GolfTEC—Milwaukee

Learning to aim the putterface correctly, trusting your line and starting the ball in the right direction are critical components to putting success, and you can only nail these essentials through dedicated putting practice. When you practice, always use a mark on the ball to help you aim your putter. A lot of players do this on the course, but very few use a mark when they're practicing. That's a problem because it's the inconsistency between play and practice that fails to properly train the eyes to see the line, thereby forcing you into a guessing game when it comes to knowing if you're set up properly or not and pointing the putterface in the direction you intend. Using a mark on the ball (it can be something as simple as a logo) can tell you if the putterface was square at impact. When you make solid contact, the ball will roll so purely that the mark or logo will blend into a solid line. That's a sign of putting success both when you practice and when you play.

DRILL 2.5

Small Target Drill

When Day 9
Where Practice facility
How Long 20 balls (about 15 mins.)

HOW TO DO IT Find a flat 15-footer on the practice green and start rolling putts. Do everything like normal, but before you pull the trigger, shift your focus from the hole (your target in this situation, since the putt is flat) to a small point at the back of the hole. Make it precise. Look for a blade of grass or a blemish on the white ring encircling the top of the cup. Forget about the hole, focus on that tiny spot, and roll the putt. Intensifying your aim like this will prep you for the limited margin of error that comes with putting when you're out on the course.

BONUS LESSONS!

Watch videos of these drills at *golftec.com/parplan.*

WINNING NUMBER 2.6

The number you get by dividing the average amateur backstroke time by the average amateur forward-stroke time. Amateurs make a slow backstroke then speed up through impact. Not good for distance control.

Source: GolfTEC

LESSON IMPROVE YOUR GREEN READING

All the clues to the break are out in the open—if you know where to look for them

Once you reach the point where you can make a consistent pendulum-like stroke and control the direction you roll putts, there's one final hill to climb to finish this section of the plan: improving your green reading. Your goal here isn't to become the best green reader you know, but simply a better one. If you can improve your slope-assessing skills to the point where you eliminate gross misreads and become proficient enough to at least always be in the ballpark, you can consider your work in this area a success. In the end, you want to get to the point where you completely eliminate three-putting from your game and, at the worst, two-putt every green. Getting in touch with and/or reviewing even the most basic of green-reading skills—paired with better speed and directional control—can make this somewhat daunting task a reality.

THE 7 KEY GREEN-READING CLUES

While a good course designer will do his best to challenge your green-reading abilities, he leaves obvious clues about how the ball will roll on different portions of the green. If you know what to look for, you'll know the general direction in which the green slopes even before you get behind your ball to assess your line.

Clue No. 1

Putts break toward the sun
The grass on the green grows all day, following the path of the sun. In the late afternoon, when the blades are at their longest, greens feature serious grain toward the setting sun. Your putts will break with the grain. This clue is especially important when playing on Bermuda grass.

Clue No. 2
Putts break away from hills
Don't forget the obvious. Putts will break away from greenside bumps, hills and rises, especially if they're extreme and/or close to your line of putt.

Clue No. 3
Putts break away from the clubhouse
While not always true, clubhouses are normally built on the highest point on the course. After all, if you build a castle you want everyone to see it. Look for home, and you'll know the general lay of the land—information that can come in handy when you can't tell exactly which way a putt falls.

Clue No. 4
Putts break toward collection areas
Those tightly mowed spots that your ball finds when you shortside the green are always below the level of the putting surface and usually house a drain at the lowest point. If you're putting near one of these areas, the break will favor that direction.

Clue No. 5
Fast greens break more
When you're on a slick putting surface, you need less force to roll the ball the same distance as on a slow green, and a ball that rolls slower is more affected by the break. The opposite happens on slow greens, where you end up generating extra speed to cover the right distance.

Clue No. 6
Putts break toward water
For obvious drainage reasons, greens will slope toward the nearest body of water. On oceanside courses, don't underestimate the natural roll of terrain toward the sea. Putts break especially hard toward the water here.

Clue No. 7
Putts break away from bunkers
The last thing a course designer—and especially the superintendent—wants is water draining into a bunker. More often than not, the green will slope away from sand to avoid extra bunker maintenance.

ASSESSMENT CHECK YOUR READS

This simple drill shows you if you tend to play too much break or too little

By applying the green-reading clues on the previous pages and using the experience you've already gained in your golfing career, you should be starting to get a good feel for speed and slope on most putting surfaces. Again, the goal is to eliminate your worst reads and slightly improve the good ones you're already making. To see if you're on the right track or still in need of some green-read fine-tuning, try the following assessment. It'll tell you immediately if you're overreading or underreading break.

STEP 1

Find a noticeably sloping area of the practice green and drop a few balls about 10 feet from the hole. Set a scorecard pencil in the ground at the point from which you'll roll putts. Go through your usual green-reading routine and mark the spot with a second pencil where your mind tells you need to start the ball in order for it to curve either to the left or right and into the cup. Next, run a string between the two pencils, tying each end high enough to allow your putts to roll under the string without any interference. The string is your start line.

Only by testing your reads will you know if you're looking at slope with the correct perspective.

YOUR READ WAS BAD.

YOUR READ WAS GOOD.

STEP 2

Roll putts using the keys for speed and directional control you learned in this section of the plan to start the ball on your chosen line (i.e., under the string). Roll about six balls and note where each one ends up in relation to the hole.

STEP 3

Assess your line. If most of the balls end up above the hole, then you've played too much break. If most of the balls end up below the hole, then you've played too little break (the typical amateur green-reading error).

STEP 4

If you overread the break, move the line closer to the hole, again using the clues you learned about slope to create a more accurate read. Move the line in the opposite direction if you underread the break. Bring the balls back to your starting point and roll them again. Assess your results like you did in step 3. This is a great exercise not only for verifying the quality of your reads, but for training your eyes to see exact amounts of break for different putts and what they look like. Experience plays a huge role in the green-reading picture, and the more you practice judging slope and assessing your results, the quicker you'll elevate your skill in this critical area of your putting game.

NOTE: Don't just use this exercise as an assessment. Perform it several times as you follow the 30-day plan as a means to improve your green-reading ability and to see how far you're progressing with your reads. Green reading is a difficult thing to teach and assess, but this drill does a good job of both.

FINAL THOUGHTS

Green reading is part science and part art form, and the players who are good at it treat it as such and, more importantly, give it the attention it deserves. Never take a read for granted or rush any read when you're on the course. This is the quick way to ruin any chance of shooting your best score ever. If you're still having difficulty nailing your reads after progressing through the plan, try the following savvy ways to get a better eye for the line.

1. Walk to the Green Ask your partner to drive the cart up and park it next to the putting surface while you walk the last 30 yards and take in the green complex as a whole, looking for the big-picture clues illustrated on pages 56 and 57. You won't get a sense for these details doing the ride-and-park routine.

2. Use Your Feet As you assess your line, walk back and forth behind your ball to get a feel for any slope. Use your feet to feel if the ground is rising or falling as you walk to the left and right. If, for example, your feet tell you the ground is rising as you walk to the right behind your ball, then it's a good bet that your ensuing putt is going to break left.

3. Make It an "Up-and-Down" Game The easiest type of slope to see is whether your putt will move uphill or downhill. This is a critical clue. If you're putting uphill, then you're going to stroke the ball with more force, and this will negate break. So read less break into uphill putts. If you're putting downhill, you're obviously not going to strike the ball as hard, so even though the putt is downhill, the ball will be rolling slower, meaning it will break more. When you're putting downhill, play more break.

GOAL 1 *Improve Your Speed Control*
Assess how good you are at making an even-length, pure pendulum stroke using My Pro To Go, then perform the Gate, Look at the Hole, and Putt From the Fringe drills using the suggested schedule on page 184.

GOAL 2 *Improve Directional Control*
Check your ability to strike putts with a square putterface and without moving the putterhead off-line using the stroke and setup keys on pages 50–54, then perform the Small Target and Arm Hang drills using the suggested schedule on page 184.

GOAL 3 *Improve Your Green Reading*
Practice reading putts and assessing your ability to judge slope using the exercise on the opposite page while continuing to familiarize yourself with green features that influence break.

CHECK YOUR PROGRESS

Decide if your stroke is where it needs to be for you to move on to the next section by uploading a video of your motion to My Pro To Go for a professional critique (plus drills that target your weaknesses). Visit *golftec.com/ parplan* to register for a 50 percent discount, available only to *The Par Plan* readers. Purchase lessons at *myprotogo.com*.

LESSONS BY golfTEC

For the ultimate experience, visit your local GolfTEC improvement center for a one-on-one lesson and hands-on instruction that guarantees lasting results. Visit *golftec.com* or consult the improvement center directory on pages 186–191.

SHORT & SWEET

A quick look at key PGA Tour wedge-shot averages:

15'10"

PGA Tour Proximity to Pin from 50–75 Yards

17'6"

PGA Tour Proximity to Pin from 75–100 Yards

25'1"

PGA Tour Proximity to Pin from 50–75 Yards (Rough)

25'11"

PGA Tour Proximity to Pin from 75–100 Yards

22.3%

PGA Tour Birdie or Better Percentage from < 125 Yards

2012 season
Source: PGATour.com

DAYS

10–13

TIGHTEN UP YOUR WEDGE SWING

Learn the easy way to dial in the right distance with each of your wedges for short shots that never leave the pin

The secret to hitting solid wedges is to strip your motion down to its roots and simply make a connected swing (arms and body moving in unison). You use the shortest clubs in your bag for these shots, and your swing should favor control over speed and power. Save the miles per hour for your driver, woods and irons and instead focus on making centered contact with the clubface pointing at your target. You'll find the advice you need to accomplish these tasks on the following pages, plus ways to adjust your motion to generate the right distance to any flag.

Your real goal in this section of the plan, however, is to eliminate your worst misses from 100 yards and in. Doing this will keep you in the game even if you don't knock down the pin on every attempt. Eradicating major wedge mishits (severely fat and thin shots) will save you at least two strokes a round. The good news is that you don't need a brand-new swing to keep these mistakes from happening. All you'll need are minor adjustments to position the low point of your wedge swing in the right spot and a few hours practicing how far to take the club back and through to dial in the right yardage.

AVOID THE BIG WEDGE MISS AT ALL COSTS

Eliminating shots that come up short or fly too far automatically makes you a better wedge player

Getting the ball on the green in regulation with one of your mid- or long irons is a great way to increase your chances of shooting a low score. But you can't expect to do this on every full swing from the fairway. When you have a wedge in your hands, however, you *should* expect to hit the green. After all, we're only talking about 60 to 100 yards of distance, and your wedges are the shortest and easiest clubs in your bag to control. Yet amateurs often fail to pounce on these shots, not only hitting the ball too far from the pin, but inexplicably missing the green altogether.

Take a look at the proximity-to-pin numbers from various distances among amateurs and pros (*chart, below*). The noticeable discrepancy between how close pros hit the ball to the pin from various short distances versus their amateur counterparts is partly fueled by the huge mistakes amateurs tend to make and good

players avoid at all costs. These are the fat shots on which you take so much turf that the resulting divots travel farther than the ball, and the ones on which you catch the ball on its equator with the leading edge of your wedge, sending it screaming through the green as it travels just a few feet off the ground. They also include the high cuts that balloon up into the air and land short and right of your target. The worst part about fat, thin, and ballooned shots from short range, in addition to the fact that they miss the putting surface from a distance you should be able to handle, is that they almost always find the most dangerous trouble spots around the green. It's not often the case that a poorly struck wedge leaves you with an easy chip or pitch to the pin. Instead, you're most often left to deal with a forced carry over a hazard (usually a bunker), an explosion shot from thick greenside rough, or a slick pitch from behind the green with the putting surface sloping away from you.

Missing the green from short range is a lost stroke. So is the one on your next swing because of the difficulty inherent in most greenside lies. Poor wedge shots, then, are as damaging to your score as an out-of-bounds drive or a three-putt.

HOW TO AVOID BIG MISSES

Like all shots, successful wedge approaches happen when you hit the ball in the right direction and the correct distance. When you worked on these issues in the driving section of this book you focused on path and angle of attack. These swing elements certainly apply to your wedge shots, but for the purposes of the plan we're going to concentrate on an additional feature of solid contact: low point. We touched briefly on low point in the discussions on angle of attack, but whereas with your driver you want to make contact with the ball after the clubhead reaches the low point of its swing arc, you want contact to happen before the clubhead reaches its low point when you're hitting one of your wedges. Moving the low point in your swing in front of the ball creates what instructors call "ball-first" impact, which is critical to hitting every club in your bag that's not a wood or a putter with a consistent strike pattern. Ball-first contact also helps generate the spin you need to produce the right kind of ballflight and to hold modern, fast greens. Catching the ball before catching the ground also helps you control distance. If you're taking too much turf before impact or, in the case of thin shots, not at all, you'll hit each of your wedges a certain distance with one swing and an entirely different distance the next. Consistent, quality strikes are the secret to wedge accuracy and distance control. While poor swing technique makes it difficult to position the low point in the right spot, you can find a way to do it by simply adjusting your setup and the way you use your hands when you swing.

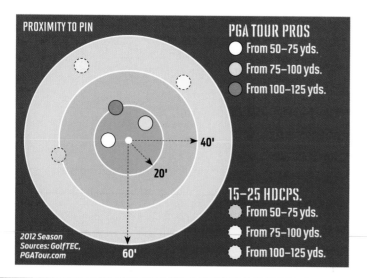

PROXIMITY TO PIN

PGA TOUR PROS
- From 50–75 yds.
- From 75–100 yds.
- From 100–125 yds.

40'

20'

60'

15–25 HDCPS.
- From 50–75 yds.
- From 75–100 yds.
- From 100–125 yds.

2012 Season
Sources: GolfTEC,
PGATour.com

"The noticeable discrepancy between how close pros hit the ball to the pin from various short distances versus their amateur counterparts is partly fueled by the huge mistakes amateurs tend to make and good players avoid at all costs."

LESSON CONTROL THE LOW POINT IN YOUR WEDGE SWING

Changing the way you use your hands and wrists when hitting short approach shots to the green can change your low point for the purest strikes possible

On every wedge swing (except the ones you make in a bunker), your goal is to hit the ball first and the ground second (which is as critical to the strike as the first part, because missing the ground creates thin contact and the type of shot that runs out of control through the green). A lot of players confuse ball-first contact with hitting down on the ball. This mistake in logic leads to overly steep downswings, slicing, and taking too much turf. You can use the same swing you use now. The only thing you need to work on as part of this plan is to move the low point in your swing forward so ball-first contact happens automatically.

THE ESSENCE OF PURE CONTACT

If the goal is to strike the ball before the clubhead reaches the low point in your swing, then the clubhead must come into impact on a descending arc (the exact opposite of what you need when hitting your driver). For a wedge or iron to move on a descending path to the ball, the shaft of the club must be leaning toward the target. It also means that your hands are ahead of the clubhead (as in closer to the target) at the point of impact. These are the telltale traits of pure contact and what you'll be looking for when you perform the assessment on the opposite page using My Pro To Go. Although your setup, backswing and downswing are important (you'll practice them a lot in this section), all that really matters is that you strike the ball with the shaft leaning toward the target. The sooner you learn how to lean the shaft forward, the quicker you'll advance in the plan.

NO! **A scooper's hands look like this: a flat right wrist and cupped left wrist.**

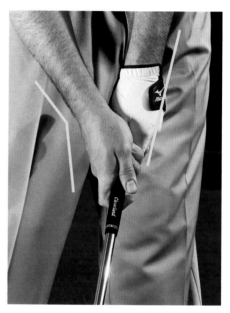

YES! **A player's hands look like this: a flat left wrist and cupped right wrist.**

HANDS AND SHAFT LEAN

Leaning the shaft away from the target with the hands behind the clubhead at impact is a typical amateur error that explains why this group struggles with wedge directional and distance control. It results from a preoccupation with getting the ball into the air at all costs. A history of low, bladed shots eventually forces players into the habit of trying to lift or scoop the ball off the turf. A history of fat shots creates "turf fear" in some players, which can also inspire scooping and lifting. Either way, flipping the club at the ball in an attempt to miss the turf or force the ball skyward immediately moves the low point in your swing backward. If the flip is severe enough, it causes the clubhead to bottom out too quickly and actually strike the ball on the upswing. Not good.

A lot of the moves that lead to a forward-leaning shaft involve the way you use your hands when you swing. Good wedge players strike the ball with their left wrist flat and their right wrist slightly cupped. Scoopers strike the ball with the exact opposite: a flat right wrist and a cupped left wrist. The drills in this section focus on helping you groove a wedge swing that relies less on your hands and more on your arms and body. You don't necessarily have to do anything special with your hands to get a flat left wrist and a cupped right wrist at impact. The secret is doing less with your hands so this arrangement happens on its own.

ASSESSMENT CHECK YOUR HAND ACTION

Use My Pro To Go to determine if you're scooping the ball or correctly hitting down before the clubhead reaches the low point in your swing

Determining the exact location of the low point in your wedge swing doesn't have to be a precise measurement. What's important is that it occur in front of the ball (good) or behind it (bad). You can locate the low point by focusing on what your hands are doing through the hitting zone, which you can easily see with the help of the My Pro To Go app. Have a friend film your full wedge swing from a face-on perspective following the guidelines on page 11. Capture your swing from address to finish (make sure you're hitting a ball on this one), then step the clip forward until the impact and look for the clues listed at right. Even the most untrained eye can spot the errors indicative of poor hand action and a misplaced low point.

> "You can locate the low point by focusing on what your hands are doing through the hitting zone."

MYPRO TOGO

Hear It From a Pro!

Upload a video of your wedge swing from both angles to a My Pro To Go coach for an in-depth analysis of your motion and receive a lesson video and customized drills to accelerate your improvement in this section of the plan. Visit *myprotogo.com* for details.

NO! LOW POINT TOO FAR BACK

You're striking the ball after your wedge has reached the low point of its arc if:

● The shaft is leaning away from the target. This exposes too much of the bounce on the bottom of the club, causing it to rebound off the turf and into the center of the ball.

● Your left wrist has a cupped look to it. This is the flip action that causes an ascending instead of a descending strike.

● Your left arm is slightly bent. This "chicken-wing" move is closely associated with an open clubface. It's also a common move following a flip of the clubhead.

YES! LOW POINT IN FRONT OF THE BALL

You're striking the ball before your wedge has reached the low point of its arc if:

● The shaft is leaning toward the target when you strike the ball.

● Your left wrist is flat. This ensures that your hands are leading the clubhead into impact and not flipping the clubhead at the ball.

● Your left arm is straight and extended. If you do it perfectly, the shaft and your left arm will form a straight line. Also, it should look like the back of your left elbow is pointing at your body and not at the target.

FIX TRY THE SLOW AND HOLD

Set the shaft lean you need at impact in the earlier sections of your swing, and then throttle down the speed to make sure it's there when you need it most

Since the secret to better wedge contact (an asset that will help you hit the ball straighter and produce consistent distances with each of your wedges) is to hit the ball first with the shaft leaning toward the target, it makes sense to set the proper impact position early in your backswing (a technique commonly referred to as "hinge and hold"). You're doing the setting part already by hinging your wrists early in your backswing. What you may not doing is the leaving-it-alone part. The reason you're losing the lean (which really is the angle created between your left arm and the shaft when you hinge your left wrist) is that you try to create too much speed and/or try to hit the ball too much with your right side. The right-side "hit" impulse is strong in most golfers, primarily because the majority of players are so right-hand-dominant. Hitting at the ball with your right hand is what reverses the hinge

in your left wrist and forces it to cup, a move that sends the clubhead racing in front of your hands and leans the shaft away from the target. Of course, this series of moves typically happens before impact, moving the low point of your swing behind (before) the ball.

Making a fast swing also is a natural impulse because, let's face it, most players are constantly on the lookout for more power and ways to stretch a few extra yards out of their clubs. In some cases, it's a smart move. For example, taking a more aggressive attitude with a driver or fairway wood can produce excellent results. But when it comes to your wedges, it's usually a bad idea. Swing too hard with a wedge and your body tends to slide out of position, resulting in poor contact or errant shots. Remember that wedge shots are all about accuracy; don't try to swing harder than 80 percent of your maximum pace. If that isn't enough to get you to

your target, take more club. You'll get better results by swinging easier.

TRACK YOUR PROGRESS

The assessment on page 67 should shed light on how adept you are at positioning the low point in your wedge swing ahead of the ball. This is an important indicator of how well you're progressing through this section of the plan as you work on the at-range and at-home drills and exercises. Use the My Pro To Go app every once in a while to see if your impact shaft lean is where it needs to be before moving on to section 4. But since the real goal of improving your wedge swing is to eliminate big misses while also getting the ball close enough to the pin for a one-putt, it's important to know if improvements in your technique are actually making this happen. The following exercise comes from Dr. Rick Jensen, a renowned performance coach and

DR. RICK JENSEN'S 11-BALL MEDIAN ASSESSMENT FOR WEDGE PLAY

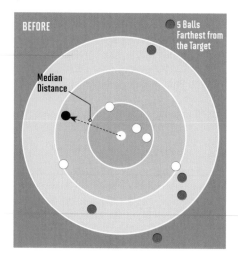

BEFORE
5 Balls Farthest from the Target
Median Distance

NO! WIDE DISPERSION
The greater your median distance from the target after 11 shots, the more you need to work on controlling the low point of your wedge swing.

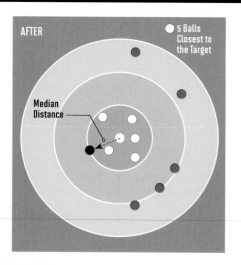

AFTER
5 Balls Closest to the Target
Median Distance

YES! TIGHT DISPERSION
Improvements in accuracy and distance control result in a shorter median distance in assessment and indicate that the plan is working.

"Swing too hard with a wedge and your body tends to slide out of position, resulting in poor contact or errant shots."

sports psychologist who helps the best players in the world get the most out of their games (*drrickjensen.com*). His 11-Ball Median Assessment (*illustrations, left*) is a great way to gauge your ability to hit more accurate wedge shots and put yourself in position to save a serious number of strokes as you fight to shoot your goal score.

To perform this assessment, find an empty area of the range where you can hit to a clear target and track where each ball lands. Hit 11 balls from any wedge distance (but all 11 balls from the same distance) to your target. When the coast is clear, walk out to

where the balls landed. (Ideally, you should perform this drill on an empty hole on the course with no other players around.) Pick up the five balls that are farthest from the target and then pick up the five closest. Mark the distance from the one remaining ball to your target. That's the median of your results, or what you can expect from your wedge swing on any given attempt from that distance. Of course, you want this median distance to be as short as possible, but that's not important right now. What is important is finding out where you stand when you begin the plan versus

where you stand at the end of 30 days. A marked improvement in this median (you'll perform this drill a few times; see schedule, page 184) means the work is paying off.

The 11-Ball Median Assessment should also tell you how you should go about selecting targets when you're out on the course. When you're facing a wedge approach, think of the typical dispersion pattern you get when performing the assessment and overlay it on the green. If any of the balls in that pattern would miss the green or find trouble, adjust your target for a wider margin of error.

PRACTICE EASY WAYS TO IMPROVE YOUR WEDGE IMPACT

Here's a succession of three drills to help you position the low point in your wedge swing where it needs to be for solid contact and better distance control

If you can hit without flipping using only your right arm, you're making big strides toward grooving a consistent and solid wedge swing.

DRILL 3.1

Left-Hand Only Drill

When Days 10 and 13
Where Practice facility
How Long 20 balls each session
(about 15 mins.)

HOW TO DO IT
Take your regular setup but with your right hand off the grip. Make smooth half swings using your left arm only (choke up on the handle) and try to catch the ball as crisply as you can. Do everything the same as in your regular swing, including rotating back and through, shifting your weight and hinging and unhinging your wrists (or wrist, in this situation). With only your left hand on the club it'll be difficult to lift or scoop the ball. Your left arm probably isn't developed enough swing-wise to actively flip the clubhead through impact. Get a feel for a balanced motion and your left wrist hinging and unhinging at an unhurried pace. Remember to rotate your left arm so you don't "chicken-wing."

Left-hand-only swings allow you to hit without scooping, because your left arm isn't strong enough to add the flip.

DRILL 3.2

Right-Hand Only Drill

When Days 10 and 13
Where Practice facility
How Long 20 balls each session
(about 15 mins.)

HOW TO DO IT
Once you finish your left-hand-only swings, make some with only your right hand on the handle and a slightly choked-up grip. Stopping the flip this time will be more difficult because your right hand is likely your dominant hand and responsible for the scoop action in your bad wedge swings. Again, make smooth half swings and try to catch the ball as crisply as possible (ball first, turf second). If you have difficulty performing this drill, focus on your right wrist. Try to retain the cup made when you hinged your wrists in your backswing all the way through impact (i.e., "hinge and hold"). Use more body than arms to negate your right-side hit impulse.

DRILL 3.3

Hinge and Hold

When Days 10 and 13
Where Practice facility
How Long 20 balls each session
(about 15 mins.)

HOW TO DO IT

Now that you've worked both hands individually (Drills 3.1 and 3.2), use this exercise to see if you can catch the ball crisply with both of them on the handle. Take your normal address position and normal hold, then make a half backswing. Stop when your left arm is parallel to the ground, and check that you've created a 90-degree angle between the clubshaft and your left arm. Also, make sure that your left wrist is flat and that your right wrist is slightly cupped. Do this a few times, then actually hit the ball (after stopping, holding, and checking the position of your left arm, wrists, and clubshaft in your backswing). The key here is to strike the ball without altering your wrist position and the angle between the clubshaft and your left arm. Have the feeling that you're making contact with the 90-degree angle still intact. Hinging and holding like this teaches you how to produce a forward-leaning shaft at impact. Once you get good at this drill, perform it without stopping at the end of your backswing.

Hinging the club in your backswing and holding on to the hinge in your downswing helps produce a forward-leaning shaft at impact.

BONUS LESSONS!

Watch videos of these drills at **golftec.com/parplan**.

TRY THIS! golfTEC

Control Your Low Point with Your Setup
Tim Sam, PGA: GolfTEC—Las Vegas

The address position you use to hit wedge shots greatly influences the consistency of your low point. If you're having difficulty controlling the low point even after performing the drills on this page, try making the following alterations in your setup.

1. **Use a narrower stance. Set your feet under the insides of your shoulders.** This will help you make a controlled swing.
2. **Set more of your weight over your left foot.** If I had to give a percentage, I'd say 60 percent of your weight should be over your front foot.
3. **Set your hands slightly forward,** tilting the shaft a few degrees toward the target. This is where you'll want to be at impact, too.
4. **Position the ball slightly left of center in your stance** to help create a forward-leaning shaft when you strike the ball.

In addition to these address-position changes, try to keep your head very still and stable while making a full turn and hinging your wrists as much as they can go. These are some of the keys that help produce the correct angle of descent.

WINNING NUMBER 2.5

The amount (in degrees) a PGA Tour player leans the shaft forward at impact when hitting an iron shot on average. Amateur players, on the other hand, average 0 degrees of shaft lean at impact when hitting an iron.

Source: GolfTEC

LESSON IMPROVE YOUR WEDGE-SHOT DISTANCE CONTROL

Change the speed of your swing by changing the length of your backswing to produce the right yardage time and again

Take the situation in which you're 75 yards from the green—the distance an average player hits his or her sand wedge. Getting the ball close in this situation is easy: put your best full swing on the ball. But what happens if you're 82 yards from the green, or 70? The obvious answer is to swing faster in the first situation and swing slower in the second, and in fact, that's correct. It's the *way* you swing faster or slower that's the hard part. Controlling speed to control distance isn't something you do by consciously speeding up or slowing down your motion. The moment you do that is the moment you disrupt the natural timing of your swing and increase the chances of catching the shot too fat or too thin.

There are only two reliable ways to control the speed in your swing and dial in the right distance for the shot you're facing: 1) making a longer backswing for more speed and 2) making a shorter backswing for less speed. The longer the swing arc, the more time the clubhead has to accelerate before impact. The shorter the swing arc, the less time the clubhead has to accelerate. So even though you're using speed to control distance, you're actually adding or removing yards by controlling the length of your swing.

The theory is similar to the one behind controlling speed with your putter. Remember the discussion about stroke length and creating constant speed by using a pendulum-like motion (page 38)? All of these elements apply to your wedge swing when you're trying to control distance. The goal is constant speed and, for the most part, producing equal swing lengths on both sides of the ball.

Regardless of how far you take the club back (longer for more speed and distance, shorter for less speed and distance), the trick is to follow through to at least the same height as your backswing. Stopping your follow-through (because you think cutting off the finish will cut off yards from the shot) increases the likelihood you'll decelerate. As it is in putting, deceleration is a killer. It leads to serious errors such as moving the low point too far back or too far forward, left wrist breakdown, and applying too much or too little body action.

ASSESSMENT CHECK YOUR SWING LENGTHS

Use My Pro To Go to determine if you're swinging long-to-short or short-to-long and producing constant speed at the moment of impact

Knowing how far you take the club back and through on a less-than-full swing sounds easy, but you'd be surprised just how difficult it is for even experienced players. Golf is a game of feel versus real—what feels short may actually be long and vice versa. The My Pro To Go app provides a crystal-clear picture of your ability to control swing length (and speed and distance as a result). Here's how:

Step 1 Have a friend capture, from a face-on perspective, the swing you'd use to hit the ball 10 yards shorter than your average sand wedge distance. Have him or her follow the guidelines on page 11, and capture the whole swing.

Step 2 Step the video forward to the end of your backswing. Select the line tool from the draw menu in the upper right-hand corner of the screen, and draw a line from your hands through the clubhead as shown.

Step 3 Step the video forward to your finish. Draw a line from your hands to the clubhead as you did in step 2. Compare the lines, which should give you a good idea about your ability to match swing lengths on a specialty wedge shot.

MY PRO TO GO
Hear It From a Pro!
Upload your wedge swing for an in-depth analysis of your ability to control swing length. Visit *myprotogo.com***.**

NO! Long-to-Short Wedge Swing

If your backswing is longer than your through-swing, then you've got serious problems. Although it makes sense that a shorter finish leads to shorter shots, mismatching swing lengths in this fashion limits your ability to create constant speed at impact—a must for every wedge swing you make, full or otherwise. Plus, going from long to short probably means you're trying to steer the ball instead of making solid contact before the low point.

YES! Shorter-to-Longer Wedge Swing

The goal is to match the length of your swing on both sides of the ball, but at the very least, always make your finish longer than your backswing, especially if you're trying to shorten your backswing to control the speed of your swing. Moving to a full finish is a good way to create constant speed through impact and avoid decelerating through the ball, a move that invariably leads to wrist breakdown and "flippy" impact.

FIX TURN YOUR WEDGE SWING INTO A CLOCK

The better you are at managing the length of your backswing to match the shot at hand, the closer you'll land the ball to the hole

Since the key to controlling distance through clubhead speed is controlling the length of your backswing, it's important to learn how to stop your clubhead at the right point for the shot you're facing. As you may have realized during the assessment on the previous page, controlling backswing length isn't as easy as it sounds. Good players, through talent and experience, instinctively know where the clubhead is at all points in their swing. Less-skilled golfers, and especially those without much experience, need a little help. While there are a number of ways to know how long a backswing you're making when you're on the course, the smartest thing to do is take a page from the lesson manual of *Golf Magazine* Top 100 Teacher Dave Pelz, the renowned short-game instructor, and use the image of a clock to help you nail the stopping point of your wedge backswing when you're at those tricky, in-between distances.

The way to do it is to imagine your left arm as the hour hand on a clock, with the 12 o'clock position above your head. If you use the same rhythm and

> **"Use the image of a clock to help you nail the stopping point of your wedge swing when you're at those tricky, in-between distances."**

Swing your arms like the hands on a clock to nail specific backswing lengths.

10:00

You've got to know the exact yardage to hit a precise wedge shot.

Invest in a range finder to get the accuracy you need to hit pinpoint wedge shots.

a slightly longer follow-through, your wedge-shot distances will increase as you lengthen your backswing from the 7:30 to 9:00 and 10:30 positions. This distance-control system guards against the biggest short-game killer: deceleration. It also creates three repeatable distances for each wedge you carry. (More on that on pages 76 and 77.) It's easy to do if you forget about the clubhead and think only about your left arm. Get your left arm to the hour on the clock that matches the length of swing you wish to make and you'll be set.

NAIL YOUR YARDAGES

All this talk about controlling your backswing to help you hit the ball various distances with each of your wedges is important stuff. Applying what you've learned thus far will immediately make you a better wedge player without your having to make serious alterations in your current motion. It won't mean much for your overall score, however, if you fail to get an accurate read of the yardage

you need on your wedge shots. A lot of recreational players get just a casual read of distance (if any), making little effort to check the yardage other than looking for the nearest sprinkler head or pacing off a few steps from a marked spot in the yardage book or course guide. Truth is, the difference between 75 yards and 72 yards is huge—the equivalent of an extra nine feet of putt if and when you pull off the shot. Lackadaisical yardage assessment, in this situation, will probably cost you a stroke, maybe two.

Make a thorough yardage book for your home course, or the one you play most frequently. Even better, invest a few hundred dollars in a quality range finder (available at any pro shop). These convenient, legal and easy-to-use devices are your best bet for learning exactly how far from the flagstick (or any other object) your ball lies on every shot. An accurate assessment of the yardage is step one in hitting a successful scoring shot and controlling wedge distance like a seasoned professional.

TRY THIS!

Connect Your Arms to Your Body for Expert Distance Control

Erik Wait, PGA: GolfTEC—Dallas

Golfers who rely too much on their arms to swing the club have a tendency to be erratic with their wedge distances. Swinging your arms out of rhythm with your body leads to inconsistencies in acceleration, speed and tempo. Learning to control your arms throughout your swing by connecting them to your body's turn will help you to better dial in your wedge distances.

A great way to learn how to connect your arms to your body's turn is to hit practice balls with a towel tucked under both armpits. Hold the towel in place with your triceps. Start with one-quarter swings using your sand wedge without actually hitting a ball. As you get comfortable with the feeling of your arms staying connected to your body, add a ball to the drill and gradually increase swing length and speed. With your arms and body working together throughout your swing you'll create a consistent speed pattern through impact. This will elevate your ability to fine-tune your wedge distances to a very high level.

WINNING NUMBER 84

The amount (in degrees) a Tour player rotates his shoulders when hitting a wedge. With an iron, this turn increases to 89 degrees. The discrepancy is a result of the fact that Tour players bend over at address four degrees more with a wedge than an iron. More bend means less turn.

Source: GolfTEC

PRACTICE EASY WAYS TO IMPROVE YOUR DISTANCE CONTROL

Try these drills on for size to create a swing in which your body and arms move in unison and allows you are able to manage the length of your backswing for pinpoint distance control

DRILL 3.4

Punisher Drill

When Days 12 and 16
Where Practice facility
How Long 20 balls each session (about 15 mins.)

HOW TO DO IT

You'll need your pitching wedge and a second iron for this drill. Set the hosel of the second club against bottom of the grip on your pitching wedge, and squeeze the two together using your normal hold (*photo, near right*). As you take your setup, sole the clubhead behind the ball and set the shaft of the second club against the left side of your torso (*photo, far right*). Make a smooth half swing at half speed and try to catch the ball with the shaft leaning forward at impact. You won't be able to make much of a follow-though, so be sure to stop your swing short and swing at half speed.

NO!
If you allow the clubhead to pass your hands and lose shaft lean, the shaft of the second club will strike the left side of your torso. Hence the name "Punisher Drill."

YES!
You know you're doing it right if the shaft of the second club doesn't hit you and instead moves forward of the left side of your torso along with your hands and arms.

DRILL 3.5

Hold and Evaluate Drill

When 12 and 21
Where Practice facility
How Long 20 balls each session (about 15 mins.)

HOW TO DO IT

Sometimes you can learn more by looking at yourself than where the ball goes. This is the goal of the Hold and Evaluate Drill. Make your best full swing with a sand wedge, and instead of focusing only on ballflight, hold your finish for a solid five seconds. Compare the quality of the shot with the quality of your finish. Do your arms feel connected to your body? Have you rotated you body all the way so that your belt buckle is facing the target? Did you make a long enough follow-through? Most important, are you in balance? This is a critical feature of your finish. If you can't hold your finish position in balance, then it's almost certain that you failed to accelerate smoothly into impact. If both your results and finish position are poor, work on making a more grounded swing. Fight the urge to lift your right heel in your downswing and try to swing more flat-footed.

BALANCE
You should be able to hold your finish position without swaying for at least five seconds.

DRILL 3.6

Mirror Drill

When Days 12 and 19
Where Home or office
How Long 18 swings each session (about 15 mins.)

Check your backswing length in a mirror to groove the feel of shorter and longer swing lengths.

HOW TO DO IT

Find a full-length mirror that allows you to make unimpeded swings directly in front of it. Grab a dry-erase marker or some masking tape and mark the 7:30, 9:00 and 10:30 left-arm positions in your backswing and the 1:30 right-arm position in your forward-swing on the mirror. Address an imaginary ball and try to produce the three backswing lengths in succession. After the completion of each backswing, look up and see how close you came to hitting the actual number on the "clock" and use the information to make the necessary adjustments on your next attempt in the event you came up too short or exceeded the desired backswing length. Try to hit each backswing position six times in each session. With a little practice, you'll learn how to stop your swing at the right spot on the course without thinking, using the feels of longer and shorter backswing lengths you grooved during this important drill. After stopping to check your backswing position, swing forward to a full finish, looking up to see you moved all the way to the tape marking the 1:30 through-swing position.

BONUS LESSONS!
Watch videos of these drills at *golftec.com/parplan*.

BONUS LESSON FINE-TUNE YOUR WEDGE DISTANCES

Mix and match backswing and finish positions to build an arsenal of ultraprecise wedge shots

There's no better method to control distance than Dave Pelz's clock positions. Nailing each backswing length while swinging through to a full finish gives you three distinct distances for each of your wedges, creating an arsenal of 9 shots if you carry three wedges and 12 distinct shots if you carry four. Pelz published the expected yardage for each club/swing combination in the August 2006 issue of *Golf Magazine*.

	60° LW	55° SW	49° PW
7:30 Swing	35 yds.	43 yds.	50 yds.
9:00 Swing	53 yds.	64 yds.	75 yds.
10:30 Swing	70 yds.	85 yds.	100 yds.

Of course, your yardages will be a little different, which is why you'll spend one range session during the plan hitting 5 balls with each wedge and each swing and create a log of distances. Use the average distance of 10 balls for each swing/wedge combination (*table, opposite page*).

Once you're comfortable with these motions, experiment by combining the three backswing lengths with two additional through-swing lengths. Try stopping your swing at the 4:30 and 3:00 positions on the target side of the ball (this time using your right arm as the big hand on the clock). Although you'll always get the best results making your through-swing longer than your backswing (or at least even) to avoid decelerating through impact, there's no harm in seeing what a shorter finish will give you in terms of distance and trajectory as long as you plan for it and keep your clubhead moving at a constant rate of speed.

The shortest backswing in your arsenal is when your left arm reaches 7:30 on the dial.

Stopping your backswing at 9:00 takes about 25 percent off the shot.

Stopping your swing here is risky, but can be helpful in producing more spin.

A great finish for shorter yardages and keeping the ball below the wind.

10:30

A full backswing stops at 10:30. Anything more and you'll disrupt your timing.

1:30

Higher and longer finishes produce higher and longer shots.

Add these swings to your log as well. With just a little bit of effort, you can develop 36 repeatable swings if you're a four-wedge player. With that kind of variety, there isn't a yardage the course can throw at you for which you won't be prepared.

How to Create a Wedge Distance Log

Spend one day during the plan (check schedule, page 184) hitting each of your wedges using the nine swings listed below. Hit five balls with each wedge/swing combination and enter the averages below. (Note the trajectory you get with each combination as well.) After all 180 balls (if you carry four wedges), you'll have a complete guide to nailing any distance you'll see on the course. Pay attention to overlaps—often you'll be able to generate the same distance with several wedge/swing combinations, giving you even more options to dial in the perfect distance.

	LW	SW	GW	PW
7:30–7:30	___	___	___	___
7:30–9:00	___	___	___	___
7:30–10:30	___	___	___	___
9:00–7:30*	___	___	___	___
9:00–9:00	___	___	___	___
9:00–10:30	___	___	___	___
10:30–7:30*	___	___	___	___
10:30–9:00*	___	___	___	___
10:30–10:30	___	___	___	___

Long-to-short swings for trajectory control

GOAL 1 *Control the Low Point*
Assess your impact position using My Pro To Go to make sure your swing is bottoming out in front of the ball, then perform the Left-Hand Only, Right-Hand-Only and Hinge and Hold drills using the suggested schedule on page 184.

GOAL 2 *Improve Your Wedge-Shot Distance Control*
Assess your ability to make a longer through-swing so that you avoid deceleration, then perform the Punisher, Hold and Evaluate, and Mirror drills using the suggested schedule on page 184. Create a wedge-shot arsenal by combining different backswing and through-swings and logging the results.

CHECK YOUR PROGRESS

Decide if your low point and ability to control distance are up to snuff by uploading a video of your swing to My Pro To Go for a professional critique (plus drills that target your weaknesses). Visit *golftec.com/parplan* to register for a 50 percent discount, available only to *The Par Plan* readers. Purchase lessons at *myprotogo.com*.

LESSONS BY golfTEC

For the ultimate experience, visit your local GolfTEC improvement center for a one-on-one lesson and hands-on instruction that guarantees success. Visit *golftec.com* or consult the improvement center directory on pages 186–191.

DAYS
14—17

THE SECRETS TO SCRAMBLING

These tried-and-true keys for expert chipping and pitching will stop your scores from ballooning when you miss greens

CHIPS & DIPS

A quick look at key PGA Tour chip- and pitch-shot averages:

56.2%
PGA Tour Scrambling

84.6%
PGA Tour Scrambling from < 10 Yards

26.9%
PGA Tour Scrambling from > 30 Yards

3' 7"
PGA Tour Proximity to Pin from < 10 Yards

7' 0"
PGA Tour Proximity to Pin from 10–20 Yards

*2012 season
Source: PGATour.com*

It's very rare for a skilled golfer to miss wildly when pitching or chipping. After all, these are short shots made with even shorter swings with the target in clear view. If a Tour pro fails to get the ball close from around the green, then he experienced a major malfunction that won't likely be repeated soon. Amateurs, on the other hand, miss short shots all the time. It's mostly a technique issue, but a lack of confidence also figures into the equation; you don't trust your technique, so you end up making a cautious stroke that more often than not puts you in a tough putting situation.

In this section of the plan, you'll learn how to improve your chip and pitch skills to a level where you'll execute these shots on the course without even thinking. Then you'll learn how to expand your short-shot arsenal by familiarizing yourself with three primary short-game clubs and the amount of carry and roll you get with each one.

Ultimately, you'll learn how to adjust your setup and swing to fine-tune trajectory, speeds and distance to match very specific short-shot situations. That's when you'll start to consistently get the ball close and earn more than your fair share of up-and-downs.

THE UPSIDE OF GETTING UP-AND-DOWN

There's no easier way to save a stroke than hitting a pitch or chip shot close

The amateur ranks have short-game problems. Sure, you might be able to pitch and chip the ball onto the green so that your next shot is a putt without much problem, but you're probably not pitching and chipping the ball close enough to the hole to shoot your goal score. For evidence, take a look at the PGA Tour statistics in the box at right. That 8' 9" distance listed at the top is important. It's the average distance from the cup a Tour pro knocks a shot that follows one that misses a green in regulation (the second shot on a par 3, the third shot on a par 4, etc.), and it takes into account every shot imaginable within 30 yards of the green. (See how you stack up by performing the 11-Ball Median Assessment on pages 66–67, but this time on a short-game shot.) What makes the distance so special is how it relates to the number directly below it. By hitting to within nine feet of the pin following a missed green, a PGA Tour player leaves himself with a putt he'll make slightly more than half of the time (hence the gaudy PGA Tour up-and-down average of 56 percent). This is important because of the third statistic in the box—if and when a chip or pitch lands outside 10 feet, the chance for an up-and-down gets cut roughly in half. Hopefully you're starting to get the picture: You don't need a decent short game to shoot your best score; you need a great one.

So far in the plan we've focused on making small improvements in several key areas of your game, the summation of which will undoubtedly fuel lower scores. We'll continue to do this as you proceed through the rest of the plan. However, when it comes

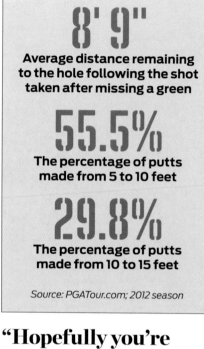

8' 9"
Average distance remaining to the hole following the shot taken after missing a green

55.5%
The percentage of putts made from 5 to 10 feet

29.8%
The percentage of putts made from 10 to 15 feet

Source: PGATour.com; 2012 season

> **"Hopefully you're starting to get the picture: You don't need a decent short game to shoot your best score; you need a great one."**

to scrambling, the bar is going to be raised. Here, the goal is *substantial* improvement and taking your short game to a completely new level. Don't worry—you can handle it. After all, chip swings and pitch swings are two of the easiest kinds of strokes you can make. In fact, if you can execute a good putting stroke, you should have no

problems nailing some of the proper mechanics for short-game shots. The real lessons in this section of the plan have more to do with how you *think* about short shots than your ability to execute them. For example, most amateurs use only one club (most commonly a sand wedge) for greenside swings, but good short-game players use at least three clubs, opting for the one that produces the appropriate combination of carry and roll for the shot at hand. Furthermore, most amateurs choose to fly the ball all the way to the pin on short shots, but the reality is that it's better to get the ball on the green as soon as possible and let it roll most of the way to your target. And the majority of recreational players believe that each short-game situation demands a unique swing, when all you really need is one that you can mix and match with different amounts of wrist hinge and various ball positions to hit every greenside shot you can imagine.

The most important thing you can learn about pitching and chipping the ball is that getting the ball on the ground as soon as possible is priority No. 1. Doing this effectively increases your margin of error, especially if you're the type of a golfer who likes to launch the ball high from short range and try to drop it next to the pin. While this sometimes is your best option (see pages 98–99), it leads to disaster if you misplay the shot (big swings lead to big misses). On the other hand, if you mishit it a bit with a less-lofted club when all you're trying to do is get the ball rolling on the green, you're probably going to end up okay. Good short-game players are smart players. Time to go to class.

LESSON LAND YOUR SHORT SHOTS IN THE RIGHT SPOT

A consistent landing area helps you select the correct trajectory for the shot at hand

The variety of greenside situations is so vast that it's impossible to learn a shot to specifically handle each one. The good news is that you don't have to. The secret to taking your short game to the level you need to post your best score ever is to apply techniques that cover the gamut of situations you'll face on the course. The most important of these is trajectory control. Developing the ability to control trajectory—and produce different kinds of trajectories on demand—allows you to hit any chip or pitch from any situation.

Trajectory is one of those words with which everyone is familiar yet has a hard time accurately defining. Basically, it's the path an object takes as it travels through the air. When you hit a pitch or chip, the shot trajectory is defined by 1) how far the ball flies through the air before it lands and starts rolling on the green, 2) how high the ball flies, and 3) where in its arc the ball reaches its apex. Each of these trajectory elements is connected to the others by the landing spot. The landing spot signals the end of the ball's carry through the air and the beginning of its roll. Its position

relative to the lie influences the height and where the apex occurs. The landing spot ties everything together and, as you'll discover, allows you to picture the correct trajectory for any short-shot situation.

A CONSISTENT LANDING SPOT

Good players use the landing spot to picture the trajectory they need to get the ball as close to the hole as possible. Although this may sound like just another extra step to worry about (especially when you're really more concerned with not skulling the ball across the green), it's not as complicated

You use only one landing spot for all pitch and chip spots— an area one to two paces from the edge of the green.

CARRY

LANDING SPOT

as it seems, because *there's only one ideal landing spot!* From now on, you should plan to land every pitch and chip shot one to two paces from the edge of the green, preferably on a flat section of the putting surface. Sticking to a single landing spot not only takes a lot of the guesswork out of your short game, but it also limits the damage if and when you fail to pull off the shot.

Every time you assess a pitch or a chip shot, check your lie and then locate the landing spot. Gauge the distance between the landing spot and the cup to see how much roll you're going to need, and gauge the distance between the landing spot and where your ball lies to see how high or low you need to flight the ball. You really don't even have to do this. If you look at the ball, the landing spot and the pin simultaneously, your mind will draw the ideal trajectory for the shot automatically. Seeing where you

need to land the ball and the distance from that spot to the hole allows you to instinctively figure out the ideal trajectory to get the ball close. This is the technique you'll be using as part of the plan and, as you practice it, you'll find that the resulting shot gives you the perfect blend of a high success rate with a high margin of error.

A few rules to keep in mind:

1. The closer the ball is to the landing spot, the less height the shot will need.
2. The greater the distance from the ball to the landing spot, the more height the shot will need.
3. The closer the landing spot is to the hole, the more you'll have to carry the ball through the air.
4. The farther the landing spot is from the hole, the more you'll have to roll the ball on the green.
5. If the ball looks like it will roll to the left once it hits, move your landing

spot to the right (and vice versa). Good short-game players read the roll on chips and pitches like they do a putt.

Visualizing the ideal trajectory is easy. The trick is in producing it with your swing. That'll be the focus of the majority of the lessons and drills in this section. On the following pages, however, you're going to go through a quick assessment of your short-game stroke using My Pro To Go to make sure there aren't any glaring errors in your motion, and then recap proven short game moves to tighten up your technique. Once that's complete, however, you'll shift your focus back to trajectory and learn how switching clubs and making alterations in your setup allow you to produce the shot you're looking for without a lot of effort. Again, the goal is changing the way you think about hitting short shots, not how you actually hit them.

Judging the distance from the ball to the landing spot and the landing spot to the hole allows you to visualize the ideal trajectory.

ROLL

"The goal is more about changing the way you think about hitting short shots."

ASSESSMENT REVIEW THE SHORT-GAME BASICS

Use My Pro To Go to spot errors that keep you from producing the correct short-game swing

Before diving into the intricacies of trajectory control, make sure your short-game motion is up to snuff by reviewing it using My Pro To Go. Have a friend capture your swing on a 10-yard chip with your sand wedge from both a face-on and down-target perspective. (Follow the guidelines on page 11.) As you play each video, keep an eye out for the short-stroke checkpoints listed below and at right.

BUMP THE GRASS

For the most consistent results, think of your short-game swing as more like a putting stroke than just a smaller version of your full swing. In fact, many players hit shot-game shots like they're putts, but with a wedge and with a wedge setup. Problems arise, however, if you haven't quite developed a solid and repeatable putting motion. You don't want to substitute one poor technique for another. If you don't feel confident enough in your putting stroke to use it on delicate short-game shots, then focus on creating more of a "bumping" motion with your wedges instead of hitting the shot like a putt. Swing the club back and through while bumping the sole of your wedge against the grass under the ball through impact. You shouldn't be making large divots here. Just a bump.

The real secret to producing a controlled strike from short range, however, is to avoid decelerating at all costs. Properly accelerating the clubhead through the ball is something most amateurs struggle with; since the shot is so short, the tendency is to slow down into impact. The key is to keep everything moving.

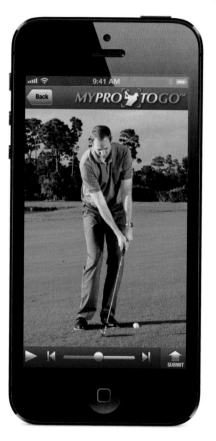

Some good advice: make sure you keep your left arm and hand moving toward the target until you finish the shot. Your left hand is the control hand for chip and pitch strokes, and if you use it correctly it should swing past your left leg in your forward-stroke. You can check to see if you're doing this by hitting practice chips and holding and evaluating your finish.

If you're having trouble consistently bumping the grass under the ball, or if your wrists are noticeably breaking down through impact, then focus on swinging the club while maintaining the Y shape formed by your arms and

the clubshaft. Adding a bit of wrist hinge is okay to increase your feel for the shot and, as you'll learn later in this section, produce more distance. However, keep in mind that you want your left wrist to be as flat as possible when you strike the ball. Keep the Y—and especially your left arm and hand—moving all the way through the shot. Stopping movement leads to deceleration and a poor result.

SHORT STROKE CHECKPOINTS

As you review your technique using the video in My Pro To Go, keep an eye out for the following. Nailing these short-stroke musts is the fast way to a consistent and reliable short game.

Setup *Shaft set more vertical at address to keep the heel from digging (stand closer to the ball). Ball back, hands at zipper, shaft leaning toward target.*

Backstroke *More shoulder turn than wrist hinge.*

Downstroke *Y formed by arms and clubshaft maintained throughout.*

Impact *Wrists firm, not "flippy!"*

Finish *Left hand finishes in front of left leg to ensure acceleration.*

THE PAR PLAN SHORT-GAME STROKE

Notice the Y formed by the arms and clubshaft. Maintain this shape from start to finish.

Hands ahead of the clubhead from start to finish. Use your core, not your hands, to power your stroke.

Left arm and hand accelerating into the ball with the lower body smoothly turning toward the target.

Y shape still intact with the wrists held firm as the clubhead bumps against the grass under the ball through impact.

PRACTICE HOW TO IMPROVE YOUR SHORT-GAME STROKE

Use these three drills to perfect your short-stroke motion

DRILL 4.1

Right Foot Up Drill

When Days 14 and 21
Where Practice facility
How Long 20 balls each session (about 15 mins.)

HOW TO DO IT

One of the biggest errors you can make when executing a short-game stroke is shifting your weight to your back foot during your downswing. Doing this usually forces you to flip the club with your hands through impact. If this is a habit of yours, then try hitting chips and pitches with your right foot pulled back (right toe even with your left heel) and raised up on its toe. Taking your right foot out of the swing like this not only forces you to set up with more weight on your left side at address, but also to keep your weight over your left side from start to finish. (You can't fall back, because your right foot isn't in a strong enough position to accommodate your weight.) Once you get the right feel, set up like normal and see if you can re-create the same swing.

Practice hitting the ball low and high to get a feel for trajectory control.

Hitting short shots with your right heel off the ground stops you from hitting it thin.

DRILL 4.2

Ping-Pong Drill

When Days 15 and 16
Where Home or office
How Long 20 balls each session (about 15 mins.)

HOW TO DO IT

You'll soon learn that you control trajectory by using different clubs and ball positions, but for now, work on launching the ball higher or lower using your sense of feel.

Since you're indoors, use Ping-Pong balls instead of golf balls. Ping-Pong balls are not only safer, but they create a helpful sound when they're struck. (You'll know you made a good swing if you hear the "bump" of the sole hitting the carpet and the "click" of the clubface striking the Ping-Pong ball at the same time.) Find an area with enough room to accommodate a short-game swing, and position a chair about five feet in front of you on your target line. Your first goal is to hit balls under the seat. Use an 8-iron and focus on keeping your wrists firm and bumping the grass (carpet, in this instance). The firmer your wrists, the lower you'll launch it. After hitting five balls under the chair, try to launch five balls over the backrest. Use your lob wedge and more wrist hinge. This will help you produce enough launch to clear the obstacle. (Although you're adding wrist hinge, don't flip your hands at the ball.) After 5 lofted shots, hit 10 more alternating between the two trajectories. Always bump the carpet and listen for the "click."

DRILL 4.3

Punisher Drill

When Days 14 and 27
Where Practice facility
How Long 20 balls each session
(about 15 mins.)

HOW TO DO IT

Like you learned on page 74, this one's called the Punisher Drill because it gives you immediate feedback if your technique fails to adhere to the keys to success. You'll need two clubs for this drill. Follow the steps below.

Step 1 Set the clubhead of one wedge against the top of the shaft of another and squeeze the two clubs together using your normal hold as shown. Sole the club behind the ball and set the shaft of the second club against the left side of your torso.

Step 2 Swing the club back using your everyday motion. Add a little wrist hinge so that the shaft of the second club separates from the left side of your body. Swing back to impact, trying to bump the grass under the ball.

NO! You Decelerated Through Imact

If you flip your wrists at the ball or fail to maintain the Y shape formed by your arms and clubshaft, the shaft of the second club will strike the left side of your torso. Hence the name "Punisher Drill."

YES! You Accelerated Through Impact

If you keep your wrists firm and swing your left arm toward the target the whole way, you'll produce a solid stroke and the shaft of the second club won't hit you. Instead, it'll move forward from the left side of your torso along with your hands and arms.

FIX THREE WAYS TO THE PERFECT TRAJECTORY

Change clubs, ball position, and wrist hinge to produce the right blend of carry and roll

When your eyes compute the distance from the ball to the landing area and the distance from the landing area to the hole, they draw a visual of the trajectory you need to get the shot close, including the amount of carry versus roll because, as previously discussed, your landing area is always in the same spot. Knowing the perfect trajectory is one thing, but producing it is another. Drill 4.2 on page 86 got you thinking about trajectory and the feels you need to launch the ball higher or lower. Even though you used different clubs for the high-lofted and low-lofted shots, you instinctively made adjustments to your setup and swing to hit the ball over or under the chair. Basically, you were already working toward a systematic way to hit the shot your mind sees when you assess the lie, landing area, and hole position. Now, we'll define the system.

You control trajectory in three ways: 1) changing clubs, 2) changing ball position, and 3) changing how much you hinge your wrists in your backswing. Over the next six pages, we'll look at each element and how to manipulate it to your advantage to produce the shot shape you need. Of these three, changing clubs is the most important because not only does it dramatically change the launch angle, it influences distance, too.

THREE CLUBS FOR ALL SHOTS

The secret to short-game success, despite the myriad situations you'll face on the course, is finding a way to produce three specific trajectories regardless of the overall distance of the shot. The trajectories are as follows:

Finding the right trio of chipping and pitching clubs preps you to produce any shot shape at will.

Carry < Roll
The ball covers more distance rolling on the green than it does flying through the air.

Carry = Roll
The ball covers the same amount of ground while in the air and on the green.

Carry > Roll
The ball covers more distance flying through the air than it does while rolling on the green.

Every short-game shot you'll need to hit on the course will require one of these shot shapes. Whereas most players attempt to change their swings to produce the three shot shapes,

8-IRON
Use an 8-iron if the shot needs more roll than carry.

PW
Use a pitching wedge if you need equal amounts of carry and roll.

LW
Use a lob wedge if the shot needs more carry than roll.

you're going to make things a lot easier on yourself by letting your clubs do the work for you. Plus, you already own three clubs that produce each of the three shot shapes automatically.

CARRY < ROLL 8-Iron
Making the basic stroke with a centered ball position using an 8-iron will produce a shot that carries 25 percent of the total distance in the air and rolls 75 percent of the total distance on the green.

CARRY = ROLL Pitching Wedge
Making the basic stroke with a centered ball position using a pitching wedge will produce a shot that carries 50 percent of the total distance in the air and rolls 50 percent of the total distance on the green.

CARRY > ROLL Lob Wedge
Making the basic stroke with a centered ball position using a lob wedge will produce a shot that carries 75 percent of the total distance in the air and rolls 25 percent of the total distance on the green.

The carry and roll percentages hold true for any distance. For example, if you have a 20-yard shot and you use a lob wedge, the ball will fly in the air for 15 yards and roll on the ground for 5 yards. If it's only an 8-yard shot, the ball will fly in the air for 6 yards and roll on the ground for 2 (assuming a less-forceful swing).

Relying on three clubs might seem strange to you since most players use one club (typically a sand wedge) for all short-game shots, but it's the right thing to do. Not only does it create the required trajectory without any work on your part, it minimizes the damage if and when you hit the ball poorly. If you blade an 8-iron using a small short-game stroke, the ball will probably stay on the green. If you blade a sand wedge making a bigger swing from the same spot, you're going to lose a few strokes.

FIX THREE WAYS TO THE PERFECT TRAJECTORY

Change clubs, ball position, and wrist hinge to produce the right blend of carry and roll

Whereas changing clubs dramatically changes launch, flight, and distance, the second part of controlling trajectory—ball position—is a little bit more of a fine-tuning mechanism.

You need this extra level of precision because you're not always going to see the 25:75, 50:50 and 75:25 carry-to-roll ratios discussed on the previous pages. Sometimes you might need something along the lines of 10 percent carry and 90 percent roll. Moving the ball

in your stance can help you nail the percentages whatever they may be. Here's how it works.

To increase the roll percentage, play the ball back. Experiment with positioning the ball one ball back of center, then two balls back, and then

A centered ball position gives you the basic carry-to-roll percentages.

The farther you move the ball back in your stance, the lower you'll hit the shot, increasing the amount of roll versus carry.

three balls back. Each successive move should cause the ball to fly lower and roll more across all distances.

To increase the carry percentage, play the ball forward. Experiment with positioning the ball one ball forward of center and then two balls forward, but don't go any farther than that, as you'll risk moving the low point of your swing too far ahead of your hands. If you need more carry than this, switch to the next higher-lofted club.

SOME NOTES ON ADDRESS
Changing ball position only works if your setup is correct. The first thing you should do is stand closer to the ball to keep the heel from digging in at impact. (The shaft should feel like it's sitting a little more vertical.) Bend forward from your hips to get your chest over your toes. If you do it correctly, you'll feel like your arms are hanging straight down without touching your torso or your legs. Set the majority of your weight over your left foot and try to keep it there during your stroke. If your weight moves to your right foot, you'll likely catch the shot thin.

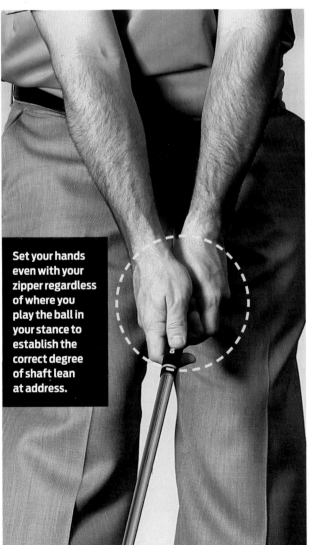

Set your hands even with your zipper regardless of where you play the ball in your stance to establish the correct degree of shaft lean at address.

IMPORTANT!
Always set your hands even with your zipper. Really keep an eye out for this. This establishes the correct amount of shaft lean to help you produce the specific carry and roll percentages. With your hands even with your zipper and the ball played back, the shaft leans more toward the target. This deflofts the club, reducing the carry percentage and overall height. Fight the urge to move your hands ahead of your zipper, as a lot of amateurs do. This moves the low point too far in front of the ball and creates a steep attack angle. Not only does this eliminate your margin of error, but it makes it almost impossible to bump the grass under the ball. The leading edge will dig in and the shot will go nowhere.

TRY THIS! golfTEC

Pick the Right Shot at the Right Time
Andy Brent, PGA: GolfTEC—Atlanta

In addition to using a consistent landing spot to visualize the ideal trajectory for the short shot you're facing, there are other factors you can use to formulate a winning shot selection. Before pulling the trigger, consider the following:

1 THE LIE
Is the ball sitting up on short grass or down in deep rough? Can you strike the ball cleanly and accurately? As a general rule, use more loft and bounce (the angle between the bottom of the sole and the leading edge) in thick grass and less loft and bounce on tight lies.

2 THE CONDITIONS
Firm conditions will allow the ball to hop through the rough and roll more on the green. Wet conditions tend to make the ball hang up in the rough and roll less on the green.

3 CONFIDENCE
Confidence level declines when the situation requires a higher trajectory. Opt for lower shorts before lofted ones.

Having a good imagination and following these simple rules will allow you to determine the best shot to go with when trying to get up and down.

WINNING NUMBER 33

The percentage difference between the PGA Tour Scrambling average from the fringe (87.7%) and the rough (54.2%). The lesson: If you're going to miss a green, miss it in the right place!

Source: PGATour.com

Data from 2012 season

FIX THREE WAYS TO THE PERFECT TRAJECTORY

Change clubs, ball position, and wrist hinge to produce the right blend of carry and roll

Visualizing trajectory and selecting the shot and club to use based on carry and roll percentages is a powerful tool. But even if you calculate the right percentages and pull the appropriate short-game club, there's still a matter of distance. As the following example shows, two shots with the same carry-to-roll ratios can demand two very different motions, even while using the same club.

Shot 1
Total Distance: 8 yards
Carry-to-Roll Ratio: 3-to-1
Carry/Roll Distances: 6 yards/2 yards

Shot 2
Total Distance: 36 yards
Carry-to-Roll Ratio: 3-to-1
Carry/Roll Distances: 27 yards/9 yards

Because these shots both require more carry than roll, you should hit them with the same club, in this case a lob wedge (or the one you use for the times you need more carry than roll). Obviously, the swing you use on the first shot has to be different from the swing on the second shot to accommodate the variance in yardage. Enter the third part of the three-part short game system: adjusting wrist hinge to create the correct distance.

A MATTER OF WRIST ACTION

In section 3 of the plan, you learned how to dial in wedge distances by overlaying your swing on a clock and taking the club back to various hours to create less speed and distance or more speed and distance. When it comes to dialing in your distances on short-game shots, the adjustments aren't nearly as severe. Here, all you'll need to do is limit or increase the amount you hinge your wrists in your backswing. Even a little amount of extra hinge can give you significantly more yards

FIRM WRISTS FOR SHORT SHOTS

When you're only a few paces from the putting surface, select the club that matches the carry-and-roll percentages you visualize in your preshot routine, then make a very firm-wristed stroke. This motion is the one that's most like your putting stroke. Make sure to maintain the triangle formed by your arms and shoulders from start to finish.

SUPPLE WRISTS FOR MEDIUM SHOTS

The farther away you are from the green, the more speed—and wrist action—you need to carry the ball all the way onto the putting surface. For medium-length shots (you'll get a better idea of "medium" on the following pages), keep your wrists soft at address and allow the momentum of the club to hinge your wrists slightly both going back and through. Don't actively engage your wrists—let the weight of the clubhead hinge them for you.

ACTIVE WRISTS FOR LONG SHOTS

When you start getting 20 yards or more from the green, you need to actively use your wrists to create the speed needed to carry the ball all the way to your landing spot, especially if you need more carry than roll. Here, purposely hinge your wrists on your backswing, forming a 90 degree angle between your left arm and the clubshaft. Don't overswing—it's still a short-game shot. Keep the same, basic motion, but add the hinge you use on normal shots. Make sure to rehinge them after impact.

relative to the overall size of the shot due to the fact you're dealing with small distances. Wrist hinge creates extra speed without your having to make a bigger swing—good news on delicate short-game shots. Keep in mind that while adding speed can increase the loft as well as the overall distance of the shot, the trajectory on short shots is mostly determined by the club you pull (more loft for more carry).

The guides below show you how to add the correct amount of hinge depending on your yardage to the pin. When you're out on the course, your plan of attack should follow this order: 1) choose the club, 2) determine the amount of wrist hinge and, 3) adjust ball position. With each successive decision you're honing in on the combination that produces a match for the shot you've visualized.

Use a firm-wristed stroke from short range.

Allow the club to hinge your wrists for more distance.

Actively hinge your wrists on long shots.

PRACTICE BUILD THE ULTIMATE SHORT-SHOT ARSENAL

Just a few hours' practice can help you produce 27 different shots on command

A single afternoon spent around the practice green experimenting with different clubs, ball positions, and swing lengths can pay huge dividends in your short game.

DRILL 4.4

Arsenal Drill

When Days 15 and 27
Where Practice facility
How Long 108 balls
(about 90 mins.)

Thus far in this section you've learned how to produce three basic trajectories by selecting one of three dedicated short-game clubs. You've also learned how adjusting ball position allows you to fine-tune trajectory and how to hit longer shots by adding wrist hinge to your backswing. If you combine these factors, you can produce 27 different short-game shots (what you get when you mix and match three swings with three clubs and three ball positions). That's a pretty solid arsenal, and you'll be surprised by how deep you get into it over the course of a season, especially if you're a golfer who misses a lot of greens. Although it's not vital to groove each swing for the purposes of the plan, we recommend that you experiment with different clubs, swings, and ball positions for a few practice sessions. The great thing about doing this is that you can pick up the balls from the practice green and use them again for full-swing work on the lesson tee, cutting the cost of that bucket in half. Plus, you can never get enough reps when it comes to your short game: The more experience you have creating different trajectories with different clubs and swings and off different lies, the more likely you'll get up and down in two shots when you miss greens on the course.

HOW TO DO IT

Grab a large bucket of practice balls, find a clear section of the short-game practice area, and make each of the 27 swings four times hitting actual shots. (Mark your landing spot with a business card or credit card). Do it in an organized fashion so that you can compare each shot with the one that came before and after it. This will allow you to note the effect each change (club, ball position, swing) has on your results. Start with your lowest-lofted short-game club (the one that gives you more roll than carry), your centered ball position, and the firm-wrist swing. Then change ball position (move it back and then move it forward). Do the same with the midsize swing and then the one that uses active wrists before switching clubs. Log the results in the yardage book beow. Since you already know the carry-to-roll percentages based on the club you're using, keep an eye out for carry distance and total distance. These are the variables that tend to trip golfers up on the course.

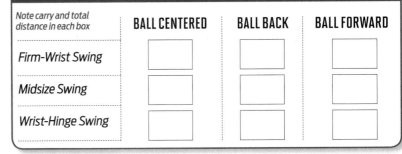

8-IRON (CARRY < ROLL CLUB)

Note carry and total distance in each box	BALL CENTERED	BALL BACK	BALL FORWARD
Firm-Wrist Swing			
Midsize Swing			
Wrist-Hinge Swing			

PITCHING WEDGE (CARRY = ROLL CLUB)

Note carry and total distance in each box	BALL CENTERED	BALL BACK	BALL FORWARD
Firm-Wrist Swing			
Midsize Swing			
Wrist-Hinge Swing			

LOB WEDGE (CARRY > ROLL CLUB)

Note carry and total distance in each box	BALL CENTERED	BALL BACK	BALL FORWARD
Firm-Wrist Swing			
Midsize Swing			
Wrist-Hinge Swing			

PRACTICE BUILD THE ULTIMATE SHORT-SHOT ARSENAL

Just a few hours' practice can help you produce 27 different shots on command

While it's a great idea to familiarize yourself with the yardages and trajectories you produce by performing the practice regimen on the previous pages, eventually you'll want to get to the point where you pull the right club, set the ball in the right spot in your stance, and add the correct amount of hinge based on feel. That will come with experience. In your quest to post your best score ever in 30 days, however, stick to the rules discussed thus far. Hitting the right kind of pitch or chip boils down to answering the following questions. By using the same landing spot on all shots (one to two paces from the edge of the green), your responses should come in a heartbeat.

1. *How far away am I from my landing spot?* The longer the ball needs to travel to reach your spot, the more wrist hinge you need in your swing. The closer you are to the landing spot, the less hinge you'll need.

2. *How much carry do you need compared with roll?* The more you need to carry the ball, the higher you need to launch it. The more you need to roll the ball, the lower you need to launch.

3. *What club should I pull?* If, based on your answer to question 2, you need to launch the ball higher, use a club with more loft. If you need to launch the ball lower, use a club with less loft.

4. *Where should I play the ball in my stance?* Odds are, if you pulled a higher-lofted club based on your answers to questions 2 and 3, you'll play the ball more forward in your stance. Pair lower-lofted clubs with a back-ball position.

The system is really quite simple, but it only works if you adhere to the short-stroke basics discussed earlier in this section. If you put in the appropriate time performing the drills on pages 86 and 87, chipping or pitching the ball close will become a true strength in your game.

> "The system is really quite simple, but it only works if you adhere to the short-stroke basics."

A GUIDE FOR YOUR SHORT GAME

The grid below shows you how to nail the correct mixture of the elements that determine the trajectory for any short shot you can imagine. Continuing to familiarize yourself with how club selection, ball position, and wrist hinge affect shot shape will make it that much easier to execute the correct moves when you're in the middle of a round. Keep in mind that pulling the right club is the most important feature to get right. Choosing the correct one based on the carry-to-roll ratio you need will, at the very least, get you on the green and *near* the cup. Speed is the next critical element. Adding the correct amount of hinge will get you *close;* fine-tuning your setup with the right ball position just might get you *in.*

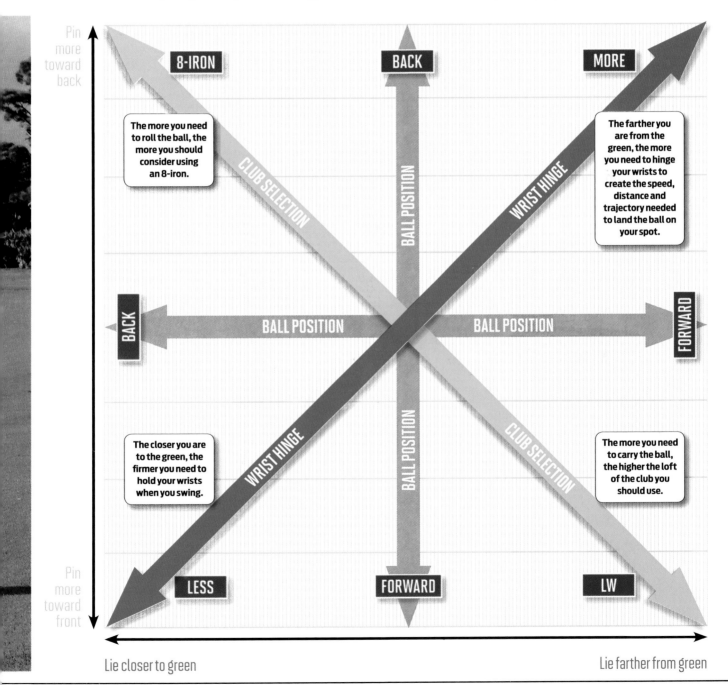

Pin more toward back

8-IRON

The more you need to roll the ball, the more you should consider using an 8-iron.

CLUB SELECTION

BACK

BALL POSITION

MORE

WRIST HINGE

The farther you are from the green, the more you need to hinge your wrists to create the speed, distance and trajectory needed to land the ball on your spot.

BACK

BALL POSITION

BALL POSITION

FORWARD

The closer you are to the green, the firmer you need to hold your wrists when you swing.

WRIST HINGE

BALL POSITION

CLUB SELECTION

The more you need to carry the ball, the higher the loft of the club you should use.

Pin more toward front

LESS

FORWARD

LW

Lie closer to green

Lie farther from green

LESSON ADAPTING TO UNIQUE SITUATIONS

At times you need to break the rules and fly the ball past your landing spot and all the way to the pin

Every lie around the green isn't perfect, and some don't fit neatly into the system presented in this section. In some instances you'll need a slightly different attack in order to get the ball close enough for a one-putt. Apart from distance, landing spot, and pin position, common bad lies require you to add as much loft as possible and fly the ball all the way to the pin with minimal roll-out. These are the situations where you see guys like Phil Mickelson pull off a lob or flop shot.

ROUGH

Because there's grass behind the ball, you won't produce decent enough contact to get the ball all the way to the pin or even to your landing spot. Here, you'll need to open up the clubface and your stance and hit the ball almost like you're exploding out of a bunker (see section 9).

MULTIPLE TIERS

Whereas you can still run the ball from the landing spot to the pin if the green features only a small series of humps or valleys, hitting to a noticeably higher area of the green can make judging the roll very difficult. This is a time when you might want to use extra loft to carry the ball closer to the hole.

CHIPPING DOWNHILL

When the green is sloping away from

THREE KEYS FOR A SUCCESSFUL LOB

1 **Aggressively thump the sole of the club on the ground.** This is a different feel than the bumping move you make through impact on standard chips. Make several "thump" practice swings before stepping into the shot.

2 **Keep an eye out for ball position.** When you open the clubface and your front foot, the ball effectively moves back in your stance. You want at least a centered ball position relative to your toe line.

3 **Even if your confidence level isn't very high, make a full swing back and through.** Most players never swing hard enough for a lob, and their shots usually come up short. Make a big, but smooth, swing.

you, the carry-to-roll ratios discussed thus far don't always work. Plus, it takes experience to control the roll on slick, downhill putting surfaces. Again, here's a spot where it makes sense to use more loft to carry the ball past your landing spot and minimize the amount of roll.

HOW TO HIT A FLOP SHOT

The situations listed here all have two things in common: maximum loft and minimal—if any—roll. You get this kind of trajectory by hitting a flop, a specialty shot that travels as high in the air as it does over the ground and stops quickly once it hits the green. Therefore, if you find yourself in heavy rough (where the standard short-stroke motion can't cut through the grass), chipping to an upper tier (where it's difficult to know how the ball will react when it's rolling on the green), or hitting to a green that slopes away from you (where the normal carry-to-roll ratios don't apply), opt for the flop.

Use your most-lofted wedge and hinge your wrists immediately as you start back. Although it's the unhinging action of your wrists through impact that gives the shot its extra height, amateurs tend to unhinge too early. The best advice is to try to keep your wrists hinged the whole way down and through. (They'll unhinge on their own, we assure you.) Do this while using mostly your arms and adding very little leg action and you should be able to produce the loft you need to escape these difficult situations.

Step 1 Open your stance and the clubface, but keep the ball centered.

Step 2 Make a big, "armsy" swing with plenty of wrist hinge.

Step 3 Release the hinge as you strike the ball for maximum loft.

Step 4 Swing to a full finish. Stopping short won't get the job done.

HITS & MISSES

A quick look at key PGA Tour iron-shot averages:

75.6%
PGA Tour Greens in Regulation from 100–125 Yards

70.4%
PGA Tour Greens in Regulation from 125–150 Yards

63.1%
PGA Tour Greens in Regulation from 150–175 Yards

54.1%
PGA Tour Greens in Regulation from 175–200 Yards

44.1%
PGA Tour Greens in Regulation from > 200 Yards

2012 season
Source: PGATour.com

DAYS
18–22

IMPROVE YOUR IRON CONTACT

You don't need a new full swing to hit solid iron shots, just one that makes the right kind of divot with every club in your bag

It feels good to hit a green in regulation, doesn't it? Doing so usually means you knocked a good drive out there and followed it up with a solid second shot on a par 4, or made a great swing with the right club on a par 3. In fact, the confidence you get from hitting a green in regulation is so high that you may not care if you make the birdie putt or not. The reason is, unless you're a card-carrying member of the PGA Tour, you probably miss more greens than you hit. Although it's unlikely you'll ever get to the point where you reverse this trend, learning how to hit just a few more greens a round will make a huge difference in your game and put you in great position to post your best score.

As it was with driving, the secret to better iron play is improving your contact, which in this case involves learning how to make the right kind of divot with a square clubface. Although the lessons and drills you'll read about in this section of the plan focus mostly on these two basic needs, learning what it takes to meet them positively affects other elements of your technique. In other words, working on your divot patterns and clubface control automatically improves things like your setup and your swing plane—a simple case of curing the disease, not just the symptoms.

LOOK FOR THE SECRET IN THE DIRT

The size and shape of your divots tell you everything you need to know about your iron swing

Ben Hogan believed that the secrets to a better iron swing are found by digging them out of the dirt—a comment about the importance of not only taking the right kind of divot, but the importance of practice, too. He was right in the fact that the quality of your results mirror the quality of your divots, but while it's a good idea to heed Hogan's advice when it comes to improving your iron play, you don't need to hold yourself up to his lofty standards. Check out the numbers in the performance chart we use at GolfTEC improvements centers to teach students roughly how many greens they'll need to hit to shoot their goal score (*below*). Funny enough, if all you want to do is break 90, you only need to hit three greens in regulation. If your goal is to shoot in the 90s, then you really don't have to hit any greens in regulation at all. Now, before you flip to the next section because you're already hitting more greens than this right now, understand that there's more behind these numbers.

This performance chart applies only if you match the number of greens hit to your goal score while also eliminating the big misses that come from poor divot patterns and open or closed clubfaces at impact (the two components of contact we'll work on in this section). The goal here, really, is to help you build a swing that consistently gets you close without losing balls wildly left and right, and short and long of your target. If doing so helps you hit more greens than you have to in order to post your number, great. That's why we waited until the middle of the plan to address iron play, because despite its importance to your overall game, eliminating penalty shots off the tee and improving your short game and putting stroke will

> ## "If your goal is to shoot in the 90s, then you really don't have to hit any greens in regulation at all."

help your score far more than hitting more greens in regulation. Not only that, the skills discussed in the first four sections of the plan are easier to master than those for, say, hitting a four-iron to 10 feet. As we stated in the introduction to this book, the belief that you have to be a shotmaking machine to post your best score is completely unfounded. In fact, you'd be better off hitting an iron you know you can control and getting the ball close to the green than pulling the one you'd normally use for that yardage but have difficulty controlling because of its length and loft.

CONTACT MATTERS

When you hear comments from great players on how the game is all about "managing mishits," keep in mind that the misses they're talking about have nothing to do with yours. Elite players miss in feet. The rest of us miss in huge chunks of yardage, and while most golfers think of misses in left or right terms, it's actually the distance miss that plagues the amateur player. If you're the kind of golfer who can hit his or her 9-iron 135 yards on one swing and 35 yards on the next (because you hit the shot fat), then you know what we're talking about. Improving your contact by working on divot pattern and face control will help you shrink this yardage differential to the point where a miss leaves you with an easy chip or pitch to the pin. (This also works if you're more likely to catch the ball thin and hit it too far.)

Your first goal in this section of the book is to learn—just as you did with your wedges—to make contact with the ball first and the ground second, and to use your divots to assess both the quality of your path and your ability to properly position the low point of your swing. The second goal is to improve your control of the clubface and ability to square it up when you make contact with the ball. Achieving both means you'll never hit a shot too far from the green again.

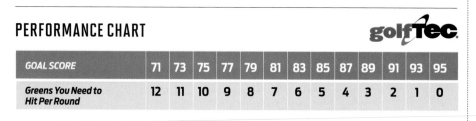

PERFORMANCE CHART

golfTEC

GOAL SCORE	71	73	75	77	79	81	83	85	87	89	91	93	95
Greens You Need to Hit Per Round	12	11	10	9	8	7	6	5	4	3	2	1	0

Discovering the number of greens you need to hit to reach your goal score shows you how much—or how little—work you need to put in to your iron game.

LESSON MAKE THE RIGHT KIND OF IRON STRIKE

Look at what's happening at impact—not before or after—to find your iron-swing miscues

When you took lessons in the past, your instructor probably had you work on hitting key positions in your swing as a way to create solid and consistent impact. This works for players who dedicate the time and resources to achieve perfection at every step of their motions. For those that don't, it's far more important to understand what *causes* the ball to do what it does—hook left, pop up to the right, fly straight at the target like a screaming bullet, etc.—and use feels and swing thoughts that make sense to you to get the ball where you want it to go.

If you take a look at many of the players on Tour both past and present, you'll notice that their swings are very unique to them. Rickie Fowler's technique is far different from Dustin Johnson's, Rory McIlroy's or Jack Nicklaus's. What the best players understand is that positions are just a variable of the shot you're trying to hit or the club you're swinging. The secret to success is controlling what's happening at impact.

LESSONS ON LEAN

The beauty of this approach is that it allows you to find your own means to produce the desired end, and for the purposes of this section, the end is iron shots hit with a forward-leaning shaft at the moment of impact. Striking the ball with the shaft leaning in the opposite direction (away from the target) produces the fats and thins that rob you of distance control and put you in positions that tax your short game. That's why looking at your divots is so important. If you're making good divots, you're probably

The secret to better iron play is in the shape of your divots.

> "If you're making good divots, you're probably making good contact with the shaft leaning forward."

making good contact with the shaft leaning forward, and the more consistent you are at achieving this position at impact, the more likely it is you'll catch the ball in the middle of the clubface. This gives you maximum energy transfer and limits clubhead twisting. Shots consistently struck in the center tend to fly the same distance with the same iron, which will go a long way toward your real goal of getting the ball close to—if not on—the green. (You'll fix directional problems by working on face control later in this section.) Therefore, step one on the path to better iron play is to assess the centeredness of your current strike and the divot pattern, then to apply the appropriate drills to get the shaft in position to deliver the appropriate blow. In order to make this happen, you *will* have to borrow a page from Ben Hogan's lesson book and look for the secrets in the dirt.

ASSESSMENT CHECK YOUR IRON IMPACT POINT

The location of your strikes says a lot about your ability to lean the shaft forward at impact

The first assessment you'll make in this section is determining where on the face you're making contact with the ball. As you can guess, shots struck in the middle of the clubface are preferred over those struck high or low on the face or out toward the heel and toe. Despite the fact that advances in equipment technology have made today's irons more forgiving than they've ever been in the past, bad strikes lead to bad shots even if you play the most forgiving irons money can buy.

HOW TO DO IT

The easiest way to determine your iron contact point is to draw a line across the equator of the ball with a dry-erase marker (*photo, above*), then set the ball on the ground with the line vertical and facing the clubface after you sole your iron on the ground. Hit the shot, then look at the clubface—the line you drew on the ball will leave a mark where impact was made. Since your swing probably isn't very consistent, do this about 10 times—that should give you a pretty good indication of where you typically make contact. Assess the quality of your strike using the checkpoints at right.

YES! Impact marks in the center of the face indicate a good swing path and forward-leaning shaft.

YES! The more ink on the face the better. This means you're compressing the ball and not just swiping at it. Again, this is a good indication that the shaft was leaning forward at impact.

YES! Turf near the bottom of the club (grooves 1 and 2) indicate you took a nice, shallow divot, which you can only do if the shaft is leaning forward at impact.

NO! Marks near the heel or toe indicate a faulty path or bad clubface angle. Notice how less defined the mark is compared with the one above.

NO! The higher the mark on the face, the more likely you came into impact on too steep an angle or with too much shaft lean.

NO! Marks toward the bottom of the clubface or the absence of dirt in grooves 1 and 2 indicate a backward-leaning shaft.

ASSESSMENT LOOK AT YOUR DIVOTS

Divot size and shape tell you what's right—and wrong—with your iron impact

The second assessment in this section tells you if you're taking solid and consistent divots. Divots are important in that they hold clues to the quality of your strike (which is why you should always practice off the turf and never on a mat). The size and shape of the divot itself can tell you a lot about your angle of attack and how good you are at getting the shaft to lean toward the target at impact. The mark in the grass you left behind when you took the divot holds a lot of information about your swing path and, in some cases, the clubface angle. Divots show you what's wrong with your technique while guiding you toward the things you should be working on.

HOW TO DO IT

Set two tees in the ground about two feet apart; an imaginary line drawn between them should run perpendicular to your target (*photo, right*). Hit several shots, starting at the right tee and continually moving toward the left tee after each swing. Make sure you set the ball on the imaginary line. After seven or eight shots, give the divots you carved in the dirt a close examination. Each one can tell you about the quality of your swing and how much work you need to put in to get the shaft consistently leaning toward the target at impact.

HIT DOWN AND THROUGH

We touched on the concept of shaft lean in section 3 and how important it was to get the low point of your wedge swing ahead of the ball and keep your left wrist from cupping through impact. These ideas also apply to your iron swing and make it easier to lean the shaft toward the target at impact and make contact in the center of the clubface while taking a nice, shallow divot. In fact, performing the wedge-swing drills on pages 68 and 69 will make positive changes in your iron swing, too (as will the iron-specific exercises on the following pages). The key concept to understand is that you hit down on the ball to get it up, and the correct way to hit down is to strike the ball first and the ground second. Your ability to do this depends a lot on where you position the ball in your stance. Golfers who allow the ball to creep forward too much aren't doing themselves any favors—the more forward the ball the more difficult it is to move the bottom of your swing in front of it.

NO!
This divot begins too far behind the ball and points a little left of the target (not as damaging for irons as it is for woods).

OK
This divot correctly starts in front of the ball, but it isn't very deep. It's more of a scuff than a divot. This swing needs more shaft lean at impact.

Golfers who play the ball back in their stance often don't have enough time to properly square the clubface and end up leaving the ball out to the right. You know this is you if your divots are large and deep. Keep things simple: Play the ball one clubhead width inside your left heel on all standard shots. (The ball will look more forward with longer clubs, but only because your stance is wider.) A consistent ball position will make it easier to lean the shaft forward at impact.

HIT WITH YOUR BODY

If you're having trouble with low point this late in

Low point

BUY A PERFECT DIVOT
Think about carving the dirt under a dollar bill when you swing to create an ideal divot.

YES!
A perfect divot—shallow, straight, and located in front of the imaginary line. These are great indications that contact was made with the shaft leaning toward the target and with the low point in front of the ball.

YES!
This divot is a good size and occurs in front of the ball.

OK
This divot starts slightly in front of the ball, but it's a bit on the deep side. It's also pointing left, and the heel side is longer than the toe side. This shot probably went right and was likely hit a little thin.

NO!
A good rectangular shape, not too shallow and not too deep. However, it starts too far behind the ball.

the plan, then stop worrying so much about hitting down. This tends to cause players to come over the top in their downswing. Think of your arms as simply attachments to all that your body is doing. They're like a couple pieces of rope loosely connected to your shoulders. They play an

important role in that they connect the club to your body, but are nonetheless followers of action, not leaders. This is a concept most players have a hard time getting their heads around because they're so used to executing motions with their hands and arms—throwing a football,

shooting a basketball, etc. But the arms' role really is to respond to your turn. Connect your arms to your chest so that they can more easily follow your body's rotation. Feel like your upper left arm is snug and across your chest as you take the club up and then back down.

Hear It From a Pro!
Upload your swing to My Pro To Go for an in-depth analysis of your iron swing and receive a lesson video and customized drills to accelerate your improvement in this section. Visit *myprotogo. com* for details.

PRACTICE LEAN THE SHAFT FOR BETTER CONTACT

Try these four drills to meet the key demand of iron play—a forward-leaning shaft at impact

DRILL 5.1

Towel Drill

When Days 18, 21 and 22
Where Practice facility
How Long 20 balls each session (about 20 mins.)

HOW TO DO IT

Spread out a golf towel on the ground about four inches behind the ball. Your goal on this drill is to hit the ball as solidly as you can without contacting the towel, and the only way you can do it is to keep your hands ahead of the clubhead through impact. Try to use more body turn than arm and hand action if you can't do it at first. Once you can miss the towel consistently, move the towel closer to the ball so that there are only two inches of space between them. With the towel this close, even minor flaws in your swing will show up—you'll strike the towel, then the ball. It's a great drill because in addition to emphasizing the need to lean the shaft, it shows you that cheating by swinging down too steeply doesn't work.

NO!
Striking the towel before striking the ball means you're losing shaft lean and allowing the clubhead to pass your hands through the hitting zone.

YES!
If you can hit the ball without hitting the towel, you're starting to groove the feels that allow you to keep your hands ahead of the clubhead through impact.

L-to-L Drill

When Day 19
Where Home or office
How Long 20 swings
(about 15 mins)

HOW TO DO IT

Make smooth swings, stopping your backswing when your left arm is parallel to the ground and stopping your through-swing when your right arm is parallel to the ground. (Check that each arm also is parallel to your target line at each stopping point.) Hinge your wrists so you create an *L* between the shaft and your left arm at the end of your backswing, and rehinge them following

impact so you create a backwards *L* between the shaft and your right arm in your finish. Nailing these positions trains you to rotate your forearms slightly both going back and coming through. (If you don't rotate your forearms, you won't be able to create the *L*'s in the right place.) Forearm rotation, especially in your left arm as you swing into impact, is critical for holding the angle in your right wrist so you don't flip the clubhead at the ball.

FORWARD-SWING *L*
Right arm parallel to ground, shaft perpendicular to right arm (and right arm rotated and parallel to target line).

Make L-to-L swings at home or in your office to groove a more unified motion.

BACKSWING *L*
Left arm parallel to ground, shaft perpendicular to left arm (and left arm rotated and parallel to target line).

BONUS LESSONS!
Watch videos of these drills at **golftec.com/parplan.**

PRACTICE LEAN THE SHAFT FOR BETTER CONTACT

Try these four drills to meet the key demand of iron play—a forward-leaning shaft at impact

YES!
Focusing on making the right divot instead of where your shots go speeds up the learning process.

DRILL 5.3

Divot Drill

When Days 20 and 24
Where Practice facility
How Long 20 balls each session
(about 15 mins.)

HOW TO DO IT

Remember the assessment on page 106? Keep doing it! Again, set two tees in the ground about two feet apart; an imaginary line drawn between them should run perpendicular to your target line. Hit several shots, starting at the right tee and moving toward the left tee after each swing. Make sure you set the ball on the imaginary line running between the two tees. After seven or eight shots, give each divot a close examination using the checkpoints on pages 106 and 107. This drill is more about assessing your divots, however. Its primary benefit is that it gets you focusing on making the right divot instead of trying to hit a good iron shot. You'll execute better moves and more easily lean the shaft forward at impact as a result.

DRILL 5.4

Business Card Drill

When Day 19
Where Home or office
How Long 20 swings (about 15 mins.)

HOW TO DO IT

Grab a Ping-Pong ball (better for indoors) and one of your business cards (a hotel-room key card also works) and set them on the ground as shown at right (card an inch and a half in front of the ball). Your goal in this drill is to make half swings at half speed and hit the Ping-Pong ball *and* the business card (sort of like the Towel Drill in reverse). You should hear two sounds: 1) the "click" of impact and 2) the "flick" of the card being struck. If you're having difficulty, try doing this drill in slow motion. Once you can do it indoors, try it on the range using regular swings for the full effect.

NO!
If you miss the card, you improperly positioned the low point, swung up too early, or allowed the club to pass your hands.

YES!
Catching the ball and the business card means you're in a great impact position, with the shaft leaning toward the target.

BONUS LESSONS!
Watch videos of these drills at **golftec.com/ parplan.**

TRY THIS! **golfTEC**

Draw Your Way to Better Contact

Nick Paez, PGA: GolfTEC—Cleveland

The euphoria (not an exaggeration) that comes with compressing the ball and getting an iron shot to fly straight at your target is one of the things that keep players coming back to the course, even after a poor round. If you're not experiencing this euphoria often enough, try this drill. It involves the use of a chalk line, which normally is for putting practice. In this situation, however, it can help you improve your iron contact, aim, and accuracy.

Snap an eight-foot chalk line on a clean area of the practice tee straight down your target line. Set a tee in the ground at the far end of the line to help you aim the clubface. Place a ball a few feet away from the tee, take your setup, confirm your aim, and swing away. Grade your contact and ballflight, then look down to see if your divot is straight over the chalk line. Compare any directional miss to the direction your divot is pointing. Place another ball behind this divot and keep at it until you reach the end of the eight-foot line. Your goal is to get 8 out of 10 divots to point straight down the line. If you can do this, you're well on your way to better iron shots.

WINNING NUMBER **2.9**

The number of strokes, on average, it took players on the 2012 PGA Tour to get the ball in the hole from 150 to 175 yards, either from the fairway or from a par-3 tee box. Tiger Woods topped the list with 2.82.

Source: PGATour.com

LESSON IMPROVE YOUR CLUBFACE CONTROL

Hitting it straight is all about striking it squarely

When it comes to amateurs and their iron swings, the majority do a pretty good job of swinging on plane. One of the reasons for this is that your irons are shorter than your driver (the club most amateurs have the most problems swinging on plane) so you tend to swing them more smoothly. Plus, you're looking to hit a certain yardage from the fairway (say, 150 yards with a 7-iron) rather than bombing it as far as you can off the tee box. The real trouble with the amateur iron game is face control, and the problem with face control, as you can easily see on the graphic below, is that a majority of ballflight errors are caused by having the clubface either too open or too closed relative to the clubhead path at the point of impact.

Although many players have forged hall-of-fame careers by wildly opening and closing the clubface during certain parts of the swing, the easiest way you can get to your goal number is by keeping clubface rotation to a minimum. You're starting to see this a lot on the Tour, because today's equipment isn't geared for shotmaking as it once was, due to the forgiveness factor built into modern irons. The name of today's game is neutrality, or keeping the clubface aligned with the swing plane from start to finish. Keeping your hands and arms from unwittingly opening or closing the face during your motion increases the odds that the clubface will be square (i.e., neutral) when you strike the ball. This will help you start more of your iron shots on line and reduce the sidespin associated with nasty slices and hooks.

In this section of the plan, you'll be asked to assess your ability to maintain a neutral clubface from start to finish, then perform a number of drills that help you do so in the event your clubface is unduly open or closed when you swing your irons. If you can pair a neutral clubface position with a solid divot pattern and forward-leaning shaft, you'll hit the kind of iron shots that give you the best chance to shoot your best score.

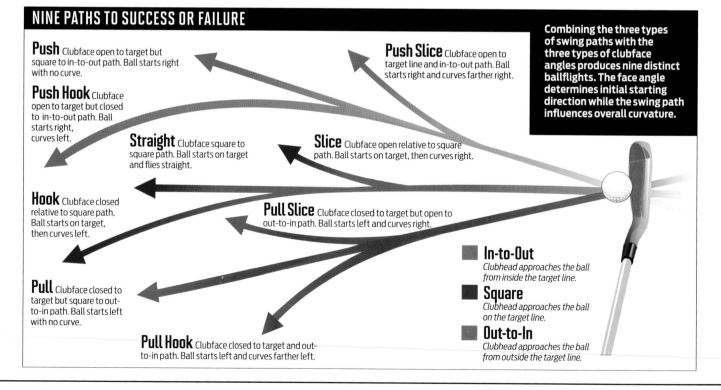

NINE PATHS TO SUCCESS OR FAILURE

Push Clubface open to target but square to in-to-out path. Ball starts right with no curve.

Push Hook Clubface open to target but closed to in-to-out path. Ball starts right, curves left.

Push Slice Clubface open to target line and in-to-out path. Ball starts right and curves farther right.

Straight Clubface square to square path. Ball starts on target and flies straight.

Slice Clubface open relative to square path. Ball starts on target, then curves right.

Hook Clubface closed relative to square path. Ball starts on target, then curves left.

Pull Slice Clubface closed to target but open to out-to-in path. Ball starts left and curves right.

Pull Clubface closed to target but square to out-to-in path. Ball starts left with no curve.

Pull Hook Clubface closed to target and out-to-in path. Ball starts left and curves farther left.

Combining the three types of swing paths with the three types of clubface angles produces nine distinct ballflights. The face angle determines initial starting direction while the swing path influences overall curvature.

In-to-Out
Clubhead approaches the ball from inside the target line.

Square
Clubhead approaches the ball on the target line.

Out-to-In
Clubhead approaches the ball from outside the target line.

ASSESSMENT CHECK YOUR CLUBFACE CONTROL

Use My Pro To Go to see if you're maintaining a neutral clubface from start to finish

How do you know if you're allowing the clubface to rotate out of control or keeping it square to your swing path? You can ask a friend, but he or she may not know what to look for. Trust what you see using My Pro To Go. Film your swing from a down-target view, following the guidelines on page 11. Capture it from address to finish, then follow the steps at right.

Setup
Launch the video from the My Swings button and select the line tool from the drawing menu in the upper right corner of the screen. At address, draw a line from the hosel through your belt buckle. This is your swing plane line, against which you'll gauge the neutrality of the clubface at key positions in your swing.

Hear It From a Pro!
Upload your swing to My Pro To Go for an in-depth analysis of your path and plane. Visit *myprotogo.com* for details.

Backswing
Step the video forward until the moment when the shaft is parallel to the ground and draw a line across the leading edge of the clubhead.
YES! The line points to about 12:30 on an imaginary clock.
NO! The line points to 1:00 or later (too closed) or 12:00 or earlier (too open) on an imaginary clock. The clubface in this photo is pointing to high noon and is slightly open.

Top of Backswing
Step the video to the end of your backswing and draw a line across the leading edge of the clubhead.
YES! The line is parallel to the plane line, and your left wrist is flat.
NO! Your left wrist is bowed (line more horizontal than the swing plane line) or cupped (line more vertical than the swing plane line). The clubface in this photo is slightly open.

Downswing
Step the video forward until the moment when the clubshaft is parallel to the ground or when the clubhead reaches your belt line, whichever comes first. Draw a line across the leading edge.
YES! The line points to about 12:30 on an imaginary clock.
NO! The line points to 1:00 or later (too closed) or 12:00 or earlier (too open) on an imaginary clock.

Release
Step the video forward until the shaft reappears out of your left side and draw a line across the leading edge.
Yes! The line is parallel to the plane line.
No! The line is more vertical than the swing plane line (face open, as in above) or the line is more horizontal than the swing plane line (face closed). If the clubface is open here, you can bet it was open at impact.

FIX USE YOUR GRIP TO SQUARE THE CLUBFACE

A better hold leads to better control

The more your clubface tends to turn open, the stronger you need to make your grip (hands rotated more to the right on the handle) so that you can get the clubface back to square at impact. You can check if you need to do this by setting up with the leading edge of your 7-iron pressed against the side of a chair (or desk, etc.). From here, turn your body into a mock impact position with the shaft leaning toward the target and your left wrist flat. If the face opens, you need to strengthen your grip and try it again. Keep strengthening your hold (turn your hands to the right) until you can rotate into your mock impact position with the face remaining square.

THE PERFECT HOLD

As with the dial on a stove, the more you turn your hands to the right on the grip, the more heat (or strength) you'll get. As in the example above, most golfers need more strength to get the clubface back to square at impact. Regardless of how strong you make your hold, it's important that you connect your hands in a way that enables them to work as a unit. This gives you the opportunity to exert total control over the club and create ample speed when you swing.

The next thing to get right is grip pressure. Ask a dozen teachers how tightly, on a scale of 1 to 10, you should squeeze the handle and six will say "8" and the other six will say "3." That's because grip pressure is relative to hand strength. Most Tour pros use a light grip pressure (the 3), which they can get away with because of the strength they've built up in their hands and wrists. Most amateur's

hands aren't that strong, which explains the firmer recommendation.

The secret to nailing your grip pressure is to squeeze the handle just hard enough so that the club doesn't move around in your hands during your swing. Remember, keep your forearms and wrists relaxed so you can swing the club with maximum speed. Think, "firm fingers, oily wrists."

Copy the positions on this page to build a hold that will give you the control and security you need to post your best score ever. Feel free to tweak it here and there using your ballflight as a guide. For example, if your slices start turning into hooks, dial back the strength and rotate your hands a little more toward the left. Do the opposite if you can't reel in your slice.

CHECKPOINT NO. 1
Wrap your left pinkie and ring and middle fingers firmly around the grip, pinching the handle into the crease at the bottom of your palm. Do it correctly and you should be able to hold the club in front of you at a 45 degree angle using these three fingers.

CHECKPOINT NO. 2
With downward pressure, the lifeline on your right palm should fit snugly over your left thumb. If there's space between them, you'll suffer.

CHECKPOINT NO. 3
Whether you use an overlapping or an interlocking grip, make sure that your right pinkie is applying pressure on your left hand, rather than simply resting on top of it. Just that little bit of pressure unifies your hands.

CHECKPOINT NO. 4
Notice how in a good grip your right palm faces the side of the grip. Apply pressure in this direction to activate your wrist hinge before you swing back.

CHECKPOINT NO. 5
If you see any space between the thumb and index finger on your right hand, pinch those digits together. Pressure here ensures a more connected grip and greater control.

CHECKPOINT NO. 6
Strengthen your grip for more control by making sure the creases between your thumbs and forefingers point more toward your right shoulder, not your chin.

CHECKPOINT NO. 7
A good grip has zero gaps. To make sure your right-hand hold is as solid as it can be, wedge a tee into the crease formed by your thumb and index finger of your right hand. Make some practice swings. Pinch the tee—it shouldn't fall out when you swing.

CHECKPOINT NO. 8
If you set your right hand on the handle correctly, you'll notice that the grip sits more in the fingers of your right hand and a bit lower in your palm. That's good! A finger grip is a speed grip.

TRY THIS! golfTEC

Use Your Knuckles as Clubface Guides
Ian Hughes, PGA: GolfTEC—Naperville, Calif.

The initial direction of the ball is mostly influenced by the direction the clubface is pointing at impact. Assuming your grip is neutral (creases formed by your thumbs and forefingers pointed at the right side of your chest), you can control the clubface at impact based on where the knuckles of your left hand point when you strike the ball, providing an easy visual to help you guide the face into proper position.

- *If you struggle with the ball starting too far right of your target,* get your knuckles to point more left of the target at impact. Feel like you're rolling your hands counterclockwise through the ball.
- *If you struggle with the ball starting too far left of the target,* get your knuckles pointing more right of the target at impact. Use more body turn then hand action through the ball since you're overrotating the clubface.
- *To start the ball on line consistently,* picture the knuckles of your left hand pointing straight at your target at the moment you strike the ball.

WINNING NUMBER 30

The average distance (in feet) remaining to the hole following all approach shots hit during the 2012 PGA Tour season, whether the ball landed on the green or not. Rory McIlroy topped the list with 28' 1".

Source: PGATour.com

PRACTICE HOW TO STRIKE IT WITH A SQUARE FACE

These three drills can solve your clubface problems and help you hit straighter iron shots

DRILL 5.5

Credit Card Drill

When Days 20 and 22
Where Practice facility
How Long 20 swings each session
(about 15 mins.)

HOW TO DO IT

This drill will help you get the clubface into a squared position at the two points in your swing where it matters the most: top of the backswing and impact. Follow the steps below.

Step 1

Get a credit card from your wallet. Open the Velcro strap on your glove and slide the credit card between the back of your left wrist and the inside of the glove (*photo, below*). Half of the credit card should be visible. Redo the strap tightly.

Step 2

Take your address. The credit card will bend due to the way your left wrist cups at setup. Make your regular backswing with the goal of keeping the credit card

Use a credit card to practice keeping your left wrist flat and the clubface square.

as flat as possible. Keeping the credit card flat is a good thing because it means that you didn't cup your left wrist and open the clubface. Make repeated backswings, stopping at the top each time to gain a better feel of a flat left wrist (and credit card).

Step 3

Swing to impact. Do it at 25 percent speed. The card should help you keep your hands from flipping the clubhead. Your left wrist should be nice and flat in your mock impact position. Notice how this gets the shaft to lean slightly toward the target at impact (*photo, right*).

Step 4

Speed up your swings and hit actual shots. If you feel the card digging into your left forearm, you're allowing your left wrist to cup either at the top of your backswing or when you strike the ball. Go back to making slow-motion swings so you can regain the right sensations.

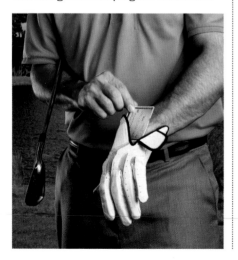

BONUS LESSONS!

Watch videos of these drills at *golftec.com/parplan*.

DRILL 5.6

Book Drill

When Day 21
Where Home or office
How Long 20 swings each session
(about 15 mins.)

HOW TO DO IT
Grab a book (about the thickness of
the one pictured here) and grip it along
its spine with your right hand above
your left as you do when you grip a golf
clubs (*photo, near right*). Next, settle in
to your address posture and follow the
steps below.

Swinging a
book as you
do your clubs
can help you
groove a square-
faced swing.

Left wrist flat here...   ...and here...   ...and here.

Step 1
Swing the book back using your normal
motion and stop when your left arm gets
parallel to the ground. Keep both of your
palms flat against the book as you do
this while flattening your left wrist and
cupping your right. If you do it correctly,
the book will rest against the inside of
your left forearm.

Step 2
Swing into a mock impact position. Get
the front (or back) of the book to directly
face the target. Again, make sure the
book is pressed snugly against the inside
of your left forearm. If you do it correctly,
the book will lean slightly toward the
target (as the clubshaft does on your
good swings).

Step 3
Rotate forward into your release while
keeping the book against the inside of
your left forearm. Get the cover (back
or front) to point more behind you.
Repeat your swing, doing it faster and
faster each time. It's critical that your left
forearm stays in contact with the book
the whole way.

PRACTICE HOW TO STRIKE IT WITH A SQUARE FACE

These three drills can solve your clubface problems and help you hit straighter iron shots

DRILL 5.7

Release Check Drill

When Day 22
Where Home or office
How Long Ten swings (about 20 mins.)

HOW TO DO IT

You'll need to go back to the mirror you've been using that allows you to take full swings without banging into walls or furniture. Set up with the mirror across from you, and make the best iron swing you can muster. Stop in your release position and, without moving anything else, look up into the mirror and assess your technique. Your release is an important area of clubface control because if the clubface is open here, then it was more than likely open when you made contact with the ball. If the clubface is overrotated in your release, then it may be the cause of your hooking or pull problems. Check for the following:

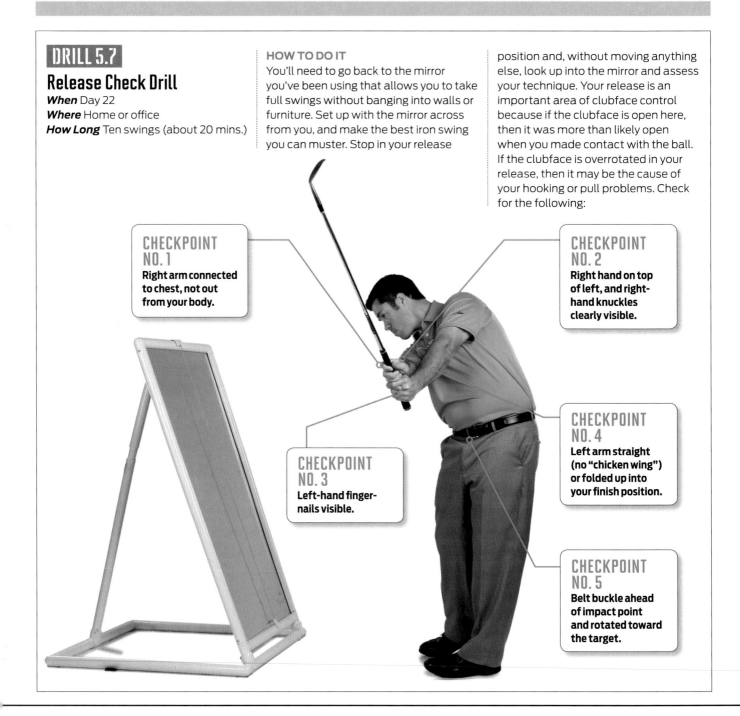

CHECKPOINT NO. 1
Right arm connected to chest, not out from your body.

CHECKPOINT NO. 2
Right hand on top of left, and right-hand knuckles clearly visible.

CHECKPOINT NO. 3
Left-hand finger-nails visible.

CHECKPOINT NO. 4
Left arm straight (no "chicken wing") or folded up into your finish position.

CHECKPOINT NO. 5
Belt buckle ahead of impact point and rotated toward the target.

DRILL 5.8

Starting Line Drill

When Days 20 and 29
Where Practice facility
How Long 10 swings each session
(about 15 mins.)

HOW TO DO IT

One way to know if you're getting the clubface pointed in the direction it needs to be at impact is to take a hard look at where your shots start in relation to your target line. Knowing this gives you important clues about the quality of your clubface angle because clubface angle pretty much determines the line on which the ball initially travels. When you're on the range, set an alignment stick directly on your target line about seven yards in front of the ball, and have a friend tape your swings using My Pro To Go from a down-target perspective using the guidelines on page 11. After a few swings, play the video and note on which side of the stick the ball starts. If the majority of your shots start out to the right of the target line, then you can bet your clubface is a little open (relative to the target line) when you strike the ball. If the majority of your shots start out to the left of the target line, than you can bet your clubface is a little closed when you strike the ball. Once you're able to flight the ball over the stick (or even hit it), you know you're really in control of the clubface and in great position to shoot your goal score.

> "Your release is an important area of clubface control because if the clubface is open here, then it was more than likely open when you made contact with the ball."

Aim at the stick and then try to hit it.

GOAL 1 *Improve Your Contact*

Assess where on the face you're impacting the ball and the quality of your divots, then perform the Towel, *L-to-L*, Divot, and Business Card drills using the schedule on page 184.

GOAL 2 *Improve Your Clubface Control*

Use My Pro To Go to see if your clubface is square, open, or closed at key moments in your swing, then perform the Credit Card, Book, Release Check, and Starting Line drills using the suggested schedule on page 184.

CHECK YOUR PROGRESS

Decide if your iron contact and clubface control are where they need to be in order to move on to the next section by uploading your swing to My Pro To Go for a professional critique of your technique (plus drills that target your weaknesses). Visit *golftec.com/ parplan* to register for a 50 percent discount, available only to *The Par Plan* readers. Purchase lessons at *myprotogo.com*.

LESSONS BY golfTEC

For the ultimate experience, visit your local GolfTEC improvement center for a one-on-one lesson and hands-on instruction that guarantees lasting results. Visit *golftec.com* or consult the improvement center directory on pages 186–191.

MYPRO TOGO

DAY 23

TAKE NEW SKILLS TO THE COURSE

How to transfer what you've learned to your actual rounds—and save a few strokes every time you play—by using your head

Good players know that shooting a competitive score involves more than putting your best swings and strokes on the ball. The game is as much mental as anything else, which is a fact you need to accept, because the round in which you're going to attempt to shoot your best score ever will be unlike any other. Most of the times you play the goal may be to enjoy your family or friends or entertain clients. Here, you're looking to shoot a number, and if you're going to be successful, you better prepare for it mentally both leading up to the big day and during the round itself.

Believe it or not, there are things you can do beyond improving your swing skills that can boost your performance on the course. Some are obvious, such as showing up at the course with enough time to properly warm up before you play. Others are more sublime, as in the *way* you warm up or the foods you eat when you play. In this section of the plan, you'll spend a day learning about the game outside the game to train your body and mind to perform at the highest level. You only have one week left. It's time to get smart and organize your skills for when the time comes to shoot your best score ever.

CARD SHARKS

A quick look at key PGA Tour scoring averages:

3.08
PGA Tour
Par 3 Scoring

4.08
PGA Tour
Par 4 Scoring

4.70
PGA Tour
Par 5 Scoring

22.6%
PGA Tour
Bounce Back

17.7%
PGA Tour Reverse
Bounce Back (scoring
over par after scoring
under par on the
previous hole)

2012 season
Source: PGATour.com

LESSON MAKE A PLAN FOR SUCCESS

Study the course to know when to play it safe or go for broke

Showing up at the course without a well-thought-out game plan is like an NFL quarterback calling signals without ever having read the offensive playbook. Even if you've never game-planned a round before, you need to do it here because it'll be the difference between success and failure. If you haven't decided where you're going to attempt to shoot your best score ever, do it now and purchase a yardage book from the pro shop. This book is your scoring map. Look for the following green-, yellow- and red-light situations.

YELLOW LIGHT PAR 5S

During this round you're going to treat every par 5 as a three-shot/two-putt hole. You're not going to go for the green in two. The reason is that it's unlikely you can follow up a big drive with an even bigger 3-wood or hybrid, and the keys to scoring are more about limiting mistakes than pulling off a miraculous shot or making the odd eagle. Take a page out of Zach Johnson's book. Johnson won the 2007 Masters by laying up on every par-5 hole at Augusta National that week, leaving about 75 yards for his third shot on each one. The plan paid off in that he birdied 11 of the 16 par 5s en route to a two-stroke victory

GREEN LIGHT MIDDLE PINS

Phone the pro shop the day before you play and ask where they plan to position the pins on the greens (or keep a keen eye for pin placement as you make your way around the course). Earmark every hole that will feature a middle pin position as a green-light situation and take dead aim at the flag.

RED LIGHT TUCKED PINS

If the pin is set anywhere but the middle, forget about it. Hit your approach to the center of the green. This is hard to do—there isn't a golfer in the world who doesn't enjoy hitting to tap-in range. You'll do more for your score, however, if you use caution in these situations and save your attacks for when the pin is in the middle.

RED LIGHT FAIRWAY BUNKERS

Most amateurs are going to suffer a bogey when they land their tee shot in a fairway bunker. Locate fairway sand in your yardage book and calculate the distance from the tees you'll be playing to both the front edge and to the back edge of any hazard within firing range of your driver. If the back edge is farther than what you can carry your driver (even if it's off to the left or right of the fairway), throttle down to the club that will land the ball just short of the front edge. This is especially critical on par 5s, where all you're looking to do is lay up with your second shot anyway.

GREEN LIGHT YOUR GAME STRENGTHS

Assess what you feel are the strengths of your game. If you're a consistent driver, for example, then look for holes where you can really take advantage of your length, like on short par 4s or holes without a lot of hazards. If you're a good bunker player, then you might want to think about breaking the rules a little and going for greens tucked behind bunkers and lean on your sand game to get up and down in the event you miss the target on your approach.

The same strategy applies to your weaknesses, too. If, for example, you're not very good at escaping

bunkers, then avoid them at all costs. If you tend to slice the most with a driver in your hand, use less club on the tee box, especially if there's trouble on the right.

KNOW YOUR YARDAGES

Jumping on green-light situations and playing it safe on red-light ones only works if you know how far you hit each of your clubs. This is critical knowledge to own in order to successfully navigate the course. If you haven't done so already, spend an afternoon at your practice facility and mark down how far you can carry the ball with each of your clubs. The carry distance is important here, especially with your driver. Hit 10 shots with each club and compute the average. If you're like most players, you'll be surprised by the discrepancy between how far you *actually* hit your clubs and how far you *think* you hit your clubs.

This also works for your putter. Spend some time on a green that rolls about the same speed as the ones on the course at which you'll attempt to shoot your best score, and find out how far you roll the ball with three different stroke lengths (using your personal tempo). Practice toe-toe strokes and ones that are six inches past each toe and, finally, a foot past each toe and you'll be set.

A NOTE ON CHIPPING

If you miss a green and have to play a short chip or pitch, try to keep the ball below the hole. You should think more about this than trying to hole out or get ultraclose, because the odds of holing out from off the green aren't very high, while the odds of missing a downhill breaker are mammoth.

"You'll be surprised by the discrepancy between how far you *actually* hit your clubs and how far you *think* you hit your clubs."

LESSON WARM UP TO GET HOT

Get your round motoring out the blocks even before you hit your first shot

If you show up at the course with only minutes to spare before your tee time, then your chances of shooting your best score ever aren't going to be very good.

Not only do you need to arrive on time, you need to show up early. Most Tour players get to the course about 90 minutes before the start of their round. That's a little excessive for the amateur ranks. If you arrive at the course 45 minutes before your tee time, you'll be able to check in and pay your green fees, switch into your spikes, use the rest room, and put in a solid 30-minute preround warm-up.

Since you never know what life will throw at you, it could be the case that there isn't enough time to engage in a proper warm-up. That's not ideal, but it's not the end of the world, either. You can still prep your body and swing for a successful round if, literally, you only have minutes to spare. Follow the guidelines below to determine your preparation routine based on how much time you have. Regardless of the situation or how early or late you arrive at the course, get into game mode as soon as possible. Once you take that first step out of the cart toward the practice green or hitting area, start focusing on the task at hand. An intent golfer is a successful golfer.

5 MINUTES TO TEE TIME

Forget about emptying that large bucket. The best you can do for your game is to roll a few long lag putts on the practice green both uphill and downhill. This will give you a feel for the speed of the greens and help you establish a rhythm for your stroke. This is important because a sizable chunk of the strokes you'll need to complete your round will take place on the putting green. Knock a few in the hole from close range after you're done lagging to get comfortable with the sound of the ball rolling into the cup, then swing two clubs at a smooth pace to loosen up your muscles.

10 MINUTES TO TEE TIME

Do the same as above, but practice about ten 15-footers that break in both directions. These are the types of putts you'll encounter the most when you're out on the course, so it'll help you to see them before you begin your round. Then, hit some short chip shots, focusing on rhythm and tempo while bumping the grass under the ball. Stretch before you hit the first tee by making full turns back and through with a club held behind your shoulders. Do some deep squats and toe-touches to further loosen up your joints and muscles.

20 MINUTES TO TEE TIME

Do the same as above, and then grab a few practice balls and hit three to five shots on the range. Swing the club you plan to use on the first tee. You don't need to go at it full throttle. Get a feel for a smooth rhythm and the swing path that will land your first shot safely in the middle of the fairway.

30 MINUTES TO TEE TIME

With a half hour remaining before you tee off, you can perform a more traditional warm-up. Again, roll lags, 15-footers, and a few short ones to get comfortable with the sound of the ball dropping into the cup, and then head to the practice range. Avoid the urge to bang driver and instead grab your sand wedge. Hit a 10-yard chip, and then try to land your next shot on top of the first ball. Without switching clubs, try to land your third shot on top of the second ball and so on. (This is a warm-up routine made famous by 1996 British Open winner Tom Lehman.) By the 15th ball, you should be making full swings. Focus on contacting the ball crisply rather than swinging for the fences. The feel of a properly struck wedge is a great one to have. It's a real confidence builder.

Next, hit three or four shots with every other iron in your bag, starting with your pitching wedge, and work your way up to your driver. Limit the number of driver swings to five. Anything more and you'll risk tiring yourself out. If you have time to spare, jump into the practice bunker and hit three sand shots. Don't worry about your results. The important thing here is to get a feel for how much sand to remove when you swing. If the conditions are soft or fluffy, you'll need to take more sand at impact. If the bunker is firm or wet, you'll need to take less.

IMPORTANT

As you're loosening up, don't fret about mechanics. Your preround warm-up is about establishing the tempo and rhythm you'll use that day. To increase the likelihood of transferring your good practice swings to the course, treat each shot you hit on the range as the real thing. Stand behind the ball, pick a target, visualize the shot, aim, and fire. Don't use alignment clubs and sticks since you won't be able to use them during the round. Simulate the real thing as you warm up so you'll be ready for it when you're out on the course.

"Once you take that first step out of the cart toward the practice green or hitting area, start focusing on the task at hand."

FIND YOUR PERSONAL PLAYING STYLE

Choose one of three ways to settle in and smoothly start back

One of the most important parts of your swing is one that happens even before you start the club back: your preshot routine. This is when you assess the situation, pick your target, picture the type of shot you want to hit, and ultimately step into your stance and begin your swing. There are as many different ways to do this as there are golfers, but there are only three types, and they each relate to a preferred style of performance. Knowing which style works best for you will help you address each shot with a high level of confidence and ensure a smoother start to your swing.

1 VISUAL PERFORMANCE

If you're really good at seeing the shape of the shot you want to hit during your preshot routine, then you're a visual performance player. While it's always a good idea to visualize shot shape, some are better at it than others. If this is you, then you'll get the most out of your game by selecting very precise targets and intensely focusing on them so you can draw the ideal shot shape in your mind's eye. This will help you produce the necessary swing path and clubface positions. Jack Nicklaus and Davis Love III are two famous examples of visual performers. They spend most of their preshot routine focusing on the target, not the ball. They see the shot and then hit it.

2 RHYTHM PERFORMANCE

Do any of your foursome move around a lot in their stance before starting the club back, as Lee Trevino did in his prime? If so, then it's likely that they're rhythm players. These golfers are most comfortable going about their preshot ritual in a controlled rhythm, the beat of which helps them move from target selection to backswing at a natural pace. If you like music, or catch yourself waggling the club back and forth or shuffling your feet at address, then you're probably a rhythm player. A good way to build on this playing style is to swing to a beat, just as you do when you practice your putting tempo (pages 42 and 43). Three-time major winner Vijay Swing (a rhythm performer) counts "13, 17" when he swings. It's an odd combination, but for him it delivers the correct pace for his motion.

3 KINESTHETIC PERFORMANCE

Some players don't feel comfortable starting the club back until they *feel* it's time to do so. The feeling can be obvious, as with the weight of the clubhead as it hovers above the ground at address. Other times it's sublime, like a tiny amount of weight shifting to the front of the right foot as a player settles into address. These types of golfers are kinesthetic performers. The best swing cue to them is a sense that everything is where it needs to be.

If you don't know which style works best for you, time your preshot routine and then try to complete it either in a slower or faster amount of time. If this makes you feel uncomfortable, then you're probably a rhythm player. You'll know if you're a kinesthetic player if you can stand over the ball without moving for a while and still hit a successful shot. Visual players know who they are in a heartbeat: they can see the ball fly through the air, even on short chips and putts.

VISUAL PLAYER
You like to see shots. Focus on the target, visualize the trajectory, and use the image to guide your swing. For the best results, pick very small targets and visualize very specific shots (how far, how high, how much curve, how much roll, etc.).

RHYTHM PLAYER

You like to move around in your setup, or waggle the club. Count a steady beat in your head as you set up and swing and take the same amount of time to complete your preshot routine on every shot.

KINESTHETIC PLAYER

You may take one minute to complete your preshot routine on one swing and 15 seconds on the next. All that matters to you is that when you feel you're ready, you go ahead and start your backswing.

LESSON PAR PLAN SCORING SECRETS

How to ensure success before you even start the club back

Fast-forward a week or so. The big day has arrived, and you're about to shoot the lowest number you ever have in your life. The hard work you've put in the last three weeks and the work you still have to complete on your shotmaking and bunker play is going to pay off in spades. There are, however, some lingering obstacles, and a lot of them have to do with *you*. Even if your new swing is firing on all cylinders, it'll fail to fuel a personal-best round if you don't do *your* part. Here's how, in seven easy steps, to control yourself, your emotions, and the way you deal with pressure to make sure your investment in the plan pays off.

1 BE FRESH

The night before you try to post your best round ever isn't the time to play in a 10-hour hold 'em tournament. Get at least eight hours of rest the night before your round. Sufficient sleep helps you to remain alert and perform at your maximum capabilities. Schedule a mid- or late-morning round (see No. 5).

2 GO IT ALONE

Sure, it'd be great to post your best score in front of your friends and family, but keep in mind that this is about you and your goal number, not the camaraderie of a typical round. Plus, you won't be able to focus on the task at hand if you're engaged in familiar conversation or playing under the pressure of having everyone you're with know what you're trying to accomplish. When you go to shoot your goal score, go it alone or, if the course requires you to play in a foursome, go in as a single.

3 PLAY IT UP

The goal is to shoot your best number, not shoot your best number from the black tees. If you're trying to shoot in the 90s or 80s, play from the white, or forward, tees. Don't stretch the course more than 6,500 yards. If you're trying to break into the 70s, then your game might be able to handle more yardage, but don't feel the need to raise your game to Tour standards. The 7,500-yard courses the pros play are cut fast. You won't get the roll they do on yours. If you happen to reach your number from the forward tees, make your *next* goal to reach it from the tips.

4 KEEP AN EYE ON MOTHER NATURE

The last thing you want to do is try to shoot your career-best round in a 30-mph wind. Or a steady rain that makes the course play longer than the yardage. Or 105 degree heat. If it looks like the weather is going to turn on you, reschedule your round. You want everything to be working your way, including the weather.

5 PLAY EARLIER, NOT LATER

Scheduling your tee time for later in the day can also stack the odds against you. As the hours pass, the grass continues to grow. This is an important factor on the greens, where longer blade lengths cause the ball to bend more and roll different than what you expect. (You'll also be dealing with more footprints.) Avoid teeing off following a busy morning at work. Shoot your goal score on a day without commitments. You probably won't get the job done if you're thinking about the e-mails you need to send and the phone calls you're missing instead of your swing and shot selection.

> ## "If you reach the point where you have a chance to post your best score ever with only three or four holes left to play, then you're going to do it sooner than later."

TRY THIS! golfTEC

Don't Forget Your Post-Shot Routine

Trevor Broesamle, PGA: GolfTEC—Santa Barbara, Calif.

SMART SHOTS

Choosing the flag as your target isn't always a good option. If the pin is tucked or guarded by a hazard, play to the fat of the green. If the pin is set in the middle, go for it. View every hole with a middle pin position as a scoring opportunity and attack the flag.

6 STAY CALM AT THE START

Short-game and scoring guru Dave Pelz published some interesting data in the October 2006 issue of *Golf Magazine.* It showed that golfers score better on the middle 10 holes than the first or last 4. It's easy to see how the pressure to shoot a certain score might make you nervous and result in poor scores at the finish. But poor play on the first 4 holes? Perhaps this is because you're not prepared to scramble when you miss the first few greens. This data emphasizes the importance of warming up your short-game feel and touch before heading to the first tee. It also indicates a need to stay calm on the opening holes. Adopt a more conservative approach at the start so you don't completely ruin your chances of posting your best number even before you reach midround. If the opening hole is a short par 4 or even a par 5, hit 3-wood instead of driver. Buck the amateur trend and tread water on the first 4 holes instead of sinking to the bottom.

7 FINISH WITH A FLAIR

The Pelz data also suggests that amateurs fall apart during the home stretch. If you find yourself in position to shoot your goal score with only a few holes remaining, then step up your attack. You've obviously played well up to this point, so keep the pedal to the metal. It's better to come up short while on the attack than failing because you played too conservatively at the end. Take solace in the fact that you came close. Truth is, if you reach the point where you have a chance to post your best score ever with only three or four holes left to play, then you're going to do it sooner than later.

You've gone through your preshot routine and executed according to your plan, but the result was substandard. What you do after less-than-desirable shots is just as important as the routine leading up to them. Follow these steps to better cope with poor results and move on to the next shot with a clear mind and a positive attitude.

1. **REACT NATURALLY** It's okay to get frustrated, but don't let it simmer for more than a few seconds. Move immediately to step 2.

2. **REDO THE SHOT** Since you can't keep hitting the shot until you get the result you want (wouldn't that be nice?), repeat the swing without a ball. This time, use a motion that "fixes" the previous shot. Go as far as visualizing the outcome while holding your finish.

3. **HIT THE RESET BUTTON** This step is the most important. When you return your club to its slot, imagine that there's a big red reset button at the bottom of the bag. Once the butt of the club hits the button, it's a cue to clear the last shot from your mind and move confidently to the next shot.

WINNING NUMBER 58

The percentage of Golf Magazine readers who admitted to drinking alcohol during rounds (online poll, February 2007). No wonder the average handicap hasn't dropped in 40 years! Alcohol (including beer) is a sedative, a diuretic, and it can impair coordination.

LESSON FUEL A SUCCESSFUL ROUND

How to eat and drink your way to your best round ever

The evolution of the athlete-golfer (Tiger Woods, Rory McIlroy, Dustin Johnson, etc.) has completely changed the way players look at fueling their bodies during play. In addition to breathing properly, exercising, and focusing on stretching both on and off the course, elite players pay careful attention to what they consume to maximize performance and shoot the best scores possible. You don't see many Tour pros slugging coffee on the first tee and breaking at the turn toward the nearest hot dog stand or beverage cart, yet that's what many amateurs do, too often to excess. You should be worried about your ability to get the ball in the hole in the fewest strokes possible, not your digestive system. Dehydration and the sugar spikes in your blood that result from eating the wrong kinds of foods and drinking the wrong kinds of liquids rob you of the concentration and energy you need to perform your best.

To post your best score ever, you'll need the right kind and right amount of nutrition and hydration during the course of play. While you don't need to carry all of the products shown at right when you're on the course, think about adding a few of them to your bag. That way you'll know that mistakes made on the course are your swing's fault, not your diet's. Here's a quick look at how some brand-name food and beverage items can fuel a more successful and healthier round.

WATER

Look on the label for a high pH value. This will help you retain the water in your body for a longer period of time. (If you're not sure of the pH value, squeeze a bit of lemon juice into the bottle for the correct effect.) Take a sip every hole for proper hydration. Water tends to leave your body faster when you chug it.

ENERGY PRODUCTS

The more you eat, the more your blood routes its way to your stomach for digestion—not good when you're trying to focus on a slick six-footer for par. Energy gels and drops provide key minerals such as magnesium, zinc, and B12 without the need for a big meal. Plus, it's better to consume liquids than solids when you're active.

Take New Skills to the Course

HEALTH BARS

These are great supplements for that burger or club sandwich you always go for at the turn. Just be sure that the bar you choose is low in sugar. (Insulin spikes cause a loss of focus.) Fruit used to be the snack of choice on Tour, but now the trend is for something with as much nutritional value but less sugar.

SUPPLEMENTS

Check with your health-store professional for information on supplements you can add to your water or juice to boost on-course performance. Some products provide just a kick of caffeine to replace your typical mug of joe. A lot of Tour players use a whey protein shake mix. This kind of nutrition can turn your swing practice into more of a workout.

GOAL 1 *Chart Your Yardage*
Spend an afternoon at the range, preferably with a range finder, to accurately determine how far you carry each of your clubs.

GOAL 2 *Discover Your Optimum Performance Style*
Look for clues that tell you if you're a visual, kinesthetic, or rhythm player so you can see your targets more clearly and start your swing smoother.

GOAL 3 *Make a Plan*
Survey the course you'll be playing and look for holes and pin positions where you can go on the attack, and locate areas that could cause havoc with your weaknesses or play to your strengths.

CHECK YOUR PROGRESS

Discover if each part of your game is keeping pace with the demands of the plan by uploading a video of your driver or iron swing, or your chipping and putting stroke, to a My Pro To Go coach for a professional critique of your technique (plus drills that target your weaknesses). Visit *golftec.com/parplan* to register for a 50 percent discount, available only to *The Par Plan* readers. Purchase lessons at *myprotogo.com*.

LESSONS BY golfTEC

If you're having trouble taking your A game to the course, visit your local GolfTEC improvement center for a one-on-one lesson and hands-on instruction that guarantees lasting results. Visit *golftec.com* or consult the center directory on pages 186–191.

LAUNCH PARTY

A quick look at key PGA Tour carry distance averages:

243
PGA Tour 3-Wood Distance (yds.)

225
PGA Tour Hybrid (15°–18°) Distance (yds.)

203
PGA Tour 4-Iron Distance (yds.)

172
PGA Tour 7-Iron Distance (yds.)

136
PGA Tour Pitching Wedge Distance (yds.)

Source: Trackman

DAY

24

FINE-TUNE YOUR GEAR FOR SCORING

How to check if your gear allows you to take full advantage of your best swings

By **DOUG RIKKERS, PGA**
Director of Clubfitting, GolfTEC

Shooting your best score doesn't just mean hitting your driver as far as possible, but as was mentioned on page 30, you should start by getting on a launch monitor and seeing if your big stick is properly fitted and tuned to your swing. You might also want to check out *Golf Magazine's* **See Try Buy** program to find out how to test and purchase the newest and best gear. (Visit golf.com/see-try-buy for more information.)

Next, spend some time analyzing the rest of your clubs to make sure you have all the distances properly gapped. Many modern sets have significant loft gaps—pay particular attention to the transition from your shortest iron to your longest wedge. Then, investigate your putter and ball fit. Using a putter with the wrong length can negatively affect your stroke, while the wrong ball can hurt you both off the tee and around the greens. It might seem a little late in the game to start worrying about your clubs, and in truth you should always stay on top of your equipment, but it's even more critical now that you make sure everything is optimized for scoring.

FIX MIND YOUR GAPS

Check your lofts to create an evenly spaced set for optimum performance

One of the most damaging mistakes you can make with your club setup is to gear everything for maximum distance. With the exception of your driver, you should think about every club in your bag in regard to a specific distance range. To begin, consider how far you typically hit your driver and what distances your alternative tee clubs should go to give you the best chance of both hitting the fairway and giving you the opportunity to successfully get on the green with your next shot (or hitting the occasional par 5 in two). For example, if you typically hit your driver 250 yards, it doesn't really help you to put a superhot, strong-lofted 3-wood in your bag that goes 240 yards when well-struck. In this case you'd be better off choosing a weaker-lofted fairway wood that's easier to hit and travels closer to 225 or 230 yards. Obviously, if you choose to carry a

third fairway wood or strong hybrid, you'll need to fit that club into a shorter distance range, probably in the neighborhood of 200 to 215 yards.

The next important consideration is how to properly transition from your hybrids to your longest iron. Unless you're a very accomplished player, you should probably have at least two hybrids in your set. The normal mid-range game-improvement iron set today typically starts with a 22 degree 4-iron or a 25-degree 5-iron. For most players, it's best to carry a strong hybrid with around 22 degrees of loft and a weaker one that measures about 25 degrees. Since hybrids carry quite a bit longer than an iron of the same loft, this setup will allow you to replace what would be 3- and 4-irons with hybrids and start your iron set with a 5-iron. Regardless, you need to pay close attention to how this transition works so you can maximize your scoring on par 5s and long par 4s.

Finally, you have to be absolutely certain that the transition from your irons to wedges is correct. Most modern iron sets have relatively strong lofts, meaning your pitching wedge probably measures about 45–46 degrees (as opposed to the 48-degree models of old). This means you must have a gap wedge with about 50 degrees of loft to go along with your sand and lob wedges. The best choices to fill out your wedge set are normally 54- and 58-degree models, or maybe 56- and 60-degree wedges. The key is to cover every distance as best you can without leaving holes that force to you try for too many touch shots.

A final thing to keep in mind is that the slower your swing speed, the larger the loft gaps you need. Conversely, if you swing fast, you can get away with smaller loft gaps. A gap analysis done on a launch monitor at GolfTEC is a great way to figure it all out and get it right.

GAPS FOR EVERY GAME

Regardless of what caliber player you are, having the right mixture of clubs in your bag is critical to scoring. Take a quick peek at the guidelines at right to see if you're on the right track.

Accomplished Player (0–9 handicap)
You're a good player who wants to take advantage of par 5s and short par 4s. You need some options off the tee that can also work as par-5 weapons.

- Driver
- Strong fairway wood (13–14.5 degrees)
- Weak-lofted fairway wood or hybrid (18–19 degrees)
- 3-iron or weak hybrid (22–24 degrees)
- 4-iron through 48-degree PW
- Strong (54-degree) sand wedge
- Lob wedge (58–60 degrees)
- Putter

Midhandicapper (10–18 handicap)
You're relatively solid all around but definitely need some help with the longer clubs as well as dialing in your scoring zone shots.

- Driver
- Traditional or weak fairway wood (15–18 degrees)
- 3-iron replacement hybrid (21–22-degrees)
- 4-iron or 4-iron replacement hybrid (25 degrees)
- 5-iron through 45-degree PW
- Gap wedge (50 degrees)
- Strong sand wedge (54–56 degrees)
- Lob wedge (58–60 degrees)
- Putter

High Handicapper (> 19 handicap)
You need as much help as possible with anything longer than a 5- or 6-iron. Don't be afraid to add as many hybrids as you like.

- Driver
- Traditional or weak loft fairway wood (15–18 degrees)
- 3-iron (21–22 degrees), 4-iron (24–25 degrees), and 5-iron (27 degrees) replacement hybrids
- 6-iron through 45-degree PW
- Gap wedge (50 degrees)
- Strong (5-degree) sand wedge
- Weak (58-degree) sand wedge
- Putter

HYBRID GAPS

Consider replacing long irons with similarly lofted hybrids, and gap them just as you would any clubs in your set.

WOOD GAPS

The shorter you carry the ball with your driver, the less there is need for a souped-up and superstrong 3-wood.

IRON GAPS

The age-old standard of having 4-degree gaps among all of your irons still holds true. Have them checked often.

WEDGE GAPS

The gap between your highest-lofted iron and your lowest-lofted wedge is the most important in your bag.

FIX GET THE RIGHT GRIPS

Your grips are your only connection to the club, so it's important that they be the right size

I f you're like most golfers, you bought your clubs and gave little thought to the grips with which they came fitted. Unfortunately, according to a *Golf Magazine* study (January 2011), 90 percent of golfers are actually using the wrong-sized grip. Launch-monitor analyses showed that 9 out of every 10 players who took part in the study performed better with a grip size different from the one on their personal clubs. Obviously, the grip is your main connection to the club and plays a major role in how well you can control both the clubhead and your shots. If you really care about shooting lower scores, you simply cannot gloss over this part of your equipment.

To begin checking your grip size, take your normal hold and note of the position of the fingers on your left hand. Ideally, the tip of your left ring finger just barely makes contact with your left thumb pad. If it's digging in, your grips are too small (*photo, right*); if there's a significant gap, your grips are too big. Although the traditional notion that smaller grips promote a better release of the club (making it easier to draw shots) or that bigger grips inhibit the release (leading to more fades and slices) has never been proved, improper grip size can cause a host of problems that will make it tough to shoot your best score.

For example, if your grips are too small, you'll need more strength to hold on to your clubs during your swing, which will increase tension, tighten your muscles, and produce a swing that lacks dynamic movement and overall smoothness. This situation not only saps power and speed from your swing, but it also makes it quite a bit more difficult to create solid contact and control the direction of your shots. Similarly, grips that are too big can also put more pressure on your hands and wrists and force you

Your fingers will dig in to your palm— and you'll lose control—if your grips are too small.

to expend more energy and strength to control the club during your swing. Clearly, both these situations are ones you want to avoid at all costs.

The only way to know what size grip to use is to experiment with as many different sizes as possible. When you decide to make the change, ask the professional who's fitting you the following questions. The answers will go a long way toward making sure the job gets done right.

1. What size grips are currently on my set? Part of a good trial is comparing your performance with new grips against what you brought to the fitting.

2. Should I test different styles? Yes. One style (velvet, cord, half cord, etc.) will certainly feel better than the rest.

3. Are grips worth the investment? A set of 14 new grips will run you anywhere from $50 to $100, plus $25 in labor. That's a small price to pay for increased performance without making a single swing change.

HAND YOURSELF NEW GRIPS

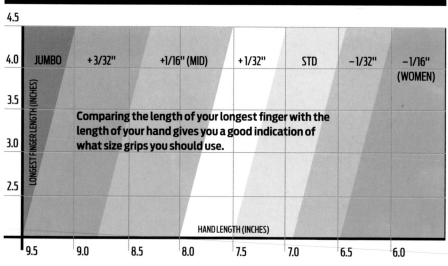

JUMBO	+3/32"	+1/16" (MID)	+1/32"	STD	−1/32"	−1/16" (WOMEN)

LONGEST FINGER LENGTH (INCHES): 4.5, 4.0, 3.5, 3.0, 2.5

Comparing the length of your longest finger with the length of your hand gives you a good indication of what size grips you should use.

HAND LENGTH (INCHES): 9.5, 9.0, 8.5, 8.0, 7.5, 7.0, 6.5, 6.0

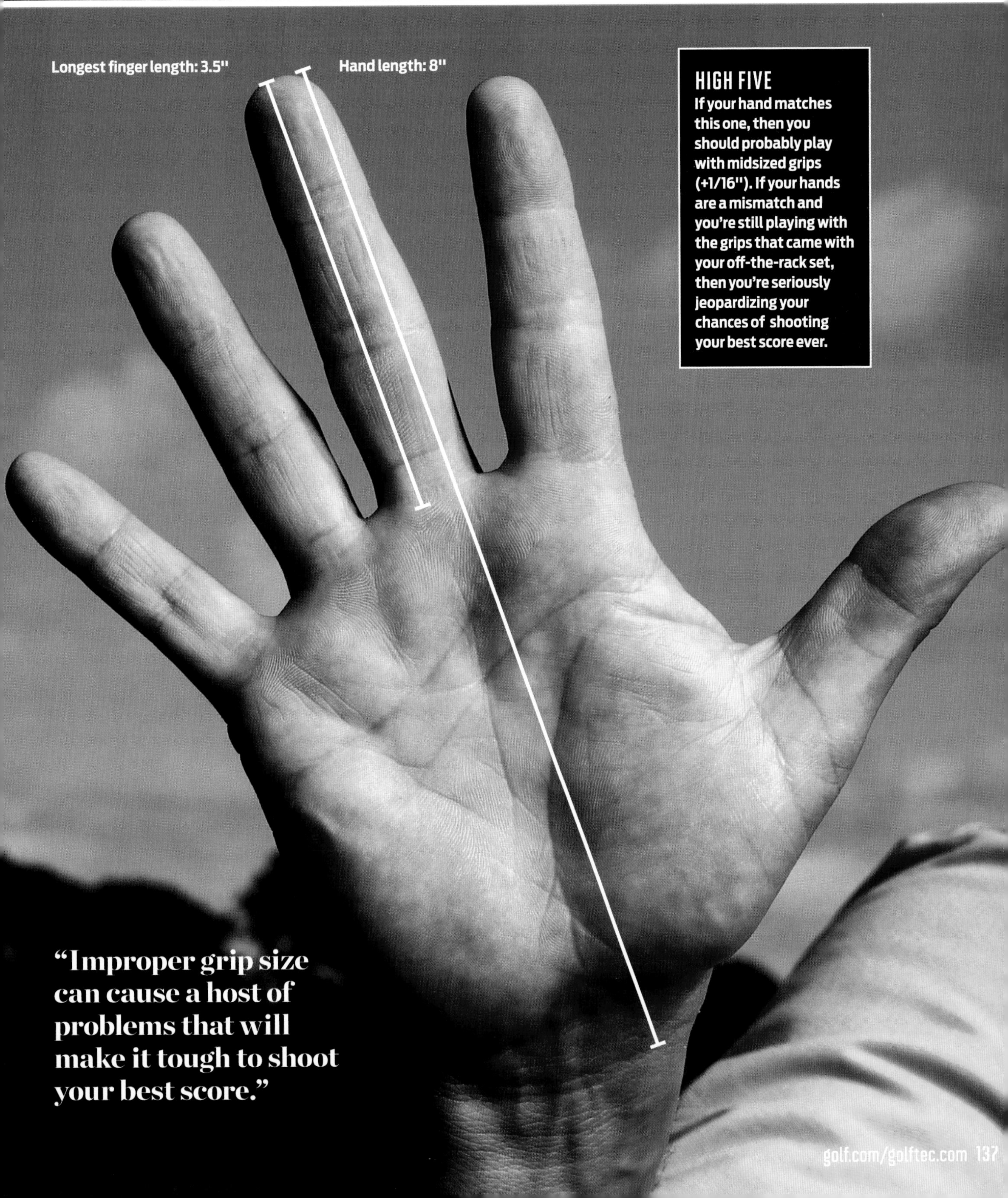

Longest finger length: 3.5"

Hand length: 8"

HIGH FIVE
If your hand matches this one, then you should probably play with midsized grips (+1/16"). If your hands are a mismatch and you're still playing with the grips that came with your off-the-rack set, then you're seriously jeopardizing your chances of shooting your best score ever.

"Improper grip size can cause a host of problems that will make it tough to shoot your best score."

FIX CHECK FOR GOOD LIES AND BAD BOUNCES

Sole shape and lie angle go a long way toward helping catch every shot clean

The proper lie angle (the angle between the shaft and the clubhead) for your build and swing has a critical effect on the direction of your shots and needs to be addressed if you hope to hit the ball at your target on a consistent basis. The bad news regarding lie angle is that if you've bought clubs off the rack, you likely do not have lie angles that are exactly right for you. The good news is that checking them is relatively simple and can be done at any GolfTEC location or with a lie board and some sole tape.

Lie angle has by far the greatest effect on your irons and wedges. Without getting into some complicated geometry, understand that the higher the loft, the more an incorrect lie angle will affect the direction of the shot. Therefore, this is where you want to focus most of your attention. If you want to do it yourself, get some masking tape (or lie tape specifically made for the procedure) and a flat piece of plastic. (You can get a lie board at any golf-equipment retailer.) All you need to do is place tape on the sole of each or your irons and wedges and then hit shots off a firm, flat surface. After each hit you should take note of the marks left on the tape. If you see marks on the toe area of the tape,

the lie angle is too flat. This error is probably the worst for an average golfer since it promotes slicing. If you're struggling with a left-to-right ballflight, especially with your irons, this could be part of the problem. Conversely, if you see marks toward the heel of the club, then your clubs are too upright. This error promotes hooks and draws, which isn't always a bad thing, particularly if you're prone to slicing. A good rule of thumb is to err on the side of too upright on the longer irons, since they're the hardest to square at impact, and on the side of too flat on your short irons and wedges.

WEDGE FINE-TUNING

A key element in the design of your wedges is bounce, which is the measurement (in degrees) of the angle from the front edge of a club's sole to the point that rests on the ground at address. With wedges, where bounce is of maximum importance, the back half of the sole is normally lower than the front edge, creating a cushion for when the club comes into contact with the ground. This feature has a massive impact on how a wedge performs from

Bounce can enhance playability from a variety of lies. ⊢

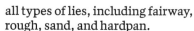

all types of lies, including fairway, rough, sand, and hardpan.

Although this might sound a bit technical and somewhat complicated, in reality, figuring out how much bounce you should have on your wedges isn't really all that difficult. The first key is to take a look at the divots you make when you hit full shots from the fairway. If your divots are shallow (or nonexistent), you should use wedges that feature a lower degree of bounce. If your divots are very deep, you should select high-bounce wedges. Obviously, if you

> ## "Typically, higher-bounce wedges perform best in softer conditions."

make moderate-depth divots, you should opt for medium-bounce wedges (*see chart, below left*).

The other factor that you need to take into account when determining wedge bounce is the playing conditions you normally encounter. Typically, higher-bounce wedges perform best in softer conditions, while lower-bounce models do best in firmer conditions. However, your technique also plays a role in selecting bounce. If you like to open the clubface when playing short shots, lower-bounce models will offer more versatility. (These are what most pros play.) Keep in mind that lower-bounce wedges tend to dig into the ground at impact quite a bit more than higher-bounce models, making them less forgiving for the average player.

BOUNCE TABLE RECOMMENDATIONS

	LOW BOUNCE	MEDIUM BOUNCE	HIGH BOUNCE
54° wedge	8°	12°	14°
56° wedge	10°	14°	16°
58° wedge	8°	12°	14°
60° wedge	8°	12°	14°

TOO FLAT
Wear or test marks near the toe are indications that your clubs are too flat. This can exacerbate a slice.

TOO UPRIGHT
Wear or test marks near the toe are indications that your clubs are too upright—not good if you struggle with hooking.

CHECK YOUR LIES OR SUFFER

CLUB	LOFT (°)	CARRY (YDS.)	DISTANCE OFF-LINE (YDS.)		
			DEGREES TOO UPRIGHT OR TOO FLAT		
			2	4	6
3-Iron	20°	190	7.2	14.5	21.7
6-Iron	30°	160	9.7	19.3	29
9-Iron	42°	130	12.3	24.5	36.7
Gap Wedge	50°	110	13.7	27.4	41.1

TRY THIS! golfTec

Demand the Truth from Your Lie Angles
Matt Carrothers, PGA (Canada): GolfTEC—Vancouver

You don't always need the trained eye of a clubfitter to know if your clubs are built with the correct lie angles for your swing. The next time you perform the Divot Drill (5.3, page 100), look for the following in addition to the size, shape, and depth of your divot marks:

1 The entry edge of the divot should be a straight line—make sure it's perpendicular to your intended target line. The depth of the divot should be even across its entire width. This means the clubs are the correct lie angles or really close.

2 If the lie angles are incorrect, one side of the divot will be deeper than the other. If the right (toe) side is deeper than the left (heel) side, then it could mean that the club is too flat. If the heel side is deeper than the right side, then it could mean that the club is too upright. If you see any of these problems, consult your fitter or the GolfTEC improvement center near you. Swinging clubs with incorrect lie angles can wreak serious havoc on your scores. Mostly, your accuracy will suffer. A lie-angle error of even 2 degrees can cause the average 9-iron shot to fly 12.3 degrees off-line.

WINNING NUMBER 10

Percentage of recreational golfers who have experienced a complete professional clubfitting from putter to driver. In comparison, most PGA Tour players have their lofts and lie angles checked every week.

Source: GolfTEC

FIX PLAY THE RIGHT KIND OF SHAFT

The shaft is the engine of the club. Are yours stalling out your swing?

Obviously, using shafts that are too short or too long for your body type can have major ill effects on your swing speed, ballstriking, and ability to square the clubface at impact. To get it right you really need to consult an experienced clubfitter, but there are some pretty basic guidelines you can follow that are based on your height and wrist-to-floor measurement. Comparing your height to the distance between your wrist and the ground when you're standing at attention gives you a pretty strong indication if your shafts are too short or too long. The average person stands 5' 11" with a wrist-to-floor measurement of 34 inches. If this is you, then the shaft of your 5-iron should be 37.5 inches. If you stand taller than six feet with a wrist-to-floor measurement greater than 34 inches, you'll need a longer club than this and throughout your set. If you're shorter than 5' 11" and have a shorter wrist-to-floor measurement, then you need to be fit with shorter shafts.

SHAFT FLEX, PROFILE AND WEIGHT

This is an area that has a huge effect on how solidly and how far you hit the ball with every club in your bag, particularly your driver. The first thing you should know when it comes to shafts is that playing with flexes that are too stiff will hurt your game about as much as any mistake you can make. Shafts that are too stiff not only force you to overexert yourself during your swing, but they also create a lot of tension that not only saps power, but also creates a lot of unnatural and difficult-to-time compensations and manipulations. A softer shaft is easier in general to control and swing comfortably. This will go a long way toward improving your consistency.

Probably the biggest misconception in regard to shaft flex is that it's based solely on swing speed. While speed is a contributing factor, tempo is actually a better basis for determining the flex. Players with a faster tempo (think Nick Price) will actually get better accuracy from a stouter, stiffer model. In contrast, players with a smoother, more rhythmic tempo (think Fred Couples) will almost always get better results from a softer flex.

Determine shaft length by measuring the distance from your wrist to the ground.

Another consideration when determining shaft flex is swing type. If you're a player who has some lag in your swing and really loads the shaft (think Sergio Garcia), then a shaft with a butt-stiff profile (stiffer in the grip end) will work to your advantage. If you tend to cast or unhinge your wrists relatively early in your downswing (think Steve Stricker), then a shaft with more stiffness in the tip (toward the hosel) will fit the bill.

Then there's weight. There are two choices here: heavier or lighter. While there are a lot of ways to add or remove weight when manufacturing a shaft, the most obvious is to use graphite for lighter models and steel for heavier models (although there are plenty of lightweight steel shafts and heavy graphite shafts on the market). Like the other shaft characteristics, weight plays an important role in making the club easier or more difficult to control. Basically, players with ample hand strength are better off using heavier shafts and players with weaker hands should play lighter shafts. A good way to check your hand strength is to take a pair of needle-nose pliers and apply them to the stem of a tee. If you can make deep marks that clearly show all of the plier's teeth, then you probably have enough hand strength for a heavier shaft. If you can only make a moderate dent in the tee or leave only one or two teeth marks, then you most likely lighter-weight graphite shafts. Another way to gauge hand strength is to grip a bathroom scale on its sides with both hands and squeeze it as hard as you can. If you can't cause the needle or display screen to read at least 75 pounds, then you should be playing with the lightest shafts possible.

TEST YOUR GRIP STRENGTH

See how many teeth marks you leave in the stem of a golf tee by squeezing the tee with a pair of pliers.

ASSESS YOUR RESULTS

The fewer teeth marks you leave in the tee stem, the lighter—and probably lighter— the shafts you should use with your irons and woods.

TRY THIS!

Nail Putter Length to Nail Your Setup

James Kinney, PGA: GolfTEC—Omaha

In order to make more putts, you must address the ball with a fundamentally solid setup and with a putter that has the right length.

Correct putter length enables you to properly set up with your eyes directly over the ball or slightly to the inside of the ball. Setting your eyes like this gives you an optical advantage to start putts on the correct line.

If you get this part of your setup right and fit your putter with the correct-length shaft, then your arms and hands will hang loosely underneath your shoulders. This is ideal because when your arms and hands hang in this fashion, they're able to swing freely back and through on a consistent arc.

The correct putter length will also help you create the proper bend in your elbows. Your elbows should be slightly bent in order to allow the putter to swing on a consistent path. Do this and you'll dramatically increase your make percentage. If your arms are too straight or too bent, you'll end up manipulating the putterhead with your hands, a mistake that leads to inconsistencies in contact, face angle, and stroke path.

WINNING NUMBER 3X

The stiffness rating of two-time Re/Max World Long Drive champion Jamie Sadlowski's driver shaft. It measures 48.25 inches and, when paired with his Adams Speedline driver head, creates a swingweight of E3.

Source: jamiesadlowski.com

FIX PLAY THE RIGHT PUTTER AND BALL

These elements are the easiest to correct to ensure success around the greens

Understanding the types of golf balls available today is key for selecting the model that will optimize you scoring potential. Most players make the understandable mistake of automatically choosing a Tour model, assuming that it's best to use the same type of ball as the pros. These models, which feature multiple-layer designs (anywhere from three to five pieces) with high-spin, low-speed urethane covers, provide an outstanding combination of low driver spin and high wedge spin, but they're not for everyone. High spin on short irons and wedges is great if you're in solid control of your shots, but if you're not, too much spin can actually make it quite a bit harder to get the ball close to the hole. If you're able to spin your greenside shots and control them, and you're in command of the trajectory of your approach shots as well, then this could be the type of ball for you. Be cautious of choosing the "X" Tour models that produce extremely low spin off the driver and long irons and are designed for higher-swing-speed players. If your clubhead speed with your driver is moderate (less than 100 mph), then you might be better off using another type of ball.

One type of golf ball that has improved greatly in recent years is the Tour-like model with a two- or three-piece design. These typically feature a softer core compression and a soft Surlyn cover. These models are not only less expensive than traditional Tour models, but they often produce a bit more distance off the tee for more moderate clubhead speeds and don't spin quite as much around the greens.

Another popular model of ball

TOUGH CHOICES Although you may want to play the same ball as your favorite Tour player, it's likely that his or her sphere of choice isn't a good fit for your swing. Unless you're capable of swinging your driver very fast and are in complete control of your irons, opt for a model with a lower spin rating.

available today is the low-compression variety, which is designed specifically for players with slower swing speeds. These golf balls are built with the softest cores and are easier to compress than firmer models. Due to advances in material technology, many of these models now offer ample short-game performance and work extremely well for a fairly wide variety of players.

PUTT WITH THE CORRECT LENGTH

For whatever reason, the stock length of most aftermarket puttershafts is 35 inches. Maybe it's because 35 inches is just long enough to keep your putter from sitting too deep in your bag.

Whatever the reason, there's a good chance that you're playing a putter that's too long for you or, in some cases, too short.

You can get an idea if you're playing the wrong-length putter by thinking about your stance. If it feels as though your arms are jammed into your sides at address, then it could be that your putter is too long. When you grip an overly long putter at the top of the handle, you're forced to bend your elbows too much, and when you swing your putter your body will get in the way. Your wrists will then take over and flip your putter back and through. Choking down will only alter swingweight and send your tempo out of whack.

If, at address, you have the feeling that your arms are too straight or too rigid, then your putter might be too short for you.

When the putter handle is so low that you have to fully straighten your arms to take your grip, it forces you to tip your shoulders up and down to make your stroke. When you do that, you'll have distance problems, because you'll contact the ball with a different amount of loft on every stroke. Plus, straight arms mean extra tension and poor tempo. Your putter is just right if your arms hang under your shoulders when you grip the top of the handle.

The perfect putter length positions your elbows just under your rib cage at address with just a slight amount of flex so your arms and shoulders can freely swing the putter under your body without excess wrist and head movement. The result from this type of setup is consistently solid contact and extra distance control.

Of course, the only way to get a

Fine-Tune Your Gear for Scoring

RIGHT ON!
If your setup is correct, finding the correct putter length is a matter of simple geometry. Your hands-to-ground and toes-to-ball distances are the sides of a right triangle. Adding their squared values gives you the square of the hypotenuse (i.e., shaft length).

GOAL 1 *Check Your Gear*
Follow the checkpoints throughout this section to get an idea if your equipment is fit for your swing and body type.

GOAL 2 *Make the Change*
If your assessment shows that your equipment is holding you back from making the best swing possible, consult an experienced clubfitter. GolfTEC offers a wide range of set analyses and clubfittings to match any budget. Visit **golf.com/see-try-buy** to review, test, and ultimately purchase the best and newest clubs on the market.

CHECK YOUR PROGRESS

Decide if your equipment is the right match for you and your swing by uploading a video to My Pro To Go. A certified My Pro To Go coach can spot errors in your gear makeup simply by looking at your address and impact positions. Visit *golftec.com/parplan* to register for a 50 percent discount, available only to *The Par Plan* readers. Purchase lessons at *myprotogo.com*.

FITTINGS BY golfTEC

For the ultimate clubfitting experience, visit your local GolfTEC improvement center for a one-on-one set analysis that can quickly get your gear—and your swing—on the right track. Visit *golftec.com/parplan* to register for a 50 percent discount on a personal fitting.

perfect putter fit is to pay a visit to an experienced clubfitter. A popular method of putterfitting was developed by *Golf Magazine* Top 100 Teacher Todd Sones. Sones's theory is based on the fact that a proper putting setup creates a right triangle between your hands, feet, and putterhead. Thus, all the fitter has to do is measure the distance from your left wrist and the ground, and the distance from that spot on the ground to your ball, and then apply simple math to determine your optimal shaft length. It's as easy as applying the Pythagorean theorem: A^2 (hands to ground distance) + B^2 (toes to ball distance) = C^2 (ball to hands distance). This only works, of course, if your putting setup is fundamentally correct.

POINTS OF ORIGIN

A quick look at key
PGA Tour approach
shot numbers:

44.1%
PGA Tour green in regulation
avg. from 200+ yards

47.8%
PGA Tour green in regulation
avg. from a fairway bunker

49.5%
PGA Tour green in regulation
avg. from the rough

74.9%
PGA Tour green in regulation
avg. from the fairway

87.9%
PGA Tour green in regulation
avg. from < 75 yards

2012 season
Source: PGATour.com

25–27

EXPAND YOUR SHOTMAKING

An easy-to-follow plan for building a basic arsenal of specialty shots to escape trouble and work the ball into scoring position

In a few days you're going to go out and shoot your best score ever. When you're on the course, however, don't expect to hit a perfect shot every time you pull a club from your bag. Accidents are going to happen, and shooting your goal number will depend heavily on how you react to these situations. In the past you might have tried to make up for an errant swing by attempting a shot you're not capable of hitting. It's this kind of misguided shotmaking that has kept you from your true scoring potential.

This section focuses on shot control and intentionally curving the ball to the left or right—and flying it higher or lower—to escape or avoid trouble. Since there are only a few days left in the plan, you'll learn just the basics. The basics, however, are really all you need to shoot your goal number. (Hopefully you'll continue to work on ball-control keys to improve your skill in this area as you play and enjoy the game in the years to come.) If you've developed your swing to the point where it produces a consistent shot shape, then learning how to generate the opposite shot shape will double your shotmaking arsenal. That will be sufficient to navigate your way to your best score ever.

THROW YOUR GAME A CURVE BALL

Straight shots are nice, but ones you can shape to your advantage are better

Whether you know it or not, you own a stock shot. If you hit a hundred balls at your practice facility, the majority will fly on the same trajectory (minus the variance in distance you get when you switch to a longer or shorter club) and in the same direction. Not all of them, but *most*. This is your signature shot shape. Yours could be a pull fade or it could be a low draw. That doesn't matter. What does is recognizing that you have one. It's also important to realize that one stock shot isn't necessarily better—or worse—than the others when it comes to shooting the lowest possible score. You can outplay the straightest hitter on earth with, for example, a low draw, but only if you plan for it.

As you've been working on your technique in different parts of the game and performing the drills using the schedule on page 184, you've been seeing some exciting improvements in your full swing, short game, and putting. At the same time, you've been tightening up your dispersion patterns, which means that you're hitting your stock shot more consistently with both your woods and irons. The plan is working, even if you're curving the ball more than

> "Use curvature to your advantage to avoid trouble off the tee and hit approach shots closer to the pin."

you'd like to. Keep in mind that the goal isn't to hit a dead-straight shot on every swing. If your stock shot is a straight ball, great. If it isn't, no big deal. Every player has a stock shot, and most of the time it features some sort of curvature. Jack Nicklaus hit a high fade. Rory McIlroy primarily plays a draw. In many ways, your stock shot defines you as a player, and having one actually means you're in control of your game.

THE POWER OF CONTROL

On the following pages we'll show you how to identify your stock shot and ultimately use it to your advantage. That's an important first step. The next one is to learn how to produce its opposite, which we'll do by covering quick-and-easy moves for curvature and trajectory control. Doing this will effectively double your shotmaking options. As an example, take the situation where you hit your tee ball into the right rough on a dogleg-right hole (one that curves to the right). If your stock shot is a low draw, then it's highly unlikely you'll get the ball on the green with your next shot—your stock curve bends in the opposite direction of the dogleg. But if you know what to do to produce a high fade (the opposite of a low draw), then you have the option to go for broke, potentially saving you a stroke as you make your way toward posting your goal score.

As you proceed through these lessons, you'll come to understand that shotmaking isn't just for recovery situations. The true benefit of being able to work the ball either way on demand is that it allows you to avoid trouble in the first place. If there's

danger on the right, then owning the skills to hit a left-biased shot eliminates it as well as the potential for penalty strokes. Shotmaking also is a great way to get the ball closer to the hole even when you're in the middle of the fairway, especially if your stock shot isn't a match for the situation you're facing (as when your stock shot is a fade but the pin is cut close to the left edge of the green). As soon as you start seeing shotmaking in these terms, you're starting to play like a pro. The best players in the world rarely hit a straight shot to the fairway or at the pin. They curve the ball to the part of the fairway or the green that gives them the greatest advantage on the next shot. So if you're curving it already, don't get too caught up with straightening your ballflight (minus excessive slices and hooks). Instead, use curvature to your advantage to avoid trouble off the tee and hit approach shots closer to the pin.

As mentioned previously, because you only have limited time to work on this area of the game, this section will focus on the basics. You're only going to learn how to hit the ball more to the left (if your stock shot is right-biased) or more to the right (if your stock shot is left-biased). After you practice these techniques, you'll work on hitting the ball higher or lower than your stock ballflight. The great thing about adding this skill to your repertoire is that it's easy to grasp. More important, it exponentially increases your shotmaking options. Learn to adjust height as well as curve and suddenly you're a *shotmaker*, the type of player who saves three or four shots with various specialty shots pulled from his or her bag of tricks.

There's more than one way to land the ball close to your target. Often, the best way involves curving the ball rather than hitting it straight. Shotmaking is as important to scoring as it is to your recovery game.

LESSON THE SECRET TO SHAPING SHOTS

Shotmaking skill starts with controlling the clubface at impact

As was touched on in section 5, both the path of your swing through impact and the clubface angle relative to the path dictate the initial direction and curvature of your shots. Instructors have known this for ages, but up until recently, they overemphasized path's role in determining starting direction and underemphasized the influence of the clubface. As it turns out, the angle of the clubface at impact (relative to the target line) is mostly what determines starting direction (straight, left of target, or right of target) and that it's the swing path that ultimately determines whether the ball bends to the left or right.

These are important concepts to get your head around because they're the building blocks for your shotmaking development. In order to consistently curve the ball to the left or right as you make your way around the course, you have to be able to consistently match the face angle at impact to the type of shot you want to hit. Things like swing speed, impact location, and attack angle all contribute to shot curvature and starting direction, but when it comes to simple shotmaking, the most important thing to worry about is the face angle. In other words, making the ball obey your commands begins with getting the clubface to do likewise.

> **"The clubface angle relative to the target line tells the ball initially where to go."**

The ballflight diagram on page 112 provided you with a basic understanding of the nine basic shot types. The one on the right will prove more useful to you as you proceed through this section of the plan and develop the skills required to shape shots. Here, you can see that the clubface angle relative to the target line tells the ball initially where to go and that the clubface angle's relationship to the path tells the ball which way it should curve. The basic lesson is that if you want to start the ball out to the left, then you need to point the clubface to the left when you strike the ball. If you want the ball to start out to the left and then curve back to the right or even farther to the left, you'll have to pair your left-biased clubface with the appropriate swing path. This isn't as complicated as it seems, because changing the swing path when trying to hit a specialty shot is simply a matter of pointing your stance in the right direction at address. You'll learn about this on pages 154–157.

COMMON CURVES

A *Golf Magazine* (November, 2006 study that analyzed shots hit by 276 amateur golfers on 69 different courses on a single Saturday morning proves that the tendency to curve the ball to the right increases with handicap. It also shows that better players tend to curve the ball with more of a left bias. This may give you an idea about the shape of your stock shot even before you perform the assessment on the following pages. It also sheds light on how you'll adjust the clubface and your path to produce the opposite ballflight.

BALLFLIGHT OF 276 PLAYERS

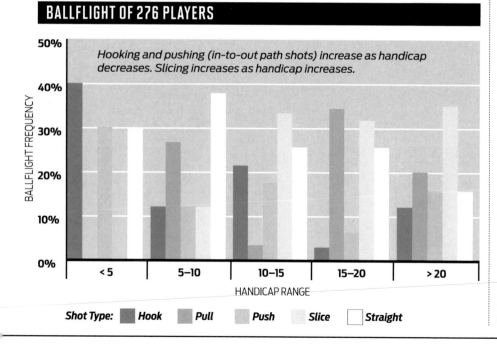

Hooking and pushing (in-to-out path shots) increase as handicap decreases. Slicing increases as handicap increases.

BALLFLIGHT FREQUENCY

HANDICAP RANGE

Shot Type: ■ Hook ■ Pull ■ Push ■ Slice □ Straight

THE NEW RULES OF BALLFLIGHT

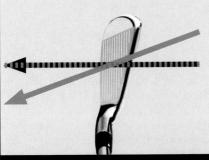

Clubface Square/Path Left
Ball starts on line and curves a little to the right because the face is slightly open relative to the path.

Clubface Square/Path Straight
Ball starts straight and stays straight because the face is square to the path.

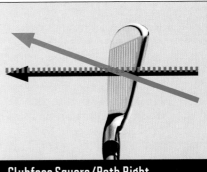

Clubface Square/Path Right
Ball starts on line but curves to the left because the face is closed relative to the path.

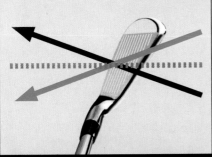

Clubface Right/Path Left
Ball starts out to the right and curves farther to the right because the face is open relative to the path.

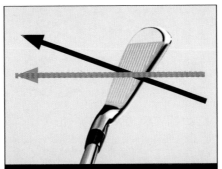

Clubface Right/Path Straight
Ball starts out to the right and curves a little to the right because the face is slightly open relative to the path.

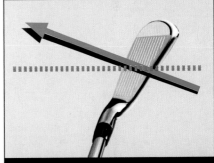

Clubface Right/Path Right
Ball starts out to the right and flies straight in that direction because the face is square to the path.

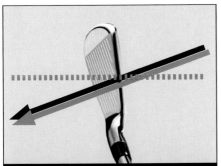

Clubface Left/Path Left
Ball starts out to the left and flies straight in that direction because the face is square to the path.

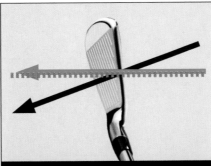

Clubface Left/Path Straight
Ball starts out to the left and curves a little to the left because the face is slightly closed to the path.

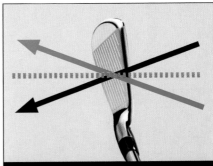

Clubface Left/Path Right
Ball starts out to the left and curves farther left because the face is closed relative to the path.

ASSESSMENT DISCOVER YOUR STOCK SHOT

Use My Pro To Go to discover the true shape of your swing

Although you're probably aware of your typical ballflight, it's important that you know its exact shape, especially since you've spent the last three weeks improving your motion. Follow the steps at right.

Step 1
Set an alignment stick in the ground on your target line about 20 feet in front of the ball. Lay a tee next to your ball to make sure you hit shots from the same place, and set a club on the ground parallel to the target line near your toes so you can take dead aim at the stick every time.

Step 2
Grab a 5-iron (less-lofted clubs provide a more realistic indication of your stock shot) and have a friend capture

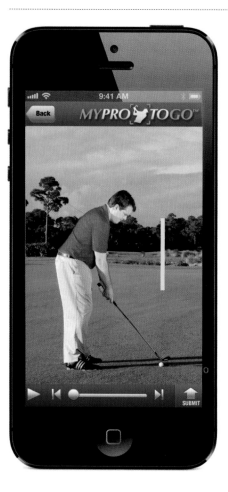

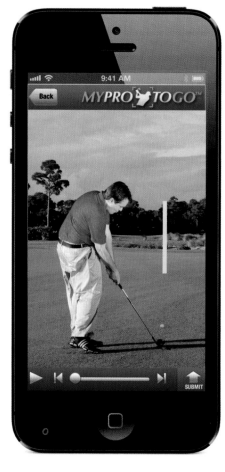

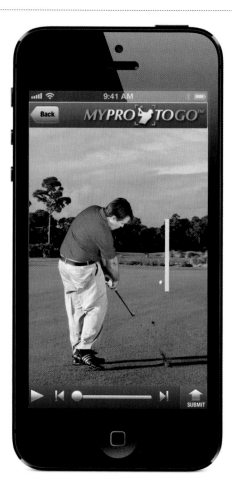

Setup
Draw a line over the alignment stick and step the video forward all the way to your impact position.

Swing
Stop just after the moment you strike the ball and follow the ball's trajectory by slowly stepping the video forward.

Assess Face Angle
If the ball starts to the left of the line, then the face was pointing to the left at impact (vice versa if it starts to the right).

your swing from start to finish from a down-target perspective. (Follow the guidelines on page 11.) Have him or her capture 20 swings.

Step 3

Launch the video, but before you play it, draw a line over the alignment rod. Run each video and keep an eye out for two things:

1. *Starting Direction* Take note of the side of the line on which the ball starts. This will tell you where your clubface is pointing at impact. If the ball starts left of the line, then it's pointing to the left at impact (and vice versa if it starts right of the line). If the ball sails over the line, then it's a safe bet that your clubface was square at impact.

2. *Landing Spot* Take note of where the ball hits the ground relative to the line. This will tell more about your swing path. If, for example, the ball starts out straight but lands on the right side of the line, then you probably swung on an outside-in path.

As you perform this drill, don't expect to produce your stock shot on every swing. If you're like most recreational players, 5 of the balls will fly in one direction, and 5 will travel in the opposite direction. The shots you're concerned with are the remaining 10. These will define your signature shot pattern.

Also, keep in mind that there are a million different ways to combine face and path to hit a million different shots. In assessing your stock swing, make sure you do it with an understanding that it's the *relationship* between the path and face that ultimately determines curvature. This can be tricky business for an amateur. If you're really interested in knowing your stock swing, get on a launch monitor. This machine computes your exact path and face numbers so you know what to expect on most swings and what you need to work on to produce the opposite shot. Consult the GolfTEC improvement center directory on page 186 to find the location nearest you. Each center is equipped with the latest in ballflight- and swing-measuring technologies.

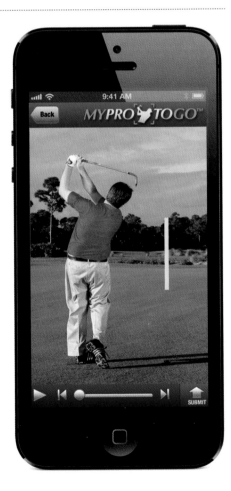

Assess Swing Path

Step the video forward until the ball lands on the ground. The total curve provides clues about your swing path.

Hear It From a Pro!

Upload your swing to My Pro To Go for an in-depth video analysis of your path and plane. Details at *myprotogo.com*.

TRY THIS!

Check the Rough for Your Signature Miss

Patrick Nuber, PGA: GolfTEC, Denver

Whether they hit a left-to-right fade or a right-to-left draw, the game's best players strive to master their signature shot shape. In doing so they naturally tend to create a signature miss that allows them (to some degree) to eliminate one side of the course. Understanding your signature miss is just as important as understanding your signature shot shape because it's vital to good course management.

Two statistics that the PGA Tour tracks is left rough tendency and right rough tendency off the tee. These figures allow players to know whether they miss more to the left or more to the right off the tee box. Since the PGA Tour doesn't track your shots when you play, do it yourself by keeping tabs on where you land your tee and approach shots during your rounds. Add the number of left misses and the number of right misses. Comparing the two values should give you your signature miss. Once you know this, make sure to select targets that accommodate your signature miss without doing too much damage to your scores.

WINNING NUMBER 63

The percentage of drives hit by Trevor Immelman in 2012 that ended up right of the center of the fairway. The fact that he hit 63% of his greens shows that great players have a signature shot and miss and know how to manage both.

Source: PGATour.com

LESSON MANAGE YOUR MISS PATTERN

It's okay to hit bad shots, but only if they fly in one direction

The assessment on the previous pages and the usefulness of its results took for granted that you were able to discern a noticeable shot pattern with only a few wild misses. If, after hitting the 20 balls in the assessment, you weren't able to determine a stock shot because your misses were both frequent and varied, then it might be time for you to tone down your expectations when you attempt to shoot your career-best score. As was stated at the beginning of this book, the goal of the par plan isn't to make you a shotmaking machine but to help you improve a little in each of the nine key areas of the game so that the summation of these improvements drops your score to your goal number. Regardless of the improvements you're making in the other areas of your game, it'll be impossible to formulate a plan to keep your tee shots in the fairway (so you can avoid penalty shots) or get the ball close to the pin with your approach shots (without hitting into severely penal areas near the green) if you're producing different types of misses with your full swing. The reason most Tour players are capable of shooting low numbers isn't only that they strike the ball perfectly swing after swing, because they miss a lot. It's more about how they manage their misses, which is easy for them to do because usually they only have a one-way miss. Ben Hogan's miss was a hook, but that's all he had to worry about. When Rory McIlroy misses, the shot almost always goes too far to the left. His game plan is built around avoiding the right side of the golf course. But when you start generating multiple misses (bad shots that travel in more than one direction), then it's impossible to avoid trouble, because there's trouble all around you. It's no use trying to avoid the left side of the golf course, because your bad miss is to the left when a lot of your shots go to the right, too.

If this is sounding all too familiar to you, then it's likely that you have lingering swing path and clubface issues to deal with, and it might be to your benefit to extend the schedule and go back to the earlier sections of this book. Even if you technically have one miss or stock shot, it won't do you any good if the dispersion of these shots is wider than, say, the width of a fairway. And while a good short game and putting stroke can save you from time to time, adding pressure by missing in more than one direction will make it extremely difficult to shoot your best score. The advice here is to take a look at your results from your initial 11-Ball Median Assessment and compare them with the results of your last assessment. If you don't see noticeable improvement in your median distance, then reboot the plan. The reason is that if you're not seeing improvement with your wedge-shot dispersion, then the situation is probably worse with the longer clubs in your bag.

The beauty of the plan is that it allows you the freedom to improve at your own pace. Sure, it's designed to help you shoot your best score in 30 days, but if you need more time, fine. If you decide to start again, double the amount of time required to complete each drill. Make it a 60-day plan. You'll reap a better reward with this adjustment than if you try to force improvement you're just not ready for. Plus, the thought of shooting your best score ever in 60 days is much nicer than never shooting it at all, and the more time you dedicate to elevating your game, the more likely the changes will stick.

NEXT STEPS

If you have a good idea of your stock shot, your next goal is to learn how to produce a shot that travels in the opposite direction. This will double the shots available to you to attack the course. If your stock shot is a fade, you'll need to learn how to draw the ball. If you're already curving the ball consistently to the left, then you need to develop a fade. This is more important at this stage of the plan than continuing to grind on mechanics, because you're pretty much going to attempt to shoot your best score with the stock swing you have right now. Again, if it's a consistent stock swing, then it doesn't matter what shape it is, and if you learn to hit its opposite, you'll be in great shape to save a few extra strokes.

> **"It'll be impossible to formulate a plan to keep your tee shots in the fairway or get the ball close to the pin with your approach shots if you're producing different types of misses with your full swing."**

your swing from start to finish from a down-target perspective. (Follow the guidelines on page 11.) Have him or her capture 20 swings.

Step 3
Launch the video, but before you play it, draw a line over the alignment rod. Run each video and keep an eye out for two things:

1. *Starting Direction* Take note of the side of the line on which the ball starts. This will tell you where your clubface is pointing at impact. If the ball starts left of the line, then it's pointing to the left at impact (and vice versa if it starts right of the line). If the ball sails over the line, then it's a safe bet that your clubface was square at impact.

2. *Landing Spot* Take note of where the ball hits the ground relative to the line. This will tell more about your swing path. If, for example, the ball starts out straight but lands on the right side of the line, then you probably swung on an outside-in path.

As you perform this drill, don't expect to produce your stock shot on every swing. If you're like most recreational players, 5 of the balls will fly in one direction, and 5 will travel in the opposite direction. The shots you're concerned with are the remaining 10. These will define your signature shot pattern.

Also, keep in mind that there are a million different ways to combine face and path to hit a million different shots. In assessing your stock swing, make sure you do it with an understanding that it's the *relationship* between the path and face that ultimately determines curvature. This can be tricky business for an amateur. If you're really interested in knowing your stock swing, get on a launch monitor. This machine computes your exact path and face numbers so you know what to expect on most swings and what you need to work on to produce the opposite shot. Consult the GolfTEC improvement center directory on page 186 to find the location nearest you. Each center is equipped with the latest in ballflight- and swing-measuring technologies.

Assess Swing Path
Step the video forward until the ball lands on the ground. The total curve provides clues about your swing path.

Hear It From a Pro!
Upload your swing to My Pro To Go for an in-depth video analysis of your path and plane. Details at *myprotogo.com*.

LESSON MANAGE YOUR MISS PATTERN

It's okay to hit bad shots, but only if they fly in one direction

The assessment on the previous pages and the usefulness of its results took for granted that you were able to discern a noticeable shot pattern with only a few wild misses. If, after hitting the 20 balls in the assessment, you weren't able to determine a stock shot because your misses were both frequent and varied, then it might be time for you to tone down your expectations when you attempt to shoot your career-best score. As was stated at the beginning of this book, the goal of the par plan isn't to make you a shotmaking machine but to help you improve a little in each of the nine key areas of the game so that the summation of these improvements drops your score to your goal number. Regardless of the improvements you're making in the other areas of your game, it'll be impossible to formulate a plan to keep your tee shots in the fairway (so you can avoid penalty shots) or get the ball close to the pin with your approach shots (without hitting into severely penal areas near the green) if you're producing different types of misses with your full swing. The reason most Tour players are capable of shooting low numbers isn't only that they strike the ball perfectly swing after swing, because they miss a lot. It's more about how they manage their misses, which is easy for them to do because usually they only have a one-way miss. Ben Hogan's miss was a hook, but that's all he had to worry about. When Rory McIlroy misses, the shot almost always goes too far to the left. His game plan is built around avoiding the right side of the golf course. But when you start generating multiple misses (bad shots that travel in more than one direction), then it's impossible to avoid trouble, because there's trouble all around you. It's no use trying to avoid the left side of the golf course, because your bad miss is to the left when a lot of your shots go to the right, too.

If this is sounding all too familiar to you, then it's likely that you have lingering swing path and clubface issues to deal with, and it might be to your benefit to extend the schedule and go back to the earlier sections of this book. Even if you technically have one miss or stock shot, it won't do you any good if the dispersion of these shots is wider than, say, the width of a fairway. And while a good short game and putting stroke can save you from time to time, adding pressure by missing in more than one direction will make it extremely difficult to shoot your best score. The advice here is to take a look at your results from your initial 11-Ball Median Assessment and compare them with the results of your last assessment. If you don't see noticeable improvement in your median distance, then reboot the plan. The reason is that if you're not seeing improvement with your wedge-shot dispersion, then the situation is probably worse with the longer clubs in your bag.

The beauty of the plan is that it allows you the freedom to improve at your own pace. Sure, it's designed to help you shoot your best score in 30 days, but if you need more time, fine. If you decide to start again, double the amount of time required to complete each drill. Make it a 60-day plan. You'll reap a better reward with this adjustment than if you try to force improvement you're just not ready for. Plus, the thought of shooting your best score ever in 60 days is much nicer than never shooting it at all, and the more time you dedicate to elevating your game, the more likely the changes will stick.

NEXT STEPS

If you have a good idea of your stock shot, your next goal is to learn how to produce a shot that travels in the opposite direction. This will double the shots available to you to attack the course. If your stock shot is a fade, you'll need to learn how to draw the ball. If you're already curving the ball consistently to the left, then you need to develop a fade. This is more important at this stage of the plan than continuing to grind on mechanics, because you're pretty much going to attempt to shoot your best score with the stock swing you have right now. Again, if it's a consistent stock swing, then it doesn't matter what shape it is, and if you learn to hit its opposite, you'll be in great shape to save a few extra strokes.

> **"It'll be impossible to formulate a plan to keep your tee shots in the fairway or get the ball close to the pin with your approach shots if you're producing different types of misses with your full swing."**

You can shoot your goal score with any kind of stock shot and a singular miss...

...but you can't shoot your goal score if you're still missing in multiple directions.

FIX HOW TO CURVE THE BALL TO THE RIGHT

If your stock shot is a draw, work on a fade to double your shot options

Golfers with a left-biased stock shot need to develop a fade. Although a fade usually doesn't travel as far as a draw, it's a great shot to own because it typically flies higher and lands softer, a good thing to have when hitting into modern, fast greens. The basic situations where you need a fade are when you're on the tee of a dogleg-right or when there's trouble lining the left side of the fairway. Or you're in the fairway, but there are trees on the right that you need to curve the ball around in order to land the ball safely on the green. Or it could be that you're attacking a front-right pin position. In any of theses situations, your play is a fade, a shot that curves softly from left to right.

Step 1

Use a slightly weaker hold (hands rotated more to the left). This will help produce a more open clubface at impact and a fading ballflight. Also, consider using more club, because a fade doesn't travel as far.

Step 2

Aim the clubface at your target, then

Point the clubface at your target.

Set your stance open to the target line (more open for more curve).

open your stance by shifting your feet counterclockwise so that your hips face more toward the target and your toe line points in the direction you want the ball to start. (Don't change the clubface as you do this.) This shifts your swing path (which should follow your toe line) to the left, and since you left the face alone as you opened up to the target, it's now open relative to your swing path. It's the perfect recipe for a left-to-right curve. Keep an eye out for ball position when you open your stance, because opening up moves the effective ball position back relative to your toe line. You may have to reposition the ball so that it's more forward in your stance.

Step 3

When you swing, forget where the clubface is aimed and motion the club along your toe line which, due to the open setup, will be out and across the target line. (Your setup also limits hip turn going back and increases hip turn going through, which further promotes an outside-in swing path and the desired fade.) Rotate your body a little faster during your downswing than you normally would. Don't roll your forearms over through impact, because you want to hit the ball with an open clubface. In fact, if you hold off your release, you'll finish with the club pointing up and down in your finish, which is a good checkpoint.

AN EASY FADE KEY

To produce a fade, focus on your right hand. If your right palm is facing down as you enter the hitting zone, you want it to face up as you hit through the ball. It also helps if you "chicken-wing" the shot a bit and keep your left elbow bent after impact. Since you're not turning the club over, you should see some space between your forearms in your release. Practice this swing in slow motion and see if you can spot the gap.

IMPORTANT

Aim to the left more than you think you need to. Remember, the face dictates the starting direction, and in a fade setup it's pointing to the right of your toe line. Thus, the ball will start more to the right than what you expect. This is a critical consideration if you're curving the ball around trees or other obstacles.

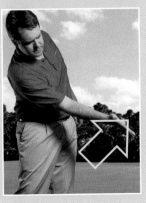

Swing along your toe line. Because the face is open relative to the path, the ball will curve to the right.

"Golfers with a left-biased stock shot need to develop a fade."

FIX HOW TO CURVE THE BALL TO THE LEFT

If your stock shot is a fade, work on a draw to double your shot options

Golfers with a right-biased stock shot need to develop a draw. The good thing about the draw is that it usually travels farther than a fade and rolls more once it hits the ground, allowing you to use a shorter and easier-to-swing club in most cases. The basic situations where you need a draw are when you're on the tee of a dogleg-left (the hole bends to the left) or when there's trouble lining the right side of the fairway. Or you're in the fairway, but there are trees on the left that you need to curve the ball around in order to hit the green. Or it could be that you're attacking a back-left pin position. In any of theses situations, your play is a draw, a shot that curves softly from right to left.

Step 1

Use a stronger grip (hands rotated to the right on the handle) and a lighter grip pressure with both hands. This will help you more easily turn the club over (toe over heel) through impact and produce a right-to-left ballflight. Remember to pull one less club, because a draw swing removes loft from the shot.

Point the clubface at your target.

Set your stance closed to the target line (more closed for more curve).

Step 2

Set up with the clubface aimed at the target and your body aligned in the direction you want the ball to start. Play the ball in its standard position for the club you're using. Again, keep an eye on ball position as you settle in, because closing your stance moves the effective ball position forward relative to your toe line. You may have to reposition the ball to make sure it's back in your stance. Setting up like this shifts your swing path (which should follow your toe line) to the right, and since you left the face alone as you rotated your body to the right, it's now closed relative to the swing path—perfect for a right-to-left curve.

Step 3

Swing along your toe line which, due to the closed setup, will move from inside the target line to the outside of the target line (from the inside out). Your setup also increases hip turn going back and limits hip turn going through, which further promotes an inside-out swing path and the desired draw. Through impact, focus on rotating your left elbow so that it points toward the ground. This will help you whip through the ball with a closed clubface. You know you did it correctly if you feel your swing ending up more around your body with the clubshaft running ear to ear behind your head.

AN EASY DRAW KEY

To produce a draw, you want your right palm to face the ground as you hit through the ball, just as it does when you enter the hitting zone. It also helps if you have the feeling that your forearms are "kissing" through impact. Because you want to turn the club over, your forearms should almost touch as you move into your release. Practice it in slow motion and see if you can catch the kiss.

IMPORTANT

Aim to the right more than you think you need to. As it does for every shot, the face dictates starting direction. Since in a draw setup it's pointing to the left of your toe line, the ball will start more to the left than what you expect. Experiment to see how far to the right you need to point your stance to produce the starting line and curvature you desire.

Swing along your toe line. Because the face is closed relative to the path, the ball will curve to the left.

"The good thing about the draw is that it usually travels farther than a fade and rolls more once it hits the ground."

FIX HOW TO HIT IT HIGHER OR LOWER

Use your setup and finish to add or remove loft

By learning how to curve the ball in the opposite direction of your stock shot, you've effectively doubled the number of shotmaking weapons at your disposal. Don't stop there. Part of the basics of shotmaking is hitting the ball higher or lower on command and to not only produce the opposite height of your stock shot but all heights. Introducing loft into the equation exponentially increases your shot arsenal.

Whereas you had to make some pretty significant changes to your setup and swing to put the clubface in position to start the ball to the left or the right, and to combine this clubface position with your swing path to generate right or left curvature, the adjustments for altering shot height aren't nearly as severe. There are five ways to hit the ball higher or lower.

1. Change the Club
This one is obvious—a club with less loft will flight the ball lower than one with more loft. If you're 150 yards away from the green, choke up on your 6-iron to cover the same distance as with your 7-iron (the club you normally use from 150 yards) and hit a noticeably lower shot.

2. Change Ball Position
As a rule, the more forward you position the ball in your stance, the more loft you can create at impact. The opposite is true for a back ball position.

3. Change Your Weight Distribution
If you want to hit the ball lower, set more of your weight on your front foot at address and keep it there when you swing. If you want to hit it higher, have the feeling that your weight is more centered from start to finish.

4. Change Shaft Lean
Moving your hands forward leans the shaft more toward the target at setup. If you can maintain this lean at impact, then you'll produce a lower ballflight. The opposite is true if you set the shaft vertical or even lean it slightly away from the target. Re-creating a backward-leaning shaft at impact requires that you add some flip to the bottom of your swing. Be careful with this one.

5. Change Your Finish
The shorter you make your through-swing, the lower the ball will fly. This is the most difficult part of height control because you always want your through-swing to be equal to or longer than your backswing.

NORMAL

BALL POSITION

A centered ball position with the shaft leaning forward produces your base height.

FINISH

Swinging through to your standard finish position produces your base shot height.

LOWER

A back ball position with more shaft lean produces a lower ballflight.

HIGHER

A forward ball position with minimal shaft lean produces a higher ballflight.

The sooner you stop your swing (i.e., the lower you finish), the lower the ball will fly.

A high-hands finish with full rotation creates a higher ballflight with less roll.

LESSON HOW TO PICK THE APPROPRIATE SHOT

Avoid trouble and hit more successful shots by drawing the right curve

As you can guess, shotmaking skill doesn't mean a thing unless you know when and how to apply it on the course. Recovery situations from trouble spots are one thing—the lie usually dictates your swing for you. What about the others? Every shot you face has a shotmaking possibility to it, and more often than not, one shot will be better than the rest for that situation. In the past you cursed your fade or draw. Now that you're a shotmaker, you can use it to your advantage.

KNOW THE RIGHT PLAY

When you're on the course, overlay the dicrection and curve of your stock shot onto what you see in front of you. Draw the line in your mind's eye and analyze how it relates to your lie and your target. Doing this should give you a fairly clear picture of where you should be aiming in order to land the ball safely in the fairway or on the green. Another trick is to imagine that you're going to hit 100 balls from your current lie, then picture the pattern that those 100 shots would fall into. This also should give you a clear picture of where you should—and shouldn't—be aiming.

These exercises also provide you clues as to which way to curve the ball to your target. Take the examples at right. In the top illustration, the pin is cut in the front-right portion of the green and guarded by a deep bunker. If your stock shot is a draw, then you have to aim right of the green and hope that the shot carries far enough and draws sufficiently to avoid the bunker. Or you can aim at the flag and draw the ball to the middle of the green, but you won't have much of a chance to make the putt. Here, you might be better served by hitting the opposite of your stock shot, starting a fade at the middle of the green (where you don't have to worry about the bunker), and letting it curve to the right and close to the pin. Since the pin is up, you'll get a better result by hitting a higher shot so that the ball rolls less once it hits the green.

In the middle illustration, you have the opposite situation. A draw is the ideal shot here because it allows you to completely avoid the water to the left of the green. The only problem is selecting the correct target. If you aim at the middle of the green, you'll be fine. If you aim at the flag, then your stock draw might end up in the hazard.

The bottom illustration shows that shot height also plays a key role in selecting the appropriate shotmaking play. If the pin is back, your best bet is to play a lower shot that lands in the middle of the green and rolls out to the hole. This is a much better option than trying to fly the ball all the way to the pin or hitting an extrahigh shot that drops next to the cup, because the penalty for flying the ball too far is so severe. The last thing you want to face is a chip shot back to the green (which likely will be sloping away from you because most greens tilt from back to front) with little room between you and the pin.

To post your best score ever, you'll need to perform these types of assessments on every shot you face. Picture your stock shot shape, determine the ideal landing spot, locate the worst spot of trouble, and then find the safest place to end up if you miss. If your stock shot isn't capable of avoiding trouble or finding the best miss location in the event you don't hit a decent shot, then go to your stock opposite. If you factor in all of these elements and take the time to adequately assess your lie and your surroundings, you'll picture the the ideal swing and trajectory with ease.

BEST SHOT: High fade.
WORST SHOT: Low draw.

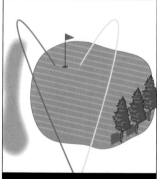

BEST SHOT: Low draw.
WORST SHOT: Any fade.

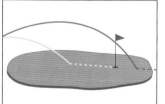

BEST SHOT: Low shot that lands in the middle.
WORST SHOT: High shot all the way to the pin.

"Every shot you face has a shotmaking possibility to it, and more often than not, one shot will be better than the rest in that situation."

LESSON TOP 10 WAYS TO SHAPE SHOTS FOR LOW SCORES

A simple shotmaking guide to make sure you're on the right path of attack

As with anything in life, shotmaking comes with its own set of rules, which are more like guidelines, really, because the essence of shotmaking is to do whatever feels most natural in a given situation. However, there's smart shotmaking and there's reckless shotmaking, and you never want to attempt a shot that blatantly bucks tried-and-true traditions. Before attempting to shoot your best score ever, consult the list below to complete your shotmaking education, and try to follow its advice when you're out on the course. You'll save a few strokes—and probably a few balls—while selecting the right shot for whatever the course throws at you.

1 Fight trouble with reliability If there's trouble surrounding the green, think twice about playing the opposite of your stock shot. When the chance for a penalty stroke reaches peak levels, you want to make sure you go with the swing that produces the most reliable results, which is your stock shot. Even if the opposite shot is technically the smarter shotmaking play, you never want to risk a blow-up score, especially when your stock shot can at least get you on the green.

2 Never curve the ball over a hazard If the pin is on the right side of the green, but playing a fade to it would require that you start the ball over a hazard, then don't play the fade. The key to scoring is to avoid hazards at all costs, both at the beginning of the ball's flight as well as at the end. This goes for your tee shots, too.

3 Be wary of carry If there's any doubt that you can successfully carry a hazard, then don't try to carry it. There's no use trying to fly the ball 165 yards over water if you're not sure you can do it. Opt for a longer club; if the longer club is one in which you don't have a lot of confidence, play short of the trouble and get on with your next swing.

4 Don't "test" shots on the course If you haven't practiced a particular shot at the range, then don't try to hit it during your rounds. Even if you have practiced it, you shouldn't consider it a shotmaking option until you can successfully execute it on the range at least 75 percent of the time.

> "There's smart shotmaking and there's reckless shotmaking, and you never want to attempt a shot that blatantly bucks tried-and-true traditions."

5 Curve it with body speed If you need to hit the ball from right to left, rotate your body a little slower on your downswing. This will make it easier to turn the clubhead over through impact. If you need to fade the ball, make a faster downswing turn. This has the tendency to keep the clubface open through impact.

6 Beware the "double-cross" Although it's never a good idea to think about what might happen if you hit the shot you plan on hitting the opposite direction, it's a savvy consideration if this "double-cross" would cause a blow-up.

7 Tee on the side of trouble If you're on a par 3 with water lining the entire right side of the hole, then tee up on the far right-hand side of the tee box and aim left. This goes for par 4s and par 5s as well.

8 Take your medicine If the lie is so bad that even your most trustworthy rescue shot isn't likely to get you on or near the green, then hack the ball back to the fairway with a wedge and get on with your next swing. You don't always need to play the hero shot, especially if there's limited chance for success.

9 Consider a low draw before high fade On a shot that requires anything longer than an 8-iron to reach your intended target, opt for a low draw shot over a high fade. The simple reason is because it's easier to draw the ball with longer clubs than it is to fade them, and it's easier to hit them lower than to launch them higher.

10 Play it back If the situation allows, play the ball back in your stance. This de-lofts the club at impact, turning your 6-iron, say, into a 5- or even a 4-iron. This allows you to use a shorter club to cover a longer distance, and shorter clubs are typically easier to manage than longer ones.

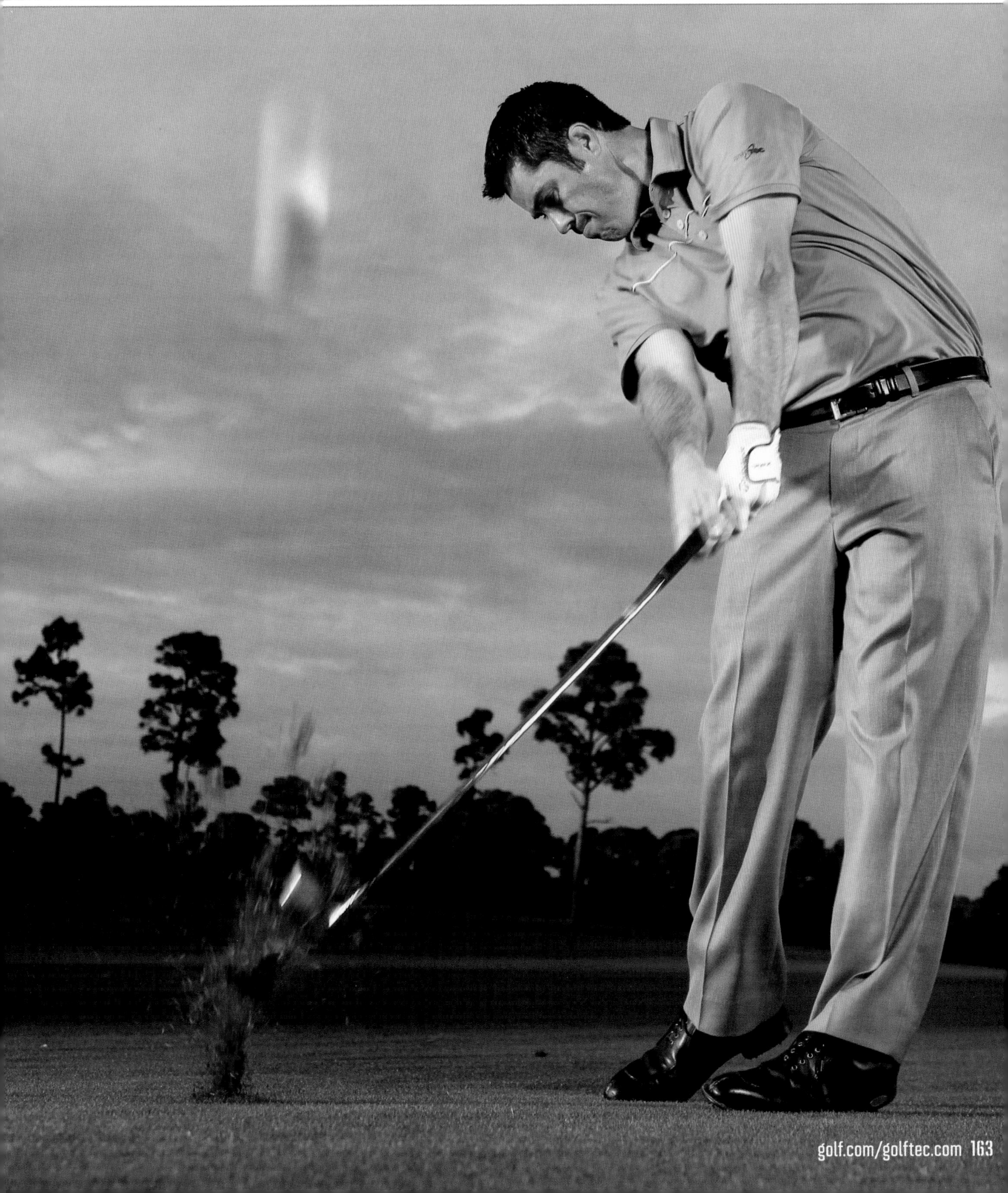

LESSON SEE YOUR SHOTS

Use your dispersion patterns to pick either the safest or most advantageous landing spot

A smart way to always make sure you're choosing the appropriate target so you avoid penalty shots and bad miss areas is to overlay your typical dispersion pattern with the club you're about to swing ontp the green or fairway. Picture the actual oval that would cover every shot out of 100 you'd hit with the club in your hands and drop it onto the center of the fairway or the flagstick (*photo below*), depending on the situation. Move the oval around the green or fairway until you find the spot that covers the widest safe-landing area or covers the least number of hazards. From the tee box, this area typically includes the center of the fairway, unless the designer has devilishly placed a hazard in the middle of the hole. On an approach shot, however, the safest and most strategic landing area may be several yards from the pin, but making the

THE SMART WAY TO PICK TARGETS

TOO CLOSE
You think you're playing it smart by aiming left of the pin toward the fat of the green, but even here your dispersion pattern doesn't give you a great enough margin for error.

JUST RIGHT
In this example, the best place to overlay your dispersion pattern is the front left portion of the green. Here, every shot out of an imaginary 100 would land safely on or near the green (and not in a hazard). Make the center of this pattern your landing point.

Expand Your Shotmaking

center of your dispersion oval your landing spot means you'll stay out of trouble and, minus a 3-putt, make par at worst. It's important to understand that the trick to hitting a successful approach shot is to eliminate worst-case scenarios, even if it doesn't get you to tap-in range every time.

If you don't exactly know what your dispersion oval looks like, or have a hard time overlaying it on the course when you're assessing targets during your preshot routine, make a goalpost with your fingers and thumbs and peer through it to the green or fairway. The distance between your fingers is the average dispersion pattern for a midhandicapped golfer. Make the goalpost narrower if you're a better player and wider if you're a novice or high handicapper. If you fail to locate a reasonable landing area with these techniques, then use the opposite of your stock shot or select a different club from your bag.

> ## "The safest and most strategic landing area may be several yards from the pin."

TOO RIGHT
Aiming right of the pin in this instance brings the back bunkers into play.

MATCH GAME
Sometimes you'll find that the best place to overlay your dispersion pattern is over the flag—the ultimate green-light, go-for-it situation.

TOO GREEDY
Aiming at the pin in this instance places too much of your dispersion pattern over the bunker. If you play this hole 100 times, a good majority of your shots will end up in the sand if you take dead aim at the flag.

Days 25–27 Action Plan

GOAL 1 *Discover Your Stock Shot*
Determine the shape of your most common shot using My Pro To Go so you know what to expect on most swings when you're out on the course.

GOAL 2 *Practice the Opposite of Your Stock Shot*
Learn to start and curve the ball in the direction opposite of your stock shot, effectively doubling the shotmaking arsenal at your disposal.

GOAL 3 *Learn How to Hit the Ball Higher or Lower*
Follow the instructions for adjusting your setup and finish to produce lower or higher shots on command. Combine these techniques with your stock and opposite shots for even more shotmaking options.

CHECK YOUR PROGRESS
Decide if your draw and fade swings are where they need to be before moving on to the next section by uploading a video of your swing to My Pro To Go for a professional critique of your technique (plus drills that target your weaknesses). Visit *golftec.com/ parplan* to register for a 50 percent discount, available only to *The Par Plan* readers. Purchase lessons at *myprotogo.com*.

LESSONS BY golfTEC
If you're having shotmaking problems, visit your local GolfTEC improvement center for a one-on-one lesson and hands-on instruction that guarantees lasting results. Visit *golftec.com* or consult the improvement center directory on pages 186–191.

DAYS
28–30

SIMPLIFY YOUR SAND GAME

How to turn a trouble situation into a scoring opportunity by focusing on the proven keys for consistent sand escapes

Here's a secret: amateurs are supposed to like the sand. It's the only place on the course where you don't have to actually hit the ball. A ball in the bunker doesn't care what your finish position looks like, and when you think of all the other nasty places the ball can find when it misses the green, the sand actually isn't a bad place to be. Yes, bunkers are penalty zones, and the only reason they exist is to make you pay for an errant shot, but they don't have to be the score-wreckers you've come to know them as.

In this section you'll learn proven techniques that make blasting the ball out of the sand easy. The real lesson, however, is more philosophical. You need to stop fearing the sand. Ramp up your confidence and begin making more aggressive swings. Easier said than done, we know, but after you assess your technique and compare it with the one you're supposed to use, you'll realize the goal of better sand play is well within reach. You'll start to make better and better sand swings and, with each one, the frustration you've built up will wane. By the time you finish the plan you might actually prefer the sand over the rough, just like the pros.

BEACH PARTY

A quick look at key PGA Tour Sand Save Averages:

48.2%
PGA Tour Sand Save Percentage

57.5%
PGA Tour Sand Saves from < 10 Yards

52.3%
PGA Tour Sand Saves from 10–20 Yards

46.9%
PGA Tour Sand Saves from 20–30 Yards

32.8%
PGA Tour Sand Saves from > 30 Yards

2012 season
Source: PGATour.com

LET THE SAND DO THE DIRTY WORK

You don't hit the ball out of a bunker—you hit the sand behind the ball

What separates the greenside bunker blast from every other shot in golf is that the clubhead doesn't contact the ball; rather, the ball moves out on a pillow of sand. In other words, the ball is just along for the ride. Once you grasp this concept and learn to slide the clubhead through the sand and hit the correct entry point, bunker play becomes easy. There are some other variables to learn, such as how to control the distance of your bunker shots, but the primary goal remains the same: hit a spot in the sand a few inches behind the ball and slide the clubhead under the ball. Once you get this part of the equation down, you can make slight adjustments in your setup and swing to really get the ball close from a variety of lies.

Those are the basics. Regardless of how well you nail them over the next three days, however, your sand play will improve dramatically with a simple change of strategy. Whereas in the past you may have tried to stop the ball as close to the pin as possible, you're going to be asked to broaden your approach. The new goal of your sand game is to limit the number of strokes it takes you to get in the hole from a bunker to three. That sounds like a lot, but think of the times when you failed to get your first shot out of the bunker (or sent it flying over the green) then followed up your next attempt with a two putt. That's *four* shots. Or say you even three-putted. That's *five* strokes. Suddenly, three strokes doesn't sound that bad, and it shouldn't. You need to be more realistic with your rescues. Check the graphic below. If Tour pros can only get sand shots to within 10 feet of the hole on average, how demanding should you be of your own sand game? For the majority of recreational players, getting the ball on the green and within 20 feet of the hole should be considered a success. For those who are simply looking to break into the double digits with their scores, just getting the ball on is the goal. In either case, you should aim for the area of the putting surface that gives you the greatest margin for error (i.e., the most room with which to work).

A big part of this strategy takes a page from Section 3, where you learned how to avoid big misses when hitting wedge shots onto the green. A big miss in the sand game is leaving the ball in the bunker. From now on, you only get one shot to escape the sand. You'll meet this standard by overcoming two of the most common bunker faults, which are 1) not creating a consistent divot in the sand under the ball or making a divot in the right place, and 2) swinging fast enough to allow the club to glide through the sand and lift the ball out. To be a good bunker player, you must learn how to slide the clubhead through the sand

> ## "The new goal is to limit the number of strokes it takes you to get in the hole from a bunker to three."

without contacting the ball. Moreover, you need to establish consistent entry and exit points. The better you are at controlling the path of the clubhead and doing it at an adequate rate of speed, the easier time you'll have escaping bunkers in one swing.

We'll attack your bunker game in three stages. In the first stage, you'll learn how to take the right amount of sand on every swing. You'll then learn how to add speed without losing control. We'll complete your bunker improvement by providing tips for handling various lies. As you'll discover, it's the lie, not your ego, that determines where you plan to land the ball on the green.

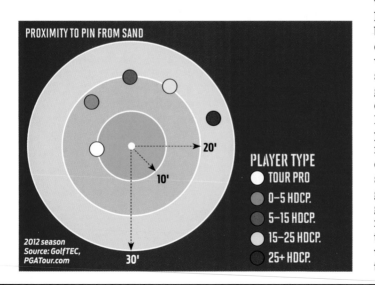

PROXIMITY TO PIN FROM SAND

20'
10'
30'

2012 season
Source: GolfTEC,
PGATour.com

PLAYER TYPE
● TOUR PRO
● 0–5 HDCP.
● 5–15 HDCP.
● 15–25 HDCP.
○ 25+ HDCP.

LESSON TAKE THE RIGHT KIND OF SAND DIVOT

To get the ball out of the sand, you need to get the sand out of the bunker

As it is with your iron swing, taking the right kind of divot in a bunker (a sand divot, in this case) is essential to success. It needs to be consistent, the right size, and located in the right spot. If you're like most amateurs, the amount of sand you blast out of the bunker, and from where this explosion takes place, varies from one shot to the next. That's why your bunker escapes vary from one attempt to the next. While the actual dimensions of the perfect sand divot changes depending to the texture of the sand (firm, fluffy, hard, wet, etc.), here's generally what you're looking for:

Entry Point Two inches behind the ball.
Exit Point Three to four inches in front of the ball.
Depth Three-quarter inch deep.

This adds up to the same amount of sand you could dig up with one hand.

Remember, in a good bunker swing you use your wedge to blast sand onto the green, and the sand carries the ball out of the bunker. The first part is the most important: Your wedge hits the hazard, not the ball. The trick is to get the second part right by taking the right amount of sand. If you don't know if you're taking a good sand divot or not, try this simple drill:

STEP 1
Draw a line in the sand from your left heel straight out away from you as shown (*photo, far left*). You don't need a ball for this one if for no other reason than it isn't important. You must convince yourself that the ball is an afterthought on these shots.

STEP 2
Make your best sand swing. Your goal is to get the clubhead to enter the sand on the line and exit about seven inches in front of the line. After this swing, make five to six more, taking a step forward each time so as to not disturb your impact marks.

STEP 3
Check your blast marks. If they show that the clubhead is entering the sand either before the line or past it, then continue to perform the drill without a ball until you can consistently start the divot in the right spot. If your blast marks are too deep, open the clubface. Deep and short divot marks are evidence that the leading edge is digging in too deep and stopping the club from gliding through the sand. It's critical that you become efficient not only in controlling the entry and exit points, but also at managing how the clubhead slides through the sand.

Try to enter the sand here.

Try to exit the sand here.

NO!
This divot starts behind the line and is much too deep. A ball hit with this swing would remain in the bunker.

PERFECT!
This divot started right on the line and is the perfect size and depth. Copy this on every swing.

OK
This divot starts close enough to the line to get the ball out. Because it's hit a little thin, this shot will roll more after it hits the green.

TARGET

ASSESSMENT MAKE SURE YOU'RE SET UP FOR SUCCESS

Use My Pro To Go to see if you're making sand-swing errors even before you start

Since your goal on most greenside bunker shots is to splash the sand out of the hazard (and let the ball ride out on the sand), the setup is a bit different from your standard wedge shot. Instead of having your hands ahead of the ball and the shaft leaning toward the target (a sure way to hit a rocket from the sand), play the ball forward in your stance, with your head, spine, and hands directly over the spot where you want to impact the sand (i.e., two inches behind the ball in normal conditions).

These adjustments alone should guarantee sand-first contact. But it's also advisable to open your stance and clubface. An open-faced club tends to glide more easily through sand because opening the face exposes more of the bounce of the club.

Bounce creates an upward force to offset the downward force of the clubface, allowing the clubhead to glide through the bunker. Most sand wedges come with anywhere between 8 and 16 degrees of bounce. Make sure to use as much of it as you can.

Since you're opening the face, open your stance about 30 degrees to the left. It's important to realize that even though you've opened up to your target, swing along the line of your toes, not toward the target itself. The open face/open stance combination produces more of a sliding action through impact. This is a much better option than the digging action you typically get with a square stance.

KEEP AN EYE ON BALL POSITION

When players open their stance in the sand, they usually do so after they've set the ball position. Doing this actually moves the effective ball position back (*photos, below*) relative to your toe line. When you take your stance, set your left foot first, then your right, and you'll do a better job of positioning the ball in the right place.

Square stances and clubfaces are not recommended for a standard bunker shot.

Open your stance and clubface. Watch out! Opening up moves the ball back in your stance relative to your toe line.

Play the ball off your left toe relative to your target line, which is centered to your toe line because your stance is open.

CHECK YOUR SETUP WITH MY PRO TO GO

To see if you've got the sand shot address position nailed, have a friend capture your setup from both a face-on and down-target perspective using the guidelines presented on page 11. In the face-on view, draw a line straight down from your nose to the sand. In the down-target view, draw a line from the ball to your target and another line across your toes (your aim line).

MYPRO TOGO

Hear It From a Pro!
Upload a video of your sand swing for an in-depth analysis of your explosion technique. Visit **myprotogo.com**.

FACE-ON ASSESSMENT

NO! Square Setup

If you can't see the entire clubface (look for the grooves), then the face is too square and the club may dig into the sand instead of gliding through it. If the ball is near or behind the line drawn from your nose, then you've allowed it to creep too far back in your stance. This also can lead to digging and a shot left short in the bunker.

DOWN-TARGET ASSESSMENT

NO! Square Setup

If the line drawn across your toes doesn't point at least 30 degrees away from the line pointing at your target, then your stance is too square. Unless you can really propel the clubhead or are an experienced bunker player, you may end up taking too much sand. Also, make sure you're not open more than 30 degrees. Aiming too far to the left relative to your target line might result in thin contact.

FACE-ON ASSESSMENT

YES! Open Setup

If you can see the entire clubface (or at least most of it), then you've opened the clubface the proper amount and have full use of the bounce on your wedge to help it glide through the sand. If the ball is noticeably in front of the line drawn from your nose, then you've successfully opened your stance while keeping the ball up in your stance.

DOWN-TARGET ASSESSMENT

YES! Open Setup

If the line drawn across your toes points about 30 degrees away from the line pointing at your target, then your stance is solid. As a final check, make sure you've dug your feet into the bunker so the soles of your shoes are under the surface of the sand. This not only helps with stability, but it also moves the bottom of your swing arc under the ball, which helps remove the fear of skulling the shot.

PRACTICE IMPROVE YOUR SAND IMPACT

Try these four drills to properly use the sand to propel the ball out of the bunker

DRILL 9.1

Thump the Grass Drill

When Day 28
Where Practice facility
How Long 20 swings
(about 15 mins.)

HOW TO DO IT

The only way your club can properly glide through the sand under the ball is if you impact the sand with the sole of your wedge, not the leading edge. This is one of the reasons for addressing bunker shots with an open clubface. To get the feel of correct sand impact, practice making an audible thump at impact. The sound is important. Listen for it the next time you watch a Tour player blast from a bunker on television—good bunker shots make a very recognizable noise. In order to magnify the thump, you'll perform this drill outside the bunker on fairway grass. Follow these steps:

Step 1

Use two clubs (or alignment sticks) to mark your target line and your stance/swing line (*inset photo*). Set your toes along the stance/swing line and point your clubface down the target line. Place a third club between your feet with the grip pointing at the spot where the ball would be.

Step 2

Make your best sand swing. Think of it as one you'd use to hit a 40-yard lob with lots of hinge and lots of speed and using mostly your upper body and arms. Thump the sole of the club against ground just to the left of the grip end of the third club (where the ball would be). Make successive swings and listen for the thump each time.

Step 3

Look at your scuff mark. You don't want a big divot here. It should feel as though you're peeling the top layer of grass off the turf. Also, you want a tight scuff pattern. This will tell you if you're making impact in the same place. This is a key to good bunker shots. The more you can impact the ground in the same place, the more consistent your results will be. Practice this drill until you get it right before trying to hit actual shots out of a bunker.

Listen for a thump and look for a tight scuff mark.

Scuff mark centered relative to toe line and forward relative to target line.

DRILL 9.2
Take Out the Oval Drill

When Day 29
Where Practice facility
How Long 20 swings (about 15 mins.)

HOW TO DO IT

Here you'll continue to work on a consistent impact pattern, but this time while making swings in the sand. Take your address without a ball, draw a line out from your left heel and another one directly along your target line. Then, trace an oval (about the size of your hand) just in front of the line drawn from your left heel. Your goal here is to swing through the sand and "remove" the oval. If any of the sand within it is still there after you swing, then keep working at it. This trains you not only to take the right kind of sand divot, but also to take it in the right place.

If you typically play bunkers that feature soft, fluffy sand, make sure to dig your feet deeper into the sand. This will help you correctly take a deeper divot. If you usually face bunkers that are firm or wet, dig in less for a shallower divot.

BONUS LESSONS!

Watch videos of these drills at **golftec.com/ parplan.**

Trace the oval here.

Swing through impact.

Make sure you "remove" the entire oval from the sand.

Make Music in a Bunker
Ty Walker, PGA: GolfTEC—Denver

The best bunker players are known for making a thump sound when splashing the ball out of the sand. In order to do this correctly, you must utilize the bounce of the sand wedge and feel as though you're scraping the bottom of the club along the sand and avoid digging too deep. By using the tines on a rake you can create a "sheet of music" to practice your divot entry and exit points to study the size and depth of the divot.

Draw the sheet perpendicular to your target line using the tines of a rake and place a ball in middle of it. Draw a line parallel to the staff lines (i.e., the ruts created by the rake) on either side of the ball to mark its location. Take a swing and inspect the divot by counting how many ruts behind the ball you entered and how far the divot extends past the entry point. The number of lines on the sheet of music blasted away in front of the ball should be about triple the number of lines erased behind the ball.

WINNING NUMBER 25

The percentage difference between the PGA Tour Sand Save average from < 10 yards (57.5%) and > 30 yards (32.5%). The longer the bunker shot, the more you must focus on using three shots to get in the hole, not two.

Source: PGATour.com

PRACTICE IMPROVE YOUR SAND IMPACT

Try these four drills to properly use the sand to propel the ball out of the bunker

DRILL 9.3

Swing & Evaluate Drill

When Day 29
Where Practice facility
How Long Ten swings (about 15 mins.)

HOW TO DO IT

Have a friend capture your bunker swing from a face-on perspective using My Pro To Go. Follow the guidelines on page 11. Whereas you used My Pro To Go earlier in this section to check the quality of your sand setup, now you're going to use it to check the quality of your sand swing. Here are the important things to look for when you play back the video:

Backswing A full wrist hinge with your left arm stopping at the 9:00 position on a clock.

Downswing Much less leg action than what you'd use for an iron swing. This improves stability in the sand. Also, check that your swing is moving along your toe line and that the sand is exploding out in the direction of the target. (You'll get a better view of this from a down-target perspective.)

Impact Clubhead entering the sand two inches behind the ball and gliding through the sand underneath the ball. If you step the video forward slowly enough, you should see the explosion of sand actually lift the ball out of the bunker.

Release Since you're hitting this shot like a flop shot and want to utilize as much of the bounce as possible, check that the face is still open after impact and not rotated over as it is in your normal full swing.

Finish The important thing here is that your forward-swing is longer than your backswing. This ensures that you create enough speed through the bunker to blast the ball out.

Use minimal leg action to power the club through sand. You'll get better results using more wrists, hands and arms.

DRILL 9.4

Thump the Carpet Drill

When Day 30
Where Home or office
How Long 20 swings (about 15 mins.)

HOW TO DO IT

In drill 9.1 on page 174 you practiced thumping the grass to improve your sand contact. This move is so important you're going to continue to practice it, but this time within the friendly confines of your home or office. Instead of thumping the grass, thump the carpet. Follow the steps on page 174, and after a while remove the clubs to get you in the habit of thumping in the right place without the help of aiming clubs and guide lines.

If you're having difficulty, check that you're not moving forward or behind the ball when you swing (My Pro To Go can help here). Address the ball with your chin, navel, hands, and clubhead all in one straight line, directly over the point you want to first impact in the sand. Your shoulders should be fairly level and your spine straight up and down, not tilted away from the target. This encourages a shallow path through the sand. Too much tilt causes the clubhead to bottom out too soon, so the club can't slide through the sand correctly.

As you swing back, keep your head steady so that your chin remains directly over the entry point. Your shoulders should turn some, but not as much as they would in a full swing. There should also be very little weight shift onto your right foot. Your left wrist should be cupped at the top, which helps you to slide the clubhead under the ball.

Through impact, maintain the cup in your left wrists and have the feeling that the clubhead is passing your hands early so you can slide it underneath the ball. The wrist action is similar to what you would experience in a flop shot since you want the clubface to remain open through impact.

Keep your nose over the area where you want the club to enter the sand.

Listen for the thump sound of the sole hitting the carpet.

BONUS LESSONS!

Watch videos of these drills at *golftec.com/parplan*.

LESSON IMPROVE YOUR SPEED THROUGH SAND

Good bunker swings are fast bunker swings

The most important thing about speed in a bunker is that you need it to get the ball out and onto the green. There's nothing slow about sand swings. Amateurs have a hard time getting used to this fact because of the proximity of most bunkers to the green—it's hard to swing fast and full when you're close to the pin. However, that's exactly what you need to do. Pretend you're hitting a 50-yard wedge shot from the fairway, making your finish longer than your backswing and accelerating from the top all the way through the ball. With a sand swing you need more hand and wrist power than you do for your other swings, but the goal is the same: speed.

If you work on the techniques discussed thus far in the section, then speed won't be a problem, and you'll start to overcome the fear of airmailing a mishit bunker shot over the green. If you make the right kind of sand divot and make it in the same place, you can swing as hard as you want without worry of this ever happening, especially if you open the clubface at address.

DISTANCE CONTROL

Even though you'll face a variety of distances from your bunker lie to the pin, you should always swing at the same fast pace. Problems happen when you try to control distance by making either a slower or extremely fast swing. The moment you try to slow down the club is the moment it digs into the sand and fails to glide all the way under and through the ball. And the moment you give your swing some extra gas is the moment you rise up out of your posture and catch the ball thin.

It doesn't matter how close you are to the flagstick. Swing as fast as you would on a 50-yard shot from the fairway.

The better way to control distance is to use the same swing and switch clubs. Because you're opening the clubface at address and swinging along your toe line, each club in your bag will produce a shot from the bunker that flies almost a third of its normal distance. If you need more yardage, use more club and keep your swing speed the same (or swing through to a full finish); if you need less yardage, use less club and keep your swing speed the same (or make a shorter through-swing). Don't rely only on your sand wedge. Your other wedges, even your 9- and 8-irons, can work wonders from the bunker and get you close from any distance without risking the mistakes that come from slowing down or speeding up your swing.

SAND CLUB SELECTION GUIDE

Club	Regular Distance	Bunker Distance
LW	60 yds.	< 15 yds.
SW	75 yds.	15–20 yds.
GW	90 yds.	20–25 yds.
PW	115 yds.	25–35 yds.
9-IRON	130 yds.	35–45 yds.
8-IRON	145 yds.	> 45 yds.

"Change clubs, not swing speed, to blast the ball the correct distance."

ASSESSMENT CHECK YOUR SWING SPEED

Use My Pro To Go to see if you're properly accelerating through the sand

Have a friend capture your swing from start to finish from a face-on perspective using the guidelines on page 11. As you step the video forward from your top-of-the-backswing position, look for the clues that indicate whether or not

you're producing enough swing speed to power the club through the sand without any digging or stopping. Use the checkpoints below.

Lower Body You shouldn't see a lot of leg action here. In fact, it's good to feel like your lower body doesn't do

very much in a bunker shot. Extra leg action and hip turn make it difficult to produce a consistent divot and to remain stable in the shifting sand.

Wrists Look for a full hinge at the top of your backswing, and then look for a release of this hinge as the clubhead

Use My Pro To Go to spot errors that rob you of swing speed in a bunker.

approaches the sand. You don't need to rehinge your wrists on the target side of the ball as you do on normal swings. In fact, it's good to delay the hinge to maintain an open clubface through impact and slightly beyond.

Head Check that your head pretty much stays in the same place as you swing down and into the sand. Draw a circle around your head at the top position for a clear assessment of any head movement. (Either toward or away form the target is bad.) The goal is to keep your head in the circle from start to impact.

TRY THIS!

Use Attack Angle For Bunker Distance Control

Brendan Locke, PGA: GolfTEC—Middleton, Wis.

In addition to switching clubs, changing the angle at which you enter the sand is an effective way to blast the ball shorter or longer. A steep angle of attack (chopping motion) will cause the ball to go higher and land softer—useful stuff from a greenside bunker when there isn't much room between you and the pin. A shallow angle of attack (basically, what you get using your normal full-swing motion) will project the ball on a lower ballflight. This allows the ball to go farther and roll more once it hits.

If adjusting angle of attack sounds complicated, then think about how you want the sand to splash out. If you need to hit the ball higher and shorter, picture the sand splashing out of the bunker higher and landing closer to your feet. This will help you produce more of a V-shaped swing, meaning one that's slightly steeper on both sides of the ball. If you need to hit the ball lower and longer, picture the sand splashing out as far away from you as possible. This will help you produce more of a flatter, U-shaped swing. Regardless of how you splash the sand, make sure to do it at full speed.

WINNING NUMBER .46

The average number of additional strokes it took PGA Tour players to get up and down from a bunker than it did to get up and down from the fringe in 2012. Hitting into sand is one of the most costliest misses, even for elite players.

Source: PGATour.com

PRACTICE INCREASE THE SPEED OF YOUR SAND SWING

Here's a light workout to help you power cleanly through any bunker

DRILL 9.5

Windmill Drill

When Day 30
Where Home or office
How Long Five minutes

> Stronger forearms give you speed and control in a bunker. Use the Windmill Drill for an effective workout.

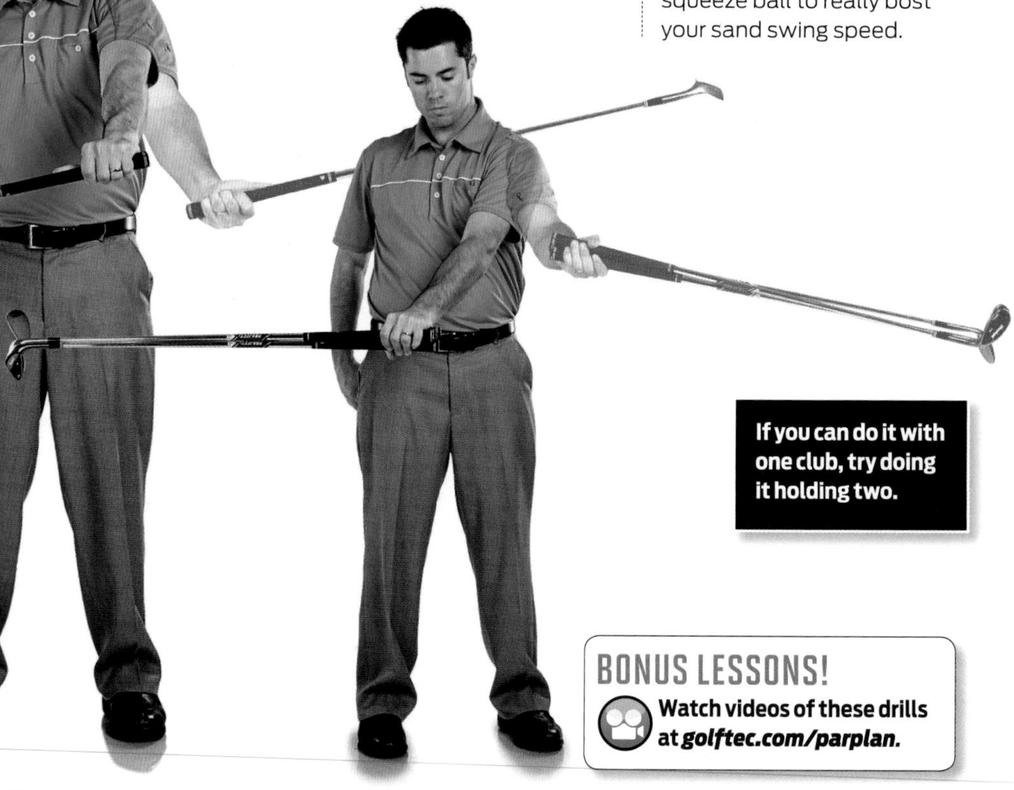

HOW TO DO IT
Because you can't rely on your legs to produce necessary speed in a bunker (excess leg action leads to inconsistent divot patterns), rely more on your arms, wrists, and hands, which in reality are some of the fastest moving parts of your body. While you won't be asked to do dumbbell curls in the gym to groove a better sand swing, it's not a bad idea to work on your forearms a little. Stronger forearms lead to more a powerful wrist action and can help you control the club as it explodes through the sand.

An easy way to work on your forearm strength is to grip a club with your left hand only and your left arm held straight out. Hold the club parallel to the ground with the clubhead on your right. Without moving anything else, slowly rotate your forearm to the left until the shaft is parallel to the ground again with the clubhead out to your left. (If you have difficulty, support your left elbow with your right hand or bring the club closer to you with your left elbow against your torso.) Go back and forth about 10 times, then switch hands. Do it slowly so you're using muscle—not momentum—to rotate the club back and forth.

Once you get to the point where rotating one club isn't a problem, do it with two. You can work on your hand and wrist strength using a squeeze ball to really bost your sand swing speed.

> If you can do it with one club, try doing it holding two.

> **BONUS LESSONS!**
> Watch videos of these drills at *golftec.com/parplan*.

LESSON ADJUST FOR DIFFERENT LIES

Use the leading edge to blast the ball from these trouble lies

The deeper the ball is buried in the sand, the less likely it is that you'll get it close. These shots are hard to control, and, in many cases, are just like being tagged with a one-stroke penalty.

The deeper the lie, the less you should open the clubface. The key on bad lies is getting the leading edge of the club under the ball. This is more difficult with a sand wedge since the bounce on the sole is designed to resist digging. Try the following methods in practice to help you with these three nasty lies:

BURIED AND SEMIBURIED LIES

If at least a quarter of the ball is below the sand (up to half of the ball), set up with most of your weight on your left side and the ball positioned in the middle of your stance. Square up the face of your sand or pitching wedge so that it can dig more easily through the sand. Pick the club up sharply on the backswing and then drive the leading edge of the clubhead hard into the sand, far enough behind the ball to get the leading edge underneath it. Provided you get the leading edge deep enough under the ball, the scooping action should create a vertical explosion of sand that pops the ball out with lots of overspin.

FRIED-EGG LIE

You'll see this lie frequently on courses with very dry, fluffy sand. The ball lands with a thud, carving out a crater and creating a ridge all the way around it, similar to an egg white surrounding its yoke. You want to employ the same technique as the buried lie shot above, scooping underneath the ball instead of sliding the club through the sand and using more of the leading edge to lodge the ball free. The difference is that you want the leading edge of the club

to enter the sand farther behind the ball, at the edge of the crater. For this reason, you may want to play the ball slightly forward of center in your stance. The only way to improve from these trouble lies is to practice and learn the interaction between the club and the sand so you can feel what adjustments will work in each situation.

SEMIBURIED

BURIED

VERY BURIED

The
Par
PLAN

YOUR DAY-BY-DAY GUIDE TO SHOOTING YOUR BEST SCORE EVER!

F ollow the schedule at right to build the skills you need to improve your performance in the nine most important areas of the game. (Alter the time frame to better fit your schedule, or to allot more practice to your weaker swing areas.) Try to maximize the time you're away from the practice facility by doing more at-home work than what's listed here. You can perform many of the indoor drills while watching your favorite TV show or movie.

If you find that some drills provide more benefit than other drills in the same part of the section, focus on those. And make sure to keep at them long after you post your best score, because your next goal is just around the corner.

DAY ZERO: PREP

0
Home/Office
Download My Pro To Go (MPTG) to your smartphone or tablet, then create an account on **myprotogo.com**

DAYS 1–5: DRIVING

1
Practice Facility
● Assess swing path using MPTG (*p. 19*)
● Drill 1.1 (*p. 22*)
● Drill 1.2 (*p. 23*)

2
Home/Office
● Drill 1.3 (*p. 23*)
Practice Facility
● Assess angle of attack (*pp. 26–27*)
● Drill 1.4 (*p. 29*)

DAYS 6–9: PUTTING (CONT'D)

8
Home/Office
● Assess directional control (*p. 51*)
● Drill 1.5 (*p. 29*)

9
Practice Facility
● Assess green reading (*p. 58*)
● Drill 2.3 (*p. 45*)
● Drill 2.4 (*p. 54*)
● Drill 2.5 (*p. 55*)

DAYS 10–13: WEDGES

10
Practice Facility
● Assess low point location using MPTG (*p. 65*)
● Drill 3.1 (*p. 68*)
● Drill 3.2 (*p. 68*)
● Drill 3.3 (*p. 69*)

DAYS 14–17: SCRAMBLING (CONT'D)

16
Home/Office
● Assess directional control (*p. 51*)
● Drill 4.2 (*p. 86*)
● Drill 3.4 (*p. 74*)

17
Practice Facility
● 11-Ball Assessment (*pp. 66–67*)
● Flop practice (*pp. 98–99*)
● Drill 1.2 (*p. 23*)

DAYS 18–22: IRONS

18
Practice Facility
● Assess impact point (*p. 105*)
● Assess divots (*pp. 106–107*)
● Drill 5.1 (*p. 108*)

DAY 24: GEAR

24
Improvement Center
● Check equipment specs (*pp. 134–143*)
Practice Facility
● Drill 5.3 (*p. 110*)
● Drill 2.3 (*p. 45*)

DAYS 25–27: SHOTMAKING

25
Practice Facility
● Determine stock shot using MPTG (*pp. 150–151*)
● Assess green reading (*p. 58*)

26
Practice Facility
● Draw/Fade practce (*p. 154*)
● High/low practice (*p. 157*)
● Personal tempo practice (*pp. 42–43*)

3
Home/Office
- Drill 1.5 (*p. 29*)
- Drill 1.3 (*p. 23*)

Improvement Center
- Driver spec check/ launch monitor

4
Practice Facility
- Drill 1.1 (*p. 22*)
- Drill 1.4 (*p. 29*)

5
Practice Facility
- Re-assess swing path using MPTG (*p. 19*)
- Re-assess angle of attack (*pp. 26-27*)

DAYS 6–9: PUTTING

6
Practice Facility
- Assess distance control using MPTG (*pp. 40–41*)
- Personal tempo practice (*pp. 42-43*)

7
Practice Facility
- Assess contact (*p. 46*)
- Drill 2.1 (*p. 44*)
- Drill 2.2 (*p. 45*)
- Drill 1.2 (*p. 23*)

11
Practice Facility
- 11-Ball Assessment (*pp. 66–67*)
- Assess swing length using MPTG (*p. 71*)
- Drill 2.2 (*p. 45*)

12
Practice Facility
- Drill 3.4 (*p. 74*)
- Drill 3.5 (*p. 75*)
- Log (*pp. 76–77*)

Home/Office
- Drill 3.6 (*p. 75*)

13
Practice Facility
- Drill 3.1 (*p. 68*)
- Drill 3.2 (*p. 68*)
- Drill 3.3 (*p. 69*)
- Drill 1.4 (*p. 29*)

DAYS 14–17: SCRAMBLING

14
Practice Facility
- Assess short-game stroke using MPTG (*pp. 84–85*)
- Drill 4.1 (*p. 86*)
- Drill 4.3 (*p. 87*)

15
Practice Facility
- Short shot arsenal (*pp. 66–67*)
- Drill 2.1 (*p. 44*)

Home/Office
- Drill 4.2 (*p. 86*)

19
Home/Office
- Drill 5.2 (*p. 109*)
- Drill 5.4 (*p. 111*)
- Drill 3.6 (*p. 75*)

20
Practice Facility
- Assess clubface control using MPTG (*p. 113*)
- Drill 5.3 (*p. 110*)
- Drill 5.5 (*p. 116*)
- Drill 5.8 (*p. 119*)

21
Practice Facility
- Drill 5.1 (*p. 108*)
- Drill 4.1 (*p. 86*)
- Drill 3.5 (*p. 75*)

Home/Office
- Drill 5.6 (*p. 117*)

22
Practice Facility
- Drill 5.1 (*p. 108*)
- Drill 5.5 (*p. 116*)
- Drill 1.1 (*p. 22*)

Home/Office
- Drill 5.7 (*p. 118*)

DAY 23: STRATEGY

23
Practice Facility
- Average carry distances (*p. 122*)

Home/Office
- Plot strategy in yardage book (*p. 122*)

27
Practice Facility
- Assess putting contact (*p. 46*)
- Short shot arsenal (*pp. 66–67*)
- Drill 4.3 (*p. 87*)

DAYS 28–30: BUNKER PLAY

28
Practice Facility
- Assess your sand divots (*pp. 170–171*)
- Assess setup using MPTG (*pp. 172–173*)
- Drill 9.1 (*p. 174*)

29
Practice Facility
- Drill 9.2 (*p. 175*)
- Assess setup using MPTG (*pp. 172–173*)
- Drill 9.3 (*p. 176*)
- Drill 5.8 (*p. 119*)

30
Practice Facility
- Assess swing speed using MPTG (*p. 180*)

Home/Office
- Drill 9.4 (*p. 177*)
- Drill 9.5 (*p. 182*)

Continually perform the various assessments using My Pro To Go each time you visit your practice facility. This is the best way to make sure you're keeping up with the plan.

MY*PRO* TO *GO*

PICK YOUR PRO

The nation's largest network of teaching professionals is at your disposal

Using the My Pro To Go app to assess your progress and uploading your swing for an expert critique of your motion will go a long way toward helping you reach your goals within the plan. To get the most out the experience and guarantee lasting improvement, however, take your game to one of 160 GolfTEC centers located across the United States and Canada. GolfTEC coaches represent the world's largest and most experienced golf-improvement group. Each and every certified personal coach is expertly trained to help you complete your improvement plan and expand your goals to take your scores lower than you ever thought possible.

For more information on individual centers and GolfTECs network of more than 500 instructors, visit **golftec.com** or **myprotogo.com.**

ALABAMA

Birmingham (Golfsmith)
Instructors: Ryan Rouch
(205) 991-1762
4604 Highway 280
Birmingham, Ala. 35242

ALBERTA

Edmonton
Manager: Clinton Schmaltz
Instructors: Clinton Schmaltz, Travis Merritt, Luke McKenzie, Michael Paulson
(780) 486-3233
17556 100 Avenue
Edmonton, Alberta
T5S 2S2

Midnapore, Calgary
Manager: Jamie Kureluk
Instructors: Jamie Kureluk, Kenneth Brown
(403) 452-7150
240 Midpark Way SE
Unit 201
Calgary, Alberta T2X 1N4

ARIZONA

Arrowhead (Golfsmith)
Manager: Kevin Self
Instructors: Jason Weiman, Kevin Self, Mitchell Moncel, Josh Watkins
(602) 288-5180
7765 W. Bell Road
Glendale, Ariz. 85382

Chandler (Golfsmith)
Managers: Thomas Gibbs, Jeff Olsen
Instructors: Chris Hantla, Derek Oesterreicher, Jeff Olsen, Thomas Gibbs
(480) 893-9029
880 N. 54th Street
Chandler, Ariz. 85226

N. Scottsdale (Golfsmith)
Manager: John Kursel
Instructors: Andrew Yang, Brian Skena, Dave Hosey, John Kursel
(480) 607-2212
15452 N. Pima Road
N. Scottsdale, Ariz. 85260

Tucson (Golfsmith)
Manager: Craig Jones
Instructors: Cody Rathbun, Craig Jones, Eric Valencia, Tyler Clark
(520) 887-4653
4439 N. Oracle Road
Tucson, Ariz. 85705

BRITISH COLUMBIA

N. Vancouver
Manager: Matt Carrothers
Instructors: Aaron Moody, Andrew Jeffers, Jamie Macintosh, Matt Carrothers, Terry Drever, Shannon Briggs
(604) 904-3677
103-788 Copping Street
N. Vancouver, British Columbia V7M 3G6

Surrey
Manager: Steve Busswood
Instructors: Matthew Bartholomew, Steve Busswood
(604) 385-4653
2411 160th Street #235
Surrey, British Columbia
V3S 0C8

Vancouver
Manager: Norman Baufeld
Instructors: James Heath, Norman Baufeld, Trevor Woynarski
(604) 683-4653
763 Terminal Avenue, 2nd Floor
Vancouver, British Columbia V6A 2M2

CALIFORNIA

Brea (Golfsmith)
Manager: Aaron Hunsaker
Instructors: Aaron Hunsaker, Eric Hird, Patrick Zamora
(714) 255-9667
835 E. Birch Street
Brea, Calif. 92821

El Segundo (Golfsmith)
Manager: Matt Newby
Instructors: Matt Newby, Rhett Delozier, Tim Leible
(310) 640-7888
2041 Rosecrans Avenue
El Segundo, Calif. 90245

Huntington Beach
Manager: Cody Botella
Instructors: Andy Thuney, Cody Botella, John Gorski
(714) 841-9608
15811 Graham Street
Huntington Beach, Calif. 92649

Irvine
Manager: Thomas Howell, Jr.
Instructors: Justin Beasley, Steve Anderson, Thomas Howell, Jr.
(949) 724-9081
17897 MacArthur Boulevard, Suite B
Irvine, Calif. 92614

Irvine–Lake Forest (Golfsmith)
Manager: Steve DeWitt
Instructors: Dean Riggs, Steve DeWitt
(949) 334-4753
16181 Lake Forest Drive
Irvine, Calif. 92618

Ontario (Golfsmith)
Manager: Mark Lyons
Instructors: Colin Dignam, Mark Lyons
(909) 987-1141
4420 Ontario Mills Parkway
Ontario, Calif. 91764

Oxnard (Golfsmith)
Manager: Ian Langford
Instructors: Adam Fox, Ian Langford, Joe Dougherty
(805) 983-1600
441 W. Esplanade
Oxnard, Calif. 93036

Palm Desert (Golfsmith)
Manager: Steven Pircher
Instructors: Chris Pritchard, Eric Sherman, Javier Silva, Steven Pircher
(760) 324-9000
72700 Dinah Shore Drive
Palm Desert, Calif. 92211

Pasadena
Manager: Andrew Loughrin
Instructors: Andrew Loughrin, Eva Sallgren, Ryan Haydis, Scott McAulay
(626) 356-0215
2245 E. Colorado Boulevard #204
Pasadena, Calif. 91107

Pleasant Hill (Golfsmith)
Manager: Bryan Patterson
Instructors: Brian McMurtrie, Bryan Patterson,
(925) 264-5047
120 Crescent Drive
Pleasant Hill, Calif. 94523

Pleasanton (Golfsmith)
Manager: Henry Coxe
Instructors: Henry Coxe, Tim Johnson
(925) 225-0444
4200 Rosewood Drive
Pleasanton, Calif. 94588

Rancho Bernardo
Manager: Scott Engelland
Instructors: David Robe, Scott Engelland, Scott Stubbs
(858) 432-7200
16779 Bernardo Center Drive
San Diego, Calif. 92128

Rocklin
Manager: Chris Woods
Instructors: Brad Heninger, Chris Woods, Elliot Hall
(916) 626-5566
1150 Sunset Boulevard Suite 156
Rocklin, Calif. 95765

San Carlos (Golfsmith)
Manager: Steve Gordon
Instructors: Josh Trimble, Nathan Bryant, Steve Gordon
(650) 595-4653
1125 Industrial Road Suite G
San Carlos, Calif. 94070

San Diego
Manager: Andrew Marr
Instructors: Andrew Marr, John Cooper, Jonathan Dyson, Neil Gram
(858) 228-5228
8935 Towne Centre Drive #105
San Diego, Calif. 92122

San Jose (Golfsmith)
Manager: Gerald Haynes
Instructors: Brent Welsh, Gerald Haynes, Meurig Morgan
(408) 243-4653
4070 Stevens Creek Boulevard
San Jose, Calif. 95129

Santa Barbara
Manager: Trevor Broesamle
Instructors: Stephen Douglas, Trevor Broesamle
(805) 884-1847
126 E. Haley, Unit A1
Santa Barbara, Calif. 93101

Santa Clarita
Manager: Matthew Hollis
Instructors: Matthew Hollis
(661) 799-7886
22947 Soledad Canyon
Santa Clarita, Calif. 91350

Santa Monica
Manager: Tony Schumacher
Instructors: Casey Wire, John Baltzersen, Kelli Ply, Mackenzie Todd, Timothy Day, Tony Schumacher
(310) 458-2636
918 Colorado Avenue
Santa Monica, Calif. 90404

South Bay
Manager: John Williams
Instructors: Michael Allred, John Williams, Paul Boyd
(310) 378-7676
22750 Hawthorne Blvd.
Torrance, Calif. 90505

Woodland Hills (Golfsmith)
Manager: Michael Katz
Instructors: David Franks, James Smith, Michael Katz, Robert Sockolich
(818) 883-7712
21494 Victory Boulevard
Woodland Hills, Calif. 91367

COLORADO

Boulder
Manager: Scott Ough
Instructors: Ben Pilon, Russ Clark, Scott Ough
(720) 379-4843
2767 Iris Avenue
Boulder, Colo. 80304

Colorado Springs
Manager: Chad Miller
Instructors: Bernie Blan, Chad Miller, Tim Fuhrer
(719) 219-3095
1727 Briargate Boulevard
Colorado Springs, Colo. 80920

Denver—Cherry Creek
Manager: Kevin Cubbage
Instructors: Arthur Patton, Brian Byrd, Jim See, Kevin Cubbage, Tim Hayes
(303) 388-4832
3773 Cherry Creek Drive North #130
Denver, Colo. 80206

Denver—Tech Center
Manager: Ty Walker
Instructors: Andrew West, Mark Kizzire, Nathan Morris, Reggie Sanchez, Steve Hockman, Troy Wilson, Ty Walker
(303) 770-5951
Marina Square Shopping Center
8101 E. Belleview Avenue, Suite H
Denver, Colo. 80237

Fort Collins South
Manager: Brad Thorberg
Instructors: Brad Thorberg, Brandon McDermott
(970) 692-5270
4637 S. Mason Street, Suite A4
Fort Collins, Colo. 80525

Golden (Golfsmith)
Manager: Josh Miller
Instructors: Erin Diegel, Josh Miller, Scott Cline
(303) 278-3589
17120 W. Colfax Avenue, Suite 108
Golden, Colo. 80401

Grand Junction
Manager: Billy Ellison
Instructors: Billy Ellison
(970) 208-1030
625 24 1/2 Road, Suite C
Grand Junction, Colo. 81505

Park Meadows (Golfsmith)
Manager: Tom Gibbs
Instructors: Charles Perry, Dan Sniffin, Mike Melena, Tom Gibbs
(303) 858-8280
9667 E. County Line Road
Englewood, Colo. 80112

Westminster (Golfsmith)
Manager: Chris Neylan
Instructors: Chris Neylan, Mark Legenza
(303) 426-6600
9440 Sheridan Boulevard
Westminster, Colo. 80030

FLORIDA

Altamonte Springs (Golfsmith)
Manager: Dustin Oakwood
Instructors: Dustin Oakwood, Steven Purviance
(407) 869-0105
297 West SR 436
Altamonte Springs, Fla. 32714

Boca Raton (Golfsmith)
Manager: Regi Starzyk
Instructors: Michael Kruzick, Regi Starzyk
(561) 483-4180
20415 State Road 7
Boca Raton, Fla. 33498

Clearwater (Golfsmith)
Manager: Brian Dyke
Instructors: Brian Dyke, Daniel Maestre, Nathan Barnes
(727) 797-2138
2753 Gulf to Bay Boulevard
Clearwater, Fla. 33759

Fort Myers
Manager: Chris Pais
Instructors: Chris Pais, Josh Jeffers
(239) 628-1653
14261 S. Tamiami Trail #7
Fort Myers, Fla. 33907

Hollywood (Golfsmith)
Manager: John Stoltz
Instructors: John Stoltz, Kris Walmer, Michael Angarano
(954) 920-6811
3300 Oakwood Boulevard
Hollywood, Fla. 33020

Jacksonville
Instructors: Kevin Lindsey, Leslie Fischer
(904) 998-4650
4372 Southside Boulevard #306
Jacksonville, Fla. 32216

Lutz (Golfsmith)
Manager: Matt Davis
Instructors: Jim Wright, Matt Davis, Rich Evans
(813) 962-8060
17649 N. Mabry Highway
Lutz, Fla. 33548

Orlando (Golfsmith)
Manager: Austen Millet
Instructors: Austen Millet, Rick Fuzesy
(407) 370-2755
4656 Millenia Plaza Way
Orlando, Fla. 32839

Naples (Golfsmith)
Manager: Nic Ondriska
Instructors: Evan Uram,
Nic Ondriska
(239) 514-4653
6428 Hollywood
Boulevard
Naples, Fla. 34109

Sarasota
Manager: Luke Stava
Instructors: Bob
Conforte, Brett Zink,
Greg Lewandrowski, Luke
Stava, Robert Hanchey
(941) 926-6025
6249 Lake Osprey Drive
Sarasota, Fla. 34240

**Sarasota—University
Town Center** (Golfsmith)
Manager: Luke Stava
Instructors: Luke Stave,
Robert Hanchey, Brett
Zink, Greg Lewandrowski,
Bob Conforte
(941) 926-6025
143 N. Cattlemen Road
Sarasota, Fla. 34243

Tampa
Manager: Don Costanzo
Instructors: Don Costanzo,
Steve Lippincott, Tony
Goff, Tyler Cole
(813) 202-8516
418 N. Dale Mabry
Highway
Tampa, Fla. 33609

W. Palm Beach (Golfsmith)
Manager: Chris Russell
Instructors: Aaron Pollak,
Chris Russell, Warren
Durbin
(561) 683-3667
785 W. Executive
Center Drive
W. Palm Beach, Fla. 33401

GEORGIA

Atlanta—Buckhead
Manager: Andy Brent
Instructors: Andy Brent,
Curt Sanders, John Coxe
(404) 467-8884
3167 Peachtree Road NE,
Suite N
Atlanta, Ga. 30305

Atlanta—Cumberland
(Golfsmith)
Manager: Joseph Charles
Instructors: Fred Hartzell,
Joseph Charles, Brent
Bonzheim
(678) 701-1802
2997 Cobb Parkway SE
#100
Atlanta, Ga. 30339

Duluth (Golfsmith)
Manager: Jason Bruce
Instructors: Andreas
Boberg, Jason Bruce,
Jason Cochran
(770) 495-9626
3960 Venture Drive
Duluth, Ga. 30096

HAWAII

Honolulu
Manager: Jason Deigert
Instructors: Bill Hunt,
Jason Deigert, Justin
Kuraoka
(808) 441-0105
510 Piikoi Street,
Suite W100
Honolulu, Hawaii 96814

ILLINOIS

Aurora—Fox Valley
(Golfsmith)
Manager: Erik Anderson
Instructors: Brady
Stuckey, Erik Anderson,
Kevin Healey
(630) 723-5215
4302 E. New York
Aurora, Ill. 60505

Chicago—Halsted Row
Manager: Ben Thulin
Instructors: Ben Thulin,
Gabe Rios, Brian Draeger,
Scott Saunders,
T.J. Sullivan
(773) 755-4653
2847 N. Halsted
Chicago, Ill. 60657

Deerfield
Manager: Ben Tinti
Instructors: Ben Tinti,
Jason Reeser
(224) 330-4020
Prairie Pointe Center
360 S. Waukegan Road,
Suite B-2
Deerfield, Ill. 60015

Des Plaines (The Golf Center)
Manager: Justin Bentley
Instructors: Ben Putka,
Chris Beedy, Justin
Bentley, Tom Portera
(847) 299-5431
353 N. River Road
Des Plaines, Ill. 60016

Downers Grove (Golfsmith)
Manager: Kevin Den Besten
Instructors: Kevin Den
Besten, Kevin Hardy
(630) 932-4653
2020 Butterfield Road
Downers Grove, Ill. 60515

Naperville
Manager: Ian Hughes
Instructors: BJ Paul,
Brandon Plowe, Ian
Hughes, James Standhardt
(630) 579-9390
Iroquois Center
1163 E. Ogden Avenue,
Suite 401
Naperville, Ill. 60563

Oak Brook
Manager: Zach Lambeck
Instructors: Garrett
Simons, Luther
Abernethy, Nick
Clearwater, Zach Lambeck
(630) 396-2020
3011 Butterfield Road
Suite #290
Oak Brook, Ill. 60523

Schaumburg (Golfsmith)
Manager: Ryan Colberg
Instructors: Meredith
Robinson, Patrick Barry,
Ryan Colberg
(847) 517-1845
905 E. Golf Road
Schaumburg, Ill. 60173

Vernon Hills
Manager: Kurt Kollmeyer
Instructors: Kurt
Kollmeyer, Leonard
Lesperance
(847) 327-0605
701 N. Milwaukee Avenue
Suite 116
Vernon Hills, Ill. 60061

INDIANA

Carmel
Manager: Ryan
Schrecongost
Instructors: Bryan Greer,
Ryan Schrecongost, Erika
Wicoff
(317) 810-0075
9873 N. Michigan Road,
Suite 140B
Carmel, Ind. 46032

Indianapolis—Castleton
(Golfsmith)
Instructors: Dean Prange,
Nicholas Lloyd, Toby
Baldwin
(317) 595-2170
8310 Castleton Corner
Drive
Indianapolis, Ind. 46250

IOWA

**Clive—Country
Club Village**
Manager: Corey Schultz
Instructors: Corey
Schultz, Josh Barnes, Nick
Busch, Nick Largent
(515) 440-4653
12951 University Avenue,
Suite 110
Clive, Iowa 50325

KANSAS

Overland Park
Manager: Dan Dolan
Instructors: Brandon
Hajek, Chad Carson, Dan
Dolan, Ray Cole
(913) 642-8881
8901 W. 95th Street
Overland Park, Kan. 66212

Wichita
Manager: Rich Maril
Instructors: Brent Beitler,
Rich Maril
(316) 295-4681
3101 N. Rock Road,
Suite 155
Wichita, Kan. 67226

KENTUCKY

Louisville
Manager: Kyle Newell
Instructors: Bryan
Montgomery, Jeff Dawson,
Kyle Newell
(502) 426-4314
102 Vieux Carre Drive
Louisville, Ky. 40223

MARYLAND

N. Bethesda
Manager: Mark Tanner
Instructors: Dave
Saunders, Kevin Tanner,
Mark Tanner
(240) 715-0291
5056-A Nicholson Lane
N. Bethesda, Md. 20852

Timonium (Golfsmith)
Manager: Todd Dennison
Instructors: Robert Oxley,
Todd Dennison
(443) 345-5118
130 W. Ridgely Road
Lutherville, Md. 21093

MASSACHUSETTS

Burlington
Manager: Ryan Skoglund
Instructors: Alex Robbins,
David Souza, Ryan
Skoglund, Todd Smith
(781) 494-4111
1 Wheeler Road
Burlington, Mass. 01803

Danvers
Manager: Brian O'Hearn
Instructors: Brian
O'Hearn, Steve Hancock,
Nick Siudela
(978) 777-2930
29 Andover Street,
Danvers, Mass. 01923

Needham
Manager: John Mescall
Instructors: Brienne
Mahon, Howie Barrow,
John Mescall
(781) 449-8222
238 Highland Avenue
Needham, Mass. 02494

MICHIGAN

Lakeside (Golfsmith)
Manager: Joe Garrisi
Instructors: Jason Jones,
Joe Garrisi,
Thomas Manial
(586) 566-7953
15300 Hall Road
Clinton Township, Mich.
48038

Novi (Golfsmith)
Manager: Stan Sall
Instructors: Andrew
Mogg, Justin Lauer,
Stan Sall
(248) 429-1600
43135 Crescent Boulevard
Novi, Mich. 48375

Troy (Golfsmith)
Instructors: Jonathan
Gallas, Jordan Kreisman,
Marlon Gisi
(248) 689-4653
790 E. Big Beaver Road
Troy, Mich. 48083

MINNESOTA

Coon Rapids—Bunker Hills
Instructors: Tim Brovold,
Marcus Wilhelm
12800 Bunker
Prairie Drive
Coon Rapids, Minn 55448

Eden Prairie
Manager: Jim McNaney
Instructors: Adam
Eggert, Brett Ledin, Jim
McNaney, Ty Armstrong
(952) 241-5100
Lariat Office Center
12200 Middleset Rd. #400
Eden Prairie, Minn. 55344

Edina (Golfsmith)
Manager: Oliver Darby
Instructors: John Kalin,
Oliver Darby,
Zachary Estridge
(952) 223-6258
2940 West 66th Street
Richfield, Minn. 55423

Minnetonka (Golfsmith)
Manager: Nick Pelle
Instructors: Jeff Orthun,
Lance West, Nick Pelle,
Randy Weigman
(952) 546-1423
14200 Wayzata Boulevard
Minnetonka, Minn. 55305

Roseville (Golfsmith)
Manager: Mickey
Soderberg
Instructors: Michael
Dolan, Mickey Soderberg,
Angela Eldred
(651) 697-4015
1800 Highway 36 West
Roseville, Minn. 55113

MISSOURI

Chesterfield
Manager: Keith Baker
Instructors: Christian
Becker, Jason Cooper,
Mike Cummings
(314) 721-4653
148 Chesterfield
Commons E. Road
Chesterfield, Mo. 63005

Clayton
Manager: Justin Hoagland
Instructors: Craig Hutson,
Justin Hoagland, Steve
Ramsey
(314) 721-4653
190 Carondelet Plaza # 178
Clayton, Mo. 63105

Columbia
Manager: Brad Benney
Instructors: Brad Benney,
Nick Germann
(573) 355-9400
3401 Broadway Business
Park Court, Suite 107
Columbia, Mo. 65203

St. Louis (Golfsmith)
Manager: Keith Baker
Instructors: Craig
Bollman, Drew Huelsing,
Keith Baker
(314) 721-4653
11955 Manchester Road
St. Louis, Mo. 63131

NEBRASKA

Omaha
Manager: James Kinney
Instructors: Cory Fletcher,
James Kinney, Jamie
Stogdill, Mark Stava, Ryan
Norman
(402) 905-2990
362 N. 114th, Suite 362
Omaha, Neb. 68154

NEVADA

Henderson
Manager: Tim Sam
Instructors: Justin Marsh,
Robert Atkinson, Tim
Sam, Will Bertz
(702) 834-6370
1570 Horizon Ridge
Parkway, Suite 100
Henderson, Nev. 89012

Reno
Manager: Nick Koch
Instructors: Bill Presse,
Gaylen Christean III, Greg
Meisner, Nick Koch
(775) 322-4653
8175 S. Virginia #B-950
Reno, Nev. 89511

NEW JERSEY

E. Brunswick (Golfsmith)
Manager:
Michael Damhoff
Instructors: Daniel
Hammer, Michael
Damhoff, Ryan Lieberum
(732) 238-1419
678 Route 18
E. Brunswick, N.J. 08816

E. Hanover
Manager: Wayne Sciscio
Instructors: Brian Bothe,
Wayne Sciscio,
Matt DiStafano
(973) 599-1993
145 Route 10 East
E. Hanover, N.J. 07936

Englewood
Manager: Dan Ashley
Instructors: Bryan Vander
May, Dan Ashley, Rich
Kwon
(201) 567-0103
380 Nordhoff Place
Englewood, N.J. 07631

Moorestown (Golfsmith)
Manager: Brad Skupaka
Instructors: Brad
Skupaka, Filindo Colace,
Pete Mangano
(877) 893-0133 x2
401 Route 38, Suite B12
Moorestown, N.J. 08057

Paramus (Golfsmith)
Manager: Tom Howard
Instructors: Gary Bates,
Ken Solar, Stuart Blasius,
Tom Howard
(201) 450-9940
240 N. State Route 17
Unit 5
Paramus, N.J. 07652

Woodbridge
Manager: Brian Gussis
Instructors: Brendan
Gorman, Brian Gussis
(732) 730-5406
181 Highway 1, Suite G
Metuchen, N.J. 08840

Woodland Park (Golfsmith)
Manager: T.J. Scillieri
Instructors: James Fox,
Rick Voegele, T.J. Scillieri
(973) 890-0817
1750 Route 46 West
Woodland Park, N.J.
07424

NEW MEXICO

Alburquerque
Manager: Kevin Amhaus
Instructors: Kevin
Amhaus, Robb Bierbaum
(505) 948-5095
6644 Indian School Road
NE, Suite R-103
Albuquerque, N.M. 87110

NEW YORK

Carle Place
Manager: Dan Benzenberg
Instructors: Dan
Benzenberg, Gerardo
Patron, Maria Oristaglio,
Richard Taliani
(516) 248-4653
233 Voice Road
Carle Place, N.Y. 11514

Lake Grove (Golfsmith)
Manager: Ryan Galloway
Instructors: Matt Berman,
Ryan Galloway, Steven
Chudyk
(631) 737-1570
3220 Middle Country
Road
Lake Grove, N.Y. 11755

New Rochelle
Instructors: Boris Busljeta,
Nicholas Banks
(914) 365-2004
130 Rhodes Street
New Rochelle, N.Y. 10801

Rochester
Manager: Scott Singer
Instructors: Eric
Sukhenko, Scott Singer
(585) 586-3090
3240 Monroe Avenue
Rochester, N.Y. 14618

White Plains
Manager: Frederick Moore
Instructors: Brad Johnson,
Frederick Moore, Tom
Sialiano
(914) 397-4820
190 E. Post Road, Suite 201
White Plains, N.Y. 10601

NORTH CAROLINA

Cary
Manager: Kevin Kohlbeck
Instructors: Glenn Payne,
John Adams, Kevin
Kohlbeck
(919) 677-8385
2020 Renaissance
Park Place
Cary, N.C. 27513

Charlotte
Manager: Andy Zachowicz
Instructors: Jim Ingram
(704) 940-0005
9571 South Boulevard
Charlotte, N.C. 28273

Greensboro—Wendover
Manager: Jim Hackett
Instructors: Scott
Duerscherl, Jim Hackett
(919) 865-2858
4217 W. Wendover Avenue
Greensboro, N.C. 27407

Raliegh (Golfsmith)
Manager: Robert Gamble
Instructors: Patrick
Holloman, Robert Gamble,
Steve Pietsch
(919) 865-2858
6254 Glenwood Avenue
Raleigh, N.C. 27612

Tyvola
Manager: Andy Zachowicz
Instructors: Andy
Zachowicz, Justin Gupton,
Paul Weber
(704) 405-1490
726 Tyvola Road
Charlotte, N.C. 28217

OHIO

Blue Ash
Instructors: Brian
Staarmann, Kirk Howard,
Matt Stotler
(513) 469-0813
11255 Reed Hartman
Highway, Suite G
Blue Ash, Ohio 45241

Brecksville
Manager: Keith Sullivan
Instructors: Keith Zabak,
Keith Sullivan
8803 Brecksville Road
Brecksville, Ohio 44141

Canton
Manager: Carl Rehm
Instructors: Carl Rehm,
Scott Campbell
(330) 433-2850
4930 Everhard Road NW
Canton, Ohio 44718

Cleveland East
Manager: Brett Smith
Instructors: Brett Smith,
Drew Farron, Mitchell
Flemming, Jason
Goodendorf
(216) 454-0074
24195 Chagrin Boulevard
Beachwood, Ohio 44122

Cleveland West
Manager: Nick Paez
Instructors: Bobby King,
Joe Meglen, Nick Paez,
Rory Albright, Scott
Masters
(440) 348-1757
26669 Brookpark
Road Extension
N. Olmsted, Ohio 44070

Columbus—Dublin
(Golfsmith)
Manager: Bradley Phillips
Instructors: Bradley
Phillips, Josh Basinger,
Matt Michallow, Paul Hobart
(614) 336-8044
7649 New Market
Center Way
Columbus, Ohio 43235

Columbus—Easton
(Golfsmith)
Manager: Pat Bernot
Instructors: Jeff
McEldowney, Joe Stago,
Pat Bernot
(614) 428-4653
3695 Easton Market
Columbus, Ohio 43219

Dayton (Golfsmith)
2720 Towne Drive
Beavercreek, Ohio 45431

OKLAHOMA

Oklahoma City
Manager: Darryl Court
Instructors: Darryl Court,
Wade Walker
(405) 749-0000
12312 N. May Ave.
Oklahoma City, Okla.
73120

Tulsa
Manager: Patrick McTigue
Instructors: Joe Hassler,
Patrick McTigue,
Paul Clagg
(918) 622-3968
6010 S. Memorial Drive
Tulsa, Okla. 74145

ONTARIO

Meadowvale, Mississauga
Manager: Ryan Klassen
Instructors: Joe Lavery,
Ryan Klassen, Will
Dempster
(905) 286-4653
2150 Meadowvale
Boulevard
Mississauga, Ontario
L5N 6R6

OREGON

Portland (Golfsmith)
Manager: Jake Bader
Instructors: Craig Hunt,
Elliot Lemley, Jake Bader
(503) 281-1842
10263 NE Cascades
Parkway
Portland, Ore. 97220

Tualatin (Golfsmith)
Manager: Chris Woods
Instructors: Ben Weyland,
Chris Woods
(503) 612-7807
7059 SW Nyberg Road
Tualatin, Ore. 97062

PENNSYLVANIA

Bridgeville
Manager: Justin Iaquinta
Instructors: Justin
Iaquinta, Justin Palermo,
Wes Vranesevic
(412) 564-9029
1597 Washington Pike A-54
Bridgeville, Pa. 15017

King of Prussia
Manager: Charles Luis
Instructors: Anthony
Napoletano, Charles Luis,
Darryl Welman
(877) 893-0133
436 W. Swedesford Road
Berwyn, Pa. 19312

Lehigh Valley
Manager/Instructor:
Steve Snyder
(610) 264-3810
1920 Catasauqua Road
Allentown, Pa. 18109

Rosemont
Instructors: Chris Young,
John Allen, Peter Carmain
(877) 893-0133
1149 W. Lancaster Avenue
Rosemont, Pa. 19010

Wexford
Manager: Matt Terry
Instructors: Doreen
Melucci, Matt Black,
Matt Terry
(724) 933-3434
1005 Wexford Plaza Drive
Wexford, Pa 15090

Willow Grove (Golfsmith)
Manager: Andy Schweppe
Instructors: Anthony
Schweppe, Ed Riordan,
Rick Flesher
(877) 893-0133
3975 Welsh Road
Willow Grove, Pa. 19090

RHODE ISLAND

Cranston
Manager: Patrick O'Leary
Instructors: Frank J.
Russo, Jr., Issac Moniz,
Patrick O'Leary, William
Schmedes
(401) 649-4653
10 Worthington Road #B
Cranston, R.I. 02910

TENNESSEE

Brentwood (Golfsmith)
Manager: Jim Stevens
Instructors: Jim Stevens,
Sean Trimble
(615) 526-6849
330 Franklin Road # 406E
Brentwood, Tenn. 37027

Franklin
Manager: Andrew Braley
Instructors: Andrew
Braley, Chris Robicheaux,
Rob Della Morte,
Travis Zimber
(615) 472-9175
615 Bakers Bridge Rd. #125
Franklin, Tenn. 37067

Knoxville
Manager: Jason Nelson
Instructors: Bobby
McCrimmon, Jason
Nelson, Kristin Price
(865) 566-0505
7240 Kingston Pike #144
Knoxville, Tenn. 37919

Memphis (Golfsmith)
Manager: Ray Sharp
Instructors: Ray Sharp,
Tony DeMarco
(901) 755-9494
7741 Winchester Road
Memphis, Tenn. 38125

TEXAS

Arlington (Golfsmith)
Manager: Robert Gordon
Instructors: Kellen
Woodfield, Robert Gordon
(817) 419-7426
1001 W. Interstate 20
Arlington, Texas 76017

Austin (Golfsmith)
Manager: Paul Thar
Instructors: Blake Sims, Dave Koenig, Mark Klement, Myron Klement, Paul Thar
(512) 231-9797
10001 Research Boulevard
Austin, Texas 78759

Dallas (Golfsmith)
Manager: Steve Kuitu
Instructors: Donald Cook, John Wagner, Michael Jordan, Steve Kuitu
(972) 239-4700
4141 L.B.J. Freeway
Dallas, Texas 75244

Dallas–Park Cities
Mockingbird
Central Plaza
Manager: Erik Wait
Instructors: Eric Reed, Erik Wait, Mark Gerhardt
(469) 334-0500
5400 E. Mockingbird #222
Dallas, Texas 75206

Fort Worth
Manager: Steven Storey
Instructors: Steven Storey, Randy Pate
(817) 524-6648
2600 W. 7th Street, #180
Fort Worth, Texas 76107

Houston–Galleria
5000 Westheimer Road
Manager: Darren Smith
Instructors: Becca Carey, Darren Smith, Thomas Baird
(713) 850-7555
Houston Galleria
5000 Westheimer Road, Suite 150
Houston, Texas 77056

Houston–Katy
Manager: Jerimey Hammersley
Instructors: Pam Dixon, Jerimey Hammersley
Check website for

Houston–Upper Kirby
Manager: Doug Strawbridge
Instructors: Doug Strawbridge, Johnny Lee, Zoran Zorkic, Ryan Thorpe
(832) 426-5650
2615 SW Freeway #270
Houston, Texas 77098

Houston–Westheimer
(Golfsmith)
Manager: Kendal Putman
Instructors: Christian Nitz, Jared Wold, Kendal Putman, Tim Wright
(713) 339-2470
10885 Westheimer
Houston, Texas 77042

Irving
Manager: Rick Beck
Instructors: Adrian Kelley, Chad Powell, Rick Beck
(972) 294-7787
114 E. John Carpenter Freeway #130
Irving, Texas 75062

Lubbock (Golf USA)
Manager: Randy Stevenson
Instructors: Randy Stevenson, Tyler Ortega
(806) 771-4653
6701 Indiana Avenue
Lubbock, Texas 79413

McAllen
Manager: James Payton
Instructors: Aswad Browning, James Payton
(956) 994-9631
2901 N. 10th Street, Suite J
McAllen, Texas 78501

N. Richland Hills (Golfsmith)
Manager: Tony Preston
Instructors: Paul Harrelson, Shane Van Kuilenburg, Tony Preston
(817) 281-7496
8701 Airport Highway
N. Richland Hills, Texas 76180

Plano (Golfsmith)
Manager: Jeff Schmiedbauer
Instructors: Eldred, Jason Cole, Michael Steckley
(972) 398-8000
900 N. Central Expwy.
Plano, Texas 75074

San Antonio (Golfsmith)
Manager: Ryan Cummings
Instructors: Jerry Trevino, Michael Ray, Ryan Cummings
(210) 519-2600
1211 N. Loop 1604 West
San Antonio, Texas 78258

Spring (Golfsmith)
Manager: Nick Camacho
Instructors: Nick Camacho, Russell Amason
(281) 419-6110
25415 N. IH-45, Suite B
Spring, Texas 77380

Webster (Golfsmith)
Instructors: Aram Hudson, Jonathan Strellow, Dustin Arnold
(281) 557-0015
19431 Gulf Freeway
Webster, Texas 77598

UTAH

Salt Lake City
Manager: Ben Knighton
Instructors: Alden Peterson, Barry Schenk, Ben Knighton
(801) 618-0399
6582 Big Cottonwood Canyon, Suite 100
Holladay, Utah 84121

VIRGINIA

Arlington
(Sport and Health)
Instructors: Craig Smith, Gary Mankulish
(703) 894-3120
1122 Kirkwood Road
Arlington, Va. 22201

McLean–Tysons Corner
(Sport & Health)
Manager: John Benkovic
Instructors: Gary Cricks, John Benkovic, Phil Bowers
(703) 942-5000
8250 Greensboro Drive
McLean, Va. 22102

Richmond
Manager: Mike Parker
Instructors: Jason Goslee, Jonathan Corbin, Mike Parker
(804) 747-7284
9017 W. Broad Street
Richmond, Va. 23294

Sterling (Golfsmith)
Manager: Craig Voudren
Instructors: Craig Voudren, Derek White
(571) 266-5082
46301 Potomac Run Plaza
Sterling, Va. 20164

WASHINGTON

Bellevue
Manager: Brett Wilkinson
Instructors: Brett Wilkinson, Eric Hambleton, Erin Menath, Nicholas Burrington
(425) 454-7956
111 108th Ave NE, Suite 150
Bellevue, Wash. 98004

Lynnwood
Manager: Lyndon Bystrom
Instructors: David McMillon, Lyndon Bystrom
(425) 412-3999
3225 Alderwood Mall Boulevard, Suite G
Lynnwood, Wash. 98036

Seattle
Manager:
Nathanael Johnson
Instructors: Nathanael Johnson, Rance Yanabu, Todd Barney
(206) 357-6885
255 Yale Ave
Seattle, Wash. 98109

Spokane
Manager: Randy Potter
Instructors: Randy Potter, Tim Connor
(509) 464-6707
1207 N. Washington Street, Suite 2
Spokane, Wash. 99201

Tukwila
Manager: Jordan Cooper
Instructors: Eric Briggs, John LeDoux, Jordan Cooper
(206) 577-3500
406 Baker Boulevard
Tukwila, Wash. 98188

WISCONSIN

Brookfield (Golfsmith)
Manager: Todd Gamroth
Instructors: Jacob Babcock, Todd Gamroth, Ryan Kraemer
(262) 782-8400
16130 W. Bluemound Road
Brookfield, Wis. 53005

Mequon
Manager: Kevin Kihslinger
Instructors: Dan Wells, Evan Hewes, Kevin Kihslinger, Victor Jacinto
(262) 240-9851
1408 W. Mequon Road
Mequon, Wis. 53092

Middleton
Manager: Brendan Locke
Instructors: Kevin Geib, McClain Gitch, Tim Boegh
(608) 831-3673
8333 Greenway Boulevard
Middleton, Wis. 53562

Wauwatosa
Manager: Brendan Locke
Instructors: Brian Jankowski, Greg Gericke, Rob Elliott
(414) 463-4653
12132 W. Capitol Drive
Wauwatosa, Wis. 53222